D0622072

STUDIES IN ROMANCE LANGUAGES: 31
John E. Keller, *Editor*

THREE COMEDIES

by Pedro Calderón de la Barca

Translated with an Introduction by

KENNETH MUIR

and

ANN L. MACKENZIE

THE UNIVERSITY PRESS OF KENTUCKY

Editorial and Sales Offices: Lexington, Kentucky 40506-0024

Library of Congress Cataloging in Publication Data

Calderón de la Barca, Pedro, 1600-1681.
    Three comedies.

    (Studies in Romance languages; 31)
    Contents: A house with two doors is difficult to
guard = Casa con dos puertas mala es de guardar—
Mornings of April and May = Mañanas de abril y mayo—
No trifling with love = No hay burlas con el amor.
    I. Muir, Kenneth.   II. Mackenzie, Ann L.   III. Title.
IV. Series
PQ6292.A2   1985   862'.3   85-5369
ISBN 0-8131-1546-9
ISBN 0-8131-0166-2 (pbk.)

c l x

Contents

Preface

In a recent review of Kurt and Roswitha Reichenberger's monumental bibliography of Calderón, the eminent Golden-Age drama scholar Hannah Bergman deeply regretted the inaccessibility of much of Calderón's theatre to English speakers ignorant of the Spanish language: "Yet Calderón is probably after Cervantes, the best-known Spanish writer in the English-speaking world." Professor Bergman concluded that "fomenting more translations into English should be one of our concerns."[1] We have been encouraged by her words to add this further volume of Calderón translations to our earlier book, *Four Comedies by Calderón.*[2]

We have again concentrated on increasing the number of comedies accessible to English-speaking readers, to departments of drama and of comparative literature in colleges and universities, and to both professional and amateur theatre companies. Traditionally Calderón's comedies have been neglected by translators in favor of serious drama such as *La vida es sueño (Life Is a Dream)* and *El alcalde de Zalamea (The Mayor of Zalamea).*[3] Yet the comedies not only form a considerable proportion of the playwright's output, they contribute substantially to his artistic achievement. Moreover, we believe that certain social and moral attitudes are less likely to alienate a modern audience as they are reflected in the comedies than as presented in Calderón's more serious drama. We have particularly in mind the treatment in the comedies of conflicts involving honor, as opposed to the relentless dramatization of blood-vengeance and cruel wife-murder in Calderón's honor-tragedies.[4]

In this present collection we have included *Casa con dos puertas mala es de guardar (A House with Two Doors Is Difficult to Guard),* acknowledged to be one of Calderón's finest comic masterpieces. Kenneth Muir first translated this play in 1962 in a free rendering published in *Tulane Drama Review* (1963).[5] He considered making it more widely accessible by republishing it, in revised form, in *Four Comedies by Calderón,* but decided against doing so because there was then a project, since abandoned, to include it in a bilingual edition. The present translation constitutes a radically different version, one which adheres much more closely to the original text. At first glance it might seem strange that we have not also chosen to include a translation of this play's companion-piece, *La dama duende (The Phantom Lady);* but an accurate and easily obtainable version of *La dama duende* by Edwin

Honig already exists in English.[6] Instead, it semed preferable to offer
Mañanas de abril y mayo (Mornings of April and May) and *No hay
burlas con el amor (No Trifling with Love)*. These two comedies have so
far received surprisingly little critical attention from scholars of Golden-
Age drama. A properly annotated modern edition of *Mañanas de abril y
mayo* is yet to be published, while a scholarly edition with detailed study
of *No hay burlas* has only recently appeared.[7] Yet, as Edward Wilson
perceptively indicated, these two comedies are "as good as, if less
famous than, the two just mentioned."[8] *Mañanas de abril y mayo* and *No
hay burlas con el amor* deserve to be both widely read and regularly
performed.[9]

We continue in this volume to follow the principles of translation
outlined in *Four Comedies*, firmly avoiding the example set by Edward
Fitzgerald, who disliked many of Calderón's dramatic devices and much
of his poetic style. "I have," he declared, "while faithfully trying to retain
what was fine and efficient, sunk, reduced, altered and replaced, much
that seemed not; simplified some perplexities, and curtailed or omitted
scenes that seemed to mar the breadth of general effect."[10] It is not, in
our opinion, the business of a translator to alter the original to suit either
his own taste or that of his age. The poetic characteristics of Calderón
deplored by Fitzgerald are those that we enjoy and have endeavored to
reproduce; his iterative imagery, his conceits, his rhetoric. Nor do we
consider it right for a translator to suppress scenes or speeches, though,
bearing in mind that seventeenth-century theatre producers never
staged a play without reducing and altering it as they then thought fit,
we naturally assume that modern producers may wish to make certain
changes for practical reasons of staging.

As in *Four Comedies*, we have chosen for the most part to render
the variety of metres used by Calderón into blank verse, this being the
poetic medium to which English-speaking audiences are most accustomed. In "Play Notes" supplied to explain his recent adaptation of
La vida es sueño, Adrian Mitchell conceded that it would be possible to
reproduce Calderón's complex verse-forms for the English stage in
exactly parallel meters. But he also pointed out that "this would result in
magnificently unspeakable English verse. The rhythms of Spanish are
not the rhythms of English. The superabundance of rhymes and echoing
word-endings in Spanish makes complicated rhyme patterns easily
acceptable in the original. But they would be turgid and strained in
English."[11] In accordance with Elizabethan and Jacobean practice, we
have varied the iambic pentameter in a number of traditional ways. We
have also inserted short lines, as did Shakespeare, when it seemed
appropriate. In certain scenes and conversations which did not appear to
us to warrant the dignity of verse, notably those involving servant
characters, we have had recourse to prose. Originally we considered the
possibility of keeping to verse throughout and of rendering the servants'

lines into doggerel, as in certain pre-Shakespearian plays. So, for instance, Calabazas' speech, in Act III, scene 2, of *Casa con dos puertas*
was initially translated in the following form:

> It's far from right
> That a master of mine
> Should be so uptight.
> They'll think it a sign
> I can't keep my mouth shut.
> You walk about,
> You come and go, but
> Always without me.
> It appears that we are
> As distant by far
> As love is from money.
> I don't find it funny!
> If a veiled lady comes,
> You shout,
> "Clear out!"
> If you go on a visit,
> You say to me "Wait!
> It won't do for you
> To accompany me."
> It isn't fair, is it?
> It's a horrible bother
> To the mother who bore me.
> What job is there for me
> In serving you further?
> I must go in quest
> Of a more human master,
> Because I have guessed
> That none could be nastier.
> An affected wit
> (Who's really a nit-wit)
> Could hardly be worse;
> Nor a man with a sound wit
> And fortune unsound;
> Nor a fussy lack-wit;
> Nor one who writes verse,
> A playwright depicting
> Both master and man
> Alike as two turnips;
> Nor a painted fop
> Who talks la-di-dar,
> Nor even the chap—
> The worst kind by far—
> Who uses the Palace
> For sexual sallies.

But we decided that it would be almost impossible for a modern actor to make such doggerel sound natural. The experiment therefore was abandoned. Instead we follow the lead given by Shakespeare in certain plays, such as *A Midsummer Night's Dream*, in which the mechanicals are made to speak in prose. It is worth remembering that in Shakespeare's later comedies characters such as Shylock, Beatrice, and Rosalind speak mainly in prose; and that, though Viola delivers some harmonious verse, much of *Twelfth Night*, the most obviusly "poetic" of Shakespeare's comedies, is written in prose.

As regards the choice of style and diction, perhaps it should be explained that though we have tried to avoid pastiche we have preferred to use a vocabulary more or less appropriate to the period of Calderón's plays because we are convinced that a modern idiom would not be at odds with the manners of the age, with the characters, and with the sentiments which they express. [12] Admittedly the ridiculous affectations of speech assumed by Beatriz in *No hay burlas con el amor* presented us with special difficulties. We decided that her affectedly latinate vocabulary might best be conveyed in English by means of some French words as well as by the use of latinisms. We point, by way of precedent, to the French terms used by Dryden's affected heroine in *Marriage à la Mode*. Beatriz's regular employment of an extraordinarily latinate syntax posed a still greater problem. Upon reflection we concluded that it was not possible to reproduce the full degree of distortion of normal word order found in the Spanish original without making much of what Beatriz says wholly incomprehensible. Consequently, we have employed some measure of hyperbaton but have been careful to avoid slavishly dogging the extraordinarily wandering movements of Beatriz's phraseology.

For the Spanish texts of these chosen comedies we have relied principally on the versions edited by Ángel Valbuena Briones. [13] We have also found it useful to consult the facsimile editions of Calderón's plays prepared by D. W. Cruickshank and J. E. Varey, [14] and the relevant volumes of Calderón edited by J. E. Hartzenbusch. [15] As a result we have been able to take some account of textual variants while trying to elucidate certain obscure passages. Even so, some difficulties of meaning proved impossible to resolve given the fact that all of the seventeenth-century printed texts are in some degree defective and that no autograph manuscripts have survived. As Hartzenbusch has pointed out, there are defects and omissions in the third acts of both *Mañanas de abril y mayo* and *No hay burlas con el amor.*

We must acknowledge also our debt to Ignacio Arellano's new edition of *No hay burlas con el amor* and to George Northup's old but still invaluable edition of *Casa con dos puertas.* Northup was the first editor to publish Félix's lengthy speech eulogizing King Philip IV and his hunting activities (Act III), which survives in the seventeenth-century Osuna manuscript of the play (Biblioteca Nacional, Madrid) but is not found in any printed text of the period.[16] Certainly the speech retards the progress of the plot, so that stage directors might well feel justified in excluding it. To make it easy for them to do so if they wish, we have printed our translation of the speech in a separate appendix following the play.

It remains for us to record our deep thanks to Ivy L. McClelland, Senior Research Fellow, Department of Hispanic Studies, University of Glasgow, who generously gave of her time and expertise to enable us to master the sense of some obstinately difficult passages which had previously resisted our best endeavors. Our gratitude is also due to the anonymous specialist readers consulted by the University Press of Kentucky, who made many helpful suggestion.

---

1. The review of *Bibliographisches Handbuch der Calderón-Forschung*, vol. 1 (Kassel: Thiele and Schwarz, 1979), and was published in *Journal of Hispanic Philology* 5, no. 1 (1980): 75-77.

2. *Four Comedies by Pedro Calderón de la Barca*, trans. with an introduction by Kenneth Muir, with notes to the individual plays by Ann L. Mackenzie (Lexington: Univ. Press of Kentucky, 1980).

3. Both these plays have recently been adapted into English by Adrian Mitchell et al. and performed very successfully at the National Theatre, at the Pit, London, and at The Other Place, Stratford-upon-Avon.

4. These tragedies are *El pintor de su deshonra* (*The Painter of His Own Dishonor*), *El Médico de su honra* (*The Surgeon of His Honor*), and *A secreto agravio, secreta venganza* (*Secret Dishonor Demands Secret Vengeance*).

5. Kenneth Muir's translation was first performed by the Drama Department, University of Pittsburgh, and afterwards (1965) at the University of California, Davis. No other English translation of this play exists, nor are there any previous versions in English of either *Mañanas de abril y mayo* or *No hay burlas con el amor.*

6. See Calderón, *Four Plays*, trans. Edwin Honig (New York: Hill and Wang, 1961).

7. Pedro Calderón de la Barca, *No hay burlas con el amor*, ed. Ignacio Arellano (Pamplona: EUNSA, 1981).

8. See Edward M. Wilson and Duncan Moir, *The Golden Age: Drama, 1492-1700* (London: Benn/New York: Barnes and Noble, 1971), p. 105.

9. A play of comparable merit which draws on the same Cervantine tale as Middleton's *The Spanish Gypsy* is the tragicomedy *No hay cosa como callar.* We hope to turn our attention to it on another occasion.

10. See *Eight Dramas of Calderón* (London/New York: Macmillan, 1906), p. 2.

11. Printed in the theatre programme for performances in Stratford and London, November 1983 and May 1984. In his translation Mitchell used iambic pentameters together with a variety of other verse-forms and including half-rhymes and assonances.

12. Some translators of plays for Penguin Books, by following E.V. Rieu's demands that they be absolutely modern, have set up a conflict between the

manners of the period and the modern English speech of their characters. In our view, an actor who talks like a Pinter or Osborne character while dressed like Celimène forfeits the willingness of his audience to take his performance seriously.

13. See Calderón de la Barca, *Obra completas*, ed. Ángel Valbuena Briones, 2nd ed., vol. 2, *Comedias* (Madrid: Aguilar, 1973).

14. See especially the facsimile reprints of *Primera parte de comedias* (Madrid, 1636), *Tercera parte de comedias* (Madrid, 1664), and *Quinta parte de comedias* (Madrid, 1677) in vols. 2, 8, and 13 of *The Comedias of Calderón* (London: Tamesis, 1973).

15. See vols. 1 and 2 of *Comedies de D. Pedro Calderón de la Barca*, Biblioteca de Autores Españoles, vols. 7 and 9 (Madrid: Rivadeneyra, 1872 and 1881).

16. See *Three Plays by Calderón*, ed. George Tyler Northup (Boston: D.C. Heath, 1926). See also his article "Some Recovered Lines from Calderón", *Homenaje ofrecido a Menéndez Pidal*, 2 (Madrid: Editorial Hernando, 1925): 495-500.

Introduction

Casa con dos puertas, Mañanas de abril y mayo, and *No hay burlas con el amor* were composed in the period 1629-1635, that is, in the early years of Calderón's dramatic career, years during which he displayed a particular enthusiasm and developed a truly extraordinary aptitude for the genre of comedy.

Critics agree that *Casa con dos puertas,* though evidently not published until 1636,[1] was written in 1629, the same year as *La dama duende,* the comedy which it strikingly resembles in basic dramatic situation, in types of conflict and confusion, and in stage devices: a brother, concerned for his honor, keeps secret his sister's presence from a friend who is a guest in his home; the sister, amorously attracted to her brother's friend, uses her personal ingenuity and the physical convenience of a concealed or extra door for easy entrance or discreet escape, to further her relationship with him. Which of these two dramatic siblings was first born, however, is still a matter for debate. Valbuena Briones is convinced by a reference to "La dama duende" in *Casa con dos puertas* that *The Phantom Lady* is the earlier work, and that *A House with Two Doors* is merely an inferior imitation.[2] Other critics have been less persuaded by the "phantom lady" reference. Stiefel speculates that there could have been an earlier play by that name to which Calderón was alluding and which he used only subsequently as a source for his own comedy.[3] F.A. De Armas wonders whether the phrase was not a topical one at the period, arising from some contemporary event now long forgotten.

It is certainly true that the phrase "dama duende" is used in at least one Golden-Age comedy known to predate both *Casa con dos puertas* and *La dama duende,* Tirso de Molina's *Quien calla, otorga (To Keep Silent Is to Condone).*[4] De Armas is one of several critics who have pointed out that *Casa con dos puertas* was definitely written before the birth in October 1629 of Prince Baltasar Carlos, first son of Philip IV and his French queen, Isabel de Borbón. Allusion is made in Act III to Queen Isabel's pregnancy, and the hope is expressed that she may live "so that the blossom / From France may yield in time fruit in Castile" ("para que flores de Francia / nos den el fruto en Castilla"). *La dama duende,* on the other hand, contains a reference to the baptism of the infant prince, which did not take place until November 1629, but this allusion may have been added by Calderón to his original text several months after its completion, in order to freshen the play's air of top-icality.[5]

Our view is that the phantom lady mentioned by Calabazas in *Casa con dos puertas* is indeed Calderón's own *Dama duende*. Given Calderón's extraordinary fondness for referring to his best comedy in plays written subsequently, we find it very difficult to believe otherwise. As we remarked in *Four Comedies*: "Almost every comedy written by Calderón after his very successful *Dama duende* contains a play of words on its title. Evidently an understanding grew between him and his audience that he would include such a reference, which became a kind of trademark, a guarantee that the comedy they attended was a genuine creation by the maker of *The Phantom Lady*" (p. 282). Among the plays alluding to *La dama duende* are *Peor está que estaba (From Bad to Worse)*, *Dicha y desdicha del nombre (Advantages and Disadvantages of a Name)*, *El secreto a voces (The Secret Spoken Aloud)*, and *Mañanas de abril y mayo*. Further support for our opinion that Calderón wrote *Casa con dos puertas* as a sequel to *La dama duende* may be found in the fact that Calabazas' remark about the "phantom lady" is prompted by his master's reference to a mysterious woman as "beautiful as an angel," for the Christian name of the angel-faced, phantom-lady protagonist ("ángel, demonio o mujer") who haunts the bemused Don Manuel in Calderón's famous comedy is Doña Ángela.[6]

Efforts to determine the date of composition of *Mañanas de abril y mayo* must also rely on internal evidence. No seventeenth-century manuscript of this play survives nor any printed version earlier than 1664 (the date of publication of Calderón's *Tercera parte de comedias*, in which the comedy is included). Yet the play was written at least twenty years before that date, for it refers to Queen Isabel, who died in 1644. Mention in the play of *La dama duende* indicates a date after 1629, while an allusion to another famous Golden-Age drama, Tirso's *El burlador de Sevilla (The Trickster of Seville)*, which was first published in 1630, seems to favor a date of composition in the early 1630s. Several key scenes of the play are set in the gardens of the new palace of the Buen Retiro. These gardens, descriptions of which are given in several passages, were not properly opened until the autumn of 1633 or the spring of 1634.[7] It is tempting to suppose that the first performance of *Mañanas de abril y mayo* may have taken place, appropriately, in April or May of 1634 as part of the court festivities celebrating the inauguration of the palace and gardens. We know that Calderón wrote an *auto* (one-act religious play) for these festivities, entitled *El nuevo palacio del Retiro*, performed in the spring of 1634.[8] It is possible that both this *auto* and Calderón's comedy *Mañanas de abril y mayo* (the latter perhaps preceded by a dance called "Las mañanitas de mayo," which has been attributed to Calderón)[9] were actually performed out of doors during that spring of 1634, in the very gardens they were composed to eulogize.

The new Buen Retiro palace evidently had several indoor theatre-rooms, but performances were also regularly staged in the palace-grounds, notably on an island in the middle of a lake.[10]

No hay burlas con el amor, of which no manuscript survives, was published in *Parte 42 de Comedias de diferentes Autores* (Zaragoza, 1650), and later under the alternative title *La crítica del amor (Love's Critic)* in Calderón's *Quinta parte de comedias* (Madrid, 1677). Tyler and Elizondo, evidently following Hilborn's somewhat unreliable evaluation of the play's verse forms, assign it to the years 1631-32.[11] Nevertheless a *loa* (comic prologue) usually attributed to Quiñones de Benavente, dated 1635 and performed by the theatre company of Antonio de Prado in that same year, names *No hay burlas con el amor* as a new play.[12] As well as this piece of external evidence, certain internal indications, notably a mention of Calderón's comedy *Con quien vengo, vengo (I'm with Who I'm With)*, written in 1635, also serve to indicate that year as the date when *No hay burlas con el amor* was composed.

It is understandable, if unfortunate, that no exact records of the first performances of our three comedies appear to have survived. Documentary evidence of subsequent performances, in both the palace and the public theatres, has, however, been preserved and is sufficient to demonstrate that all three plays were enduringly popular with seventeenth-century audiences. One might mention, for instance, a performance of *Casa con dos puertas* given at the palace in 1635 by the company of Antonio de Prado in the presence of their majesties.[13] King Philip IV and Queen Isabel must first have enjoyed this play some six years previously, but doubtless never tired of hearing repeated its fulsome eulogies of their persons. This same comedy was still being performed at the palace in the 1680s and 1690s, after Calderón's death, and in the reign of Philip IV's successor, the ill-fated last Spanish Habsburg ruler, Charles II. That *No hay burlas con el amor* was likewise still popular in the 1690s is evidenced by its performance in the Corral del Príncipe in October 1696.[14] It is worth noting that the popularity and influence of these comedies extended beyond Habsburg Spain, notably to seventeenth-century France and England. In France, Thomas Corneille, D'Ouville, Boisrobert, and Boursault all wrote plays influenced, to varying degrees, by *Casa con dos puertas*, while *No hay burlas con el amor* provided Molière with a source of inspiration for his *Les Femmes savantes* (1672). In England, William Wycherley, one of several Restoration dramatists who knew Spanish, derived a significant proportion of the plot of his first drama from *Mañanas de abril y mayo*. Wycherley changed Calderón's love-laden *Mornings of April and May*, passed in Madrid, notably in the gardens of the Buen Retiro Palace, into *Love in a Wood, or St. James's Park* (1671). He also added scenes and introduced some typically English comic characters (such as Alderman Gripe, Sir Simon Addlepot, and Lady Flippant, "in distress for a husband"), which transformed the thoughtful comedy of the Spanish original into a characteristically frivolous piece of comic Restoration theatre.

The end of the seventeenth century brought the departure of the Habsburgs from the Spanish throne but not the departure of our three plays from the Spanish theatres, or, for that matter, from theatres elsewhere in Europe. Eighteenth- and nineteenth-century manuscript copies and loose editions *(sueltas)* reveal, as do theatre records from the same period, that the comedies were regularly performed not only in Madrid but also in the provinces.[15] Translations and adaptations made in France, England, Italy, Germany, Holland, and other countries are too numerous to list in full. One might, however, select the following for mention: in France, the version of *Casa con dos puertas* made by Nicolas de la Grange (*Les Contre-temps*, 1756) and the nineteenth-century translations of Damas-Hinard; in Germany, the rendering by Zachariae and Gärtner of *No hay burlas con el amor* (*Die Liebe versteht keinen Spass*, 1770) and Konrad Pasch's adaptation of *Mañanas de abril y mayo* (*Morgen des April und Mai*, 1892); and in England, *A Tutor for the beaus: or, Love in a labyrinth. A comedy as it is acted at the Theatre Royal in Lincoln's Inn-Fields* (1737), written by John Hewitt on the basis of *Casa con dos puertas*.[16] To these might be added some of the numerous twentieth-century versions of the plays available in French, German, Italian, Russian, and Czechoslovakian. But further evidence seems scarcely necessary. Clearly these three comedies are endowed with dramatic qualities sufficiently durable to last for centuries beyond their own era and sufficiently flexible to reach into the minds and touch the sense of humor of people outside their own contemporaries. What remains necessary, therefore, is to make a critical examination of the three plays for the purpose of identifying these qualities that have traveled so well and lasted so long.

Casa con dos puertas, Mañanas de abril y mayo, and *No hay burlas con el amor,* like the majority of the innumerable comedies composed during the Spanish Golden Age, are *comedias de capa y espada* ("cloak-and-sword plays").[17] The genre derives its name from the frequency with which identities are concealed or confused (by means of cloak or veil) and the readiness with which challenges are issued and duels staged. For these are comedies of intrigue, involving various gallants and their ladies in conflicts and complications of love, jealousy, and honor. These honor-minded, love-obsessed characters are usually presented as members of contemporary upper-class Spanish society living in Spanish towns, moving about in authentically named streets, alluding to current events. *Mañanas de abril y mayo* and *No hay burlas con el amor* are both set in Madrid, while *Casa con dos puertas* takes place in and around Ocaña, near Philip IV's summer palace at Aranjuez. The palace is mentioned in several speeches, which also refer to such topical matters as the ministry of Olivares and the pregnancy of Queen

Isabel. The gardens of another royal palace, the Buen Retiro, provide a meeting-place for Clara and Hipólito, Juan and Ana in *Mañanas de abril y mayo*. Ana's house, in which other scenes of the play are enacted, is situated in the Calle de las Huertas, near the palace gardens. The real-life surroundings form a hilarious contrast with the fantastic movements of the plot, which draw the characters into a series of unlikely happenings, confront them with extraordinary combinations of coincidences, push them into sudden changes of identity, make them eavesdrop behind curtains and conceal themselves in back rooms, and bring them with dignity through one door only to impel them to leave, in comic haste, through another. Sometimes even the large supply of extra rooms and doors in "cloak-and-sword" houses proves inadequate, and the hapless gallant is reduced to seeking refuge in a china cupboard or escaping from a balcony window, as Don Alonso does in *No hay burlas con el amor*.

This type of "physical" comedy is characteristic of cloak-and-sword plays, yet it would be wrong to regard it as predominant. We should bear in mind that most of the escapes and other comic incidents of a cloak-and-sword plot are brought about by a feverishly plotting "cloak-and-sword" mind, which in many cases is that of the female protagonist. One might mention Ángela, "la dama duende," whose impish ingenuity is equalled by that of Marcela in *Casa con dos puertas* or Clara in *Mañanas de abril y mayo*. Such amusing heroines bring fine irony, subtle double meanings, witty asides, and even some delightfully rhetorical sarcasm in their exchanges with jealous lovers, preoccupied brothers or fathers, exasperated friends, and pert maidservants. Even the *graciosos* (the comic lackeys of Golden-Age plays), though they provide physical comedy in abundance by preparing to run while their masters stand to fight and by lustful advances to maidservants, even as their masters beg the leading ladies for the merest glimpse of the beauty behind their veils, are still more noteworthy for their witty remarks than for their comic actions. Some of the most entertaining comments delivered by the *graciosos* make mock of the very dramatic conventions upon which cloak-and-sword plays depend. In Act I of *Casa con dos puertas*, for instance, Calabazas warns us to expect "dos grandísimos romances" from Félix and Lisardo (Calderón's traditional method of providing us with preliminary information necessary for understanding the plot), and, indeed, to our amusement, these gallants successively bombard each other with "two enormous speeches."

A more extensive parody of *comedia* conventions is delivered by the *gracioso* Arceo in Act III of *Mañanas de abril y mayo*. Discovering a man in her room, Doña Ana is terrified for her honor and threatens to kill herself if he does not leave immediately. The man is, in fact, only the lackey, Arceo, who, however, decides to play the part of the dignified gallant which Ana has assigned to him. Arceo offers a superb parody of the type of speech frequently addressed in absolute seriousness by gallant *comedia* gentlemen to ladies whose privacy they have invaded. With an air of mock gravity he assures Ana that

Matters of import	Grandes casos de fortunas
Have brought me to your house. I did not come	A vuestra casa me traen, no a hacer mella en vuestras joyas,
To steal your jewels nor to outrage your honor.	ni a vuestra opinión ultraje.
And therefore that you may be quite assured	Y porque os aseguréis de mi término galante,
Of my discreet intentions, and be safe,	segura quedáis de mí.
Farewell! God keep you, lady!	A Dios, señora, que os guarde.

Much entertainment could be derived in performance from these words addressed to Doña Ana, not least by exploiting the dramatic contrast between the lackey's mock seriousness and the authenticity of the lady's fright.

The very variety of humor mixed into a typically Calderonian cloak-and-sword play might provide one reason why a work such as *Casa con dos puertas* or *Mañanas de abril y mayo* or *No hay burlas con el amor* retained its popularity through centuries of changing tastes and with audiences of different nationalities. But there are other factors contributing to their vitality. For instance, what we have called the "physical comedy" of the cloak-and-sword plays—the switches in identity, the dashing hide-and-seek scenes, the unexpected arrivals and panic departures through a confusion of doors—is of a type that has consistently entertained all manner of persons from the era when the comedies of Plautus triumphed in Rome to twentieth-century England with its seemingly insatiable appetite for the Whitehall farces put on by Brian Rix and company. As for Calderón's verbal humor, much of it depends on or refers to human weaknesses which would be amusingly familiar to any audience of any country at any period, inviting us to delight in the discomfiture of someone guilty of lust, pride, greed, cowardice, or deception. One might mention the discomfiture suffered by the rake Hipólito in *Mañanas de abril y mayo*, our enjoyment of which is much enhanced by a wittily sarcastic remark delivered by his exasperated friend Luis. Repeatedly Hipólito has boasted that he has a truly extraordinary "way with women" ("notable estrella con mujeres"). In Act II, however, he is contemptuously dressed down by his mistress, Doña Ana. And Luis cannot resist inviting his boastful friend to eat his favorite words, with the comment: "In all my life I've never met a man / Who has such winning manners with the ladies!" ("¡En toda mi vida he hallado / hombre de tan buena estrella / con mujeres!").

Witty repetitions are similarly employed in *No hay burlas con el amor* to increase the amusement which we derive from the crashing fall of proud Beatriz from her ostentatious pedestal of virtue. One might indicate, for instance, the scene between the sisters in Act II in the course of which Leonor becomes aware that their father is eavesdropping on their conversation. She immediately begins to play the role of virtuous sister and to accuse the astonished Beatriz of having a secret suitor, of which very offence Leonor is herself guilty. Hilariously, she delivers her accusation using the almost identically phrased exclamations of horror directed by the affectedly self-righteous Beatriz against her wayward younger sister in the previous act: "draw not nigh me" ("Tente, / no te apropincues a mí"); "Do not tarnish / The gleaming whiteness of my chaste *persona*" ("No me empañes el candor / de mi castísmo bulto"); "I cannot have / A libidinous sister" ("que tener no puedo yo / hermana libidinosa").

Admittedly, Calderón's cloak-and-sword plays always contain a proportion of witticisms which are topical in that they allude to contemporary events, social types of the period, customs, fashions, and so forth. Not all of these have traveled well across borders or down centuries. Calabazas' anecdote, in *Casa con dos puertas*, directed against unscrupulous tailors and describing the terrors of having a suit made to measure, like Moscatel's story about the amateur bull-fighter in *No hay burlas con el amor*, was doubtless uproariously received in seventeenth-century Spain but would scarcely raise a smile in twentieth- century England. Nevertheless, the majority of even such topical references are still surprisingly "topical" to this day—jokes about inflation and the cost of living, for instance, or satire on superstitions, mockery of lawyers, ridicule of doctors. *No hay burlas con el amor* even contains a jocular reference to that seemingly most modern figure of fun, the excessively long-lived mother-in-law.[18]

A list of topical witticisms in Calderón's comedies would include those numerous mocking references to his own favorite cloak-and-sword devices: lengthy explanatory monologues, veiled ladies, inquisitive servants, hidden lovers, and others. Yet, this mockery of seventeenth-century dramatic conventions appears to have lost none of its capacity to amuse along the way to our modern age. When, for example, Don Alonso in Act II, scene 5, of *No hay burlas con el amor*, having been urged by Beatriz to hide in a cupboard because her father is approaching, voices the complaint, "Is this a comedy by Calderón / In which there has to be a hidden lover / Or a veiled lady?" ("¿Es comedia de Don Pedro Calderón / donde ha de haber / por fuerza amante escondido, / o rebozada mujer?"), a twentieth-century audience might be even more amused than an audience of the playwright's own period. A modern audience would not, of course, have seen enough Calderonian comedies to appreciate fully how frequently in them lovers hide in order to avoid an encounter with honorable fathers. On the other hand, they would derive much additional entertainment by drawing a hilarious contrast between the extreme permissiveness of their own society and the strict rules regarding courtship and marriage which dominated Spanish society in the Golden Age. Moreover, it should be remembered that when Calderón mocks the *comedia* conventions in this way he is breaking the dramatic illusion, and this type of disruption is one of the most frequently used techniques of modern theatre. Audiences nowadays are conditioned to expect, and enjoy, reminders that they are witnessing not life but an imitation of life. Of course, a good proportion of such reminders in modern plays are inserted not simply to amuse us but to make us reflect seriously about the difficulty of distinguishing between reality and the illusion of reality. But it should be remembered that the Baroque age of Calderón and Cervantes was as obsessed as we are by the problems posed by the nature of truth. When Calderón shatters the illusion of reality in comedies like *No hay burlas con el amor* he expects us to think as well as to laugh; for even in his comedies the playwright is deeply concerned to convey his "serious sense of life."

The extent to which Calderón's comedies reflect his "serious sense of life" has been clearly demonstrated by Bruce W. Wardropper in an important article from the title of which we have borrowed this phrase.[19] Until now we have concentrated on the humorous aspects of Calderón's cloak-and-sword plays. But it is equally important to remember that these plays are not farces, despite the "hide-and-seek" incidents and other farcical elements of their plots. Most great comedies have some farcical content: *Twelfth Night*, *Le Misanthrope*, *The Importance of Being Earnest*, and *Playboy of the Western World*, to name a few of the most outstanding. Neither would it be accurate, despite their numerous passages of bubbling dialogue, breezy parody, airy word-play, and flashing repartee, to regard them simply as light comedies. Indeed, they might better be described as "serious comedies." It should not be forgotten that in his comedies Calderón constructs his plots upon fundamentally the same themes and issues, the same social attitudes and human predicaments, as those which form the stuff of tragedy in such works as *El pintor de su deshonra*, *El médico de su honra*, and *A secreto agravio, secreta venganza*. The theme of honor, attitudes to marriage, the question of a woman's virtue—of central significance in Calderón's wife-murder dramas—these are also key factors motivating human behavior in his comedies.[20] An outraged lover, brother, or father in a cloak-and-sword play never, of course, goes to the horrific extremes reached by Calderón's tragic wife-murderers. Nevertheless, such a character often delivers monologues in which he reveals obsessions, conflicts, and passions as violent and desperate as those to which his counterparts in tragedy give expression. So the spice of danger is added to the mixture of comedy. The audience recognizes in the speaker the capacity to murder in defense of his honor, and cannot help fearing for the safety of those he blames for his dire predicament. One might mention the soliloquy pronounced by Don Pedro, father of Beatriz and Leonor, in Act III of *No hay burlas con el amor.* This soliloquy is brief and its language might not seem particularly extreme at first impression. But the obsessive way in which Don Pedro repeats to himself the exact words spoken to him by Don Luis indicates a dangerously offended man. The latter has just withdrawn his offer for the hand of Pedro's daughter, Beatriz, and his final words were: "To marry Beatriz now conflicts with honor" ("porque hoy casar con Beatriz / no le está bien a mi honor"). These form the first words of Pedro's soliloquy, and it is plain that, however desperately he struggles to put some less terrible interpretation on them, inwardly he believes that his honor is compromised and that drastic measures may be necessary to retrieve it. Pedro's soliloquy is reminiscent of a key speech pronounced under not wholly dissimilar circumstances by the tragic hero of *A secreto agravio, secreta venganza.* Don Lope is warned by King Sebastian that rather than accompany him to war he should remain at home with his new wife. In the speech that follows, Don Lope, like Don Pedro, broods upon the words of warning spoken to him.[21] But whereas Don Pedro does not in fact move from desperate thoughts to drastic actions, Don Lope goes on to murder both his wife and the man who loves her.

Don Pedro is by no means one of the most dangerously extreme characters to figure in a Calderonian comedy. There are some men, for instance, who already have a history of violence when they first step on stage, such as Don Juan in *Mañanas de abril y mayo*, who has killed a man for reasons of jealousy and honor before the action of the play began. Then there is Félix in *Casa con dos puertas*, who not only makes violent speeches but comes perilously close to committing violent murder when he draws a dagger against his sister toward the end of the play. Her death is prevented only by the intervention of Lisardo, who restores Félix's honor by giving his hand to Marcela in marriage. Unlike the ill-fated wives of Calderón's honor-tragedies, the heroines of his comedies are invariably spinsters or widows, so that the ointment of matrimony can be liberally applied to heal wounds of honor and save threatened lives.

Despite the conventionally "happy" end bestowed by Calderón upon his cloak-and-sword plays, our awareness that these are comedies with a serious sense of life is never more acute than at their conclusion. Our knowledge of the personalities of the newly married couples is by then profound, and in most cases we are left with considerable misgivings as to their future lives together. There is usually at least one dissatisfied character at the end whose disgruntled comments intensify our unease. Don Pedro, for instance, accepts the marriage of his daughters to Alonso and Juan in *No hay burlas con el amor* only because, as he puts it: "once the damage is done / There is no other remedy" ("que ya sucedido el daño, / nada puede remediarse"). A still more deeply aggrieved person is Don Juan, who apparently agrees to marry Doña Ana at the end of *Mañanas de abril y mayo*, but does so dispiritedly ("sin alma"), while remaining depressed by some lingering doubts as to her virtue. One might well fear not simply for the happiness but for the life of Doña Ana, married to this pathologically suspicious husband.[22] Félix in *Casa con dos puertas* is another gallant who instills pessimism in the audience. Within the play he almost murders his sister. Might he not murder his wife outside it if he feels his honor threatened?[23] At the end of such plays we are left with the impression that what we have just seen enacted is a comedy-prologue that will be followed in a short space by a wife-murder tragedy of Calderonian proportions.[24]

There seems no doubt that the more serious features of Calderón's comedies, far from diminishing their popularity with audiences of his own country and period, in fact increased them. Calderón, after all, was as conscious as was Lope that "honor subjects are the best because they affect everybody deeply" ("los casos de honra son mejores / porque mueven con fuerza a toda gente").[25] His comedies reflect the characteristic preoccupations of his society: its respect for nobility of blood, its belief in male authority, its obsession with feminine virtue, its concern for personal reputation. Modern audiences may see certain aspects of the code of honor as extremely remote from their own experiences. On the other hand, they do not need a profound understanding of the nature of the honor code to appreciate its social function and implications, to realize that it forces men to behave in ways that their society finds acceptable but which may be against their emotional, moral, or spiritual development as individuals. Realizing this much, a modern audience, well accustomed to attending twentieth-century plays which dramatize the inwardly destructive effects of outer pressures upon members of their own society to conform, would surely react with thoughtful interest to the anxieties and predicaments of characters such as Don Pedro in *No hay burlas*, Don Juan in *Mañanas de abril y mayo*, and Don Félix in *Casa con dos puertas*. As for the problems of Calderón's female protagonists, who in an age of sexual inequality dare to assert their independence from male domination to the extent of seeking to choose their own marriage partners, these could hardly fail to engage the deep attention of audiences in this "liberated" era of ours, obsessed with examining the role and establishing the rights of women. Not that Calderón's fondness for portraying independently minded women is a reason for regarding him as a "feminist" ahead of his time. While he was sympathetically disposed toward women like Marcela in *Casa con dos puertas*, oppressed by a particularly domineering male guardian, the customary marriages at the end of his cloak-and-sword plays demonstrate his conviction that a woman's natural place was in the home under male supervision.

To conduct a thorough search into Calderón's stagecraft would be to move too far beyond the limits of an introductory study. Nevertheless, our attempts to explain the enduring popularity of his cloak-and-sword plays could scarcely be considered adequate if we failed to identify his principal skills as a dramatic technician. In the first place, he is a master of variations of pace and management of timing. When appropriate, he can convey an impression of leisureliness, as, for example, early in Act I of *Casa con dos puertas*, when he gives us necessary background information and sufficient time to assimilate it properly by including two unhurriedly lengthy speeches, pronounced in turn by Félix and Lisardo. He is equally adept at instilling in us an urgent sense of time's insufficiency. In the last scene of this first act we listen to an argument between Félix and Laura, she unreasonably jealous, he exasperatedly attempting to persuade her that she has no grounds. As his hasty protests are sharply countered by her accusations, as explanations are cut short by impatient innuendos, we feel the atmosphere quicken with their irritation and are made to share their uneasy awareness that her father may return at any moment. Inevitably her father suddenly does return, his arrival through one door only just preceded by Félix's exit by another. A scene in Act II brings a different pace, now not simply urgent but frenetic. The action begins to gather speed with the untimely arrival of Laura's father, Fabio, before Marcela has completed her assignation with Lisardo in Laura's house. Lisardo takes refuge in an inner room, while hard upon Fabio's arrival comes Marcela's steward to take her home. Fabio politely goes with Marcela to see her on her way, leaving the excited Laura to manage Lisardo's removal in the inadequately short space of time created by Fabio's temporary absence. The pace quickens still further when Laura's own lover, Félix, appears before Lisardo can be shown the door, and Laura must use up precious moments feverishly persuading Félix to leave. Her pressing excuse is her father's imminent return; but no sooner has Félix agreed to leave than indeed her father returns. The action is then rushed to a headlong climax when Félix attempts a hurried retreat into the very room in which Lisardo is hidden, and is impelled by jealousy to the over-hasty conclusion that his mistress has another lover.

Calderón's skills in pace and timing are more than matched by his abilities to create, manipulate, and sustain dramatic suspense, as a later scene in Act II of *Casa con dos puertas* should suffice to demonstrate. We refer to the confrontation between Félix and Laura in the former's house. This scene forms both a parallel and a contrast to the tensely argumentative scene between the same pair of lovers in the previous act: a parallel, because the lovers again engage in a furious exchange of jealous reproaches, sarcastic retorts, and injured protests of innocence, even repeating some of the phrases used on the earlier occasion; a contrast, because this time it is Félix who is violently jealous and Laura who is trying to convince him of her devotion, and this time their

argument is overheard by Marcela, secretly listening behind the tapestry. Marcela is in a state of fearful uncertainty lest Laura reveal to Félix
that the man he saw in Laura's room was his own sister's lover. The
audience are as conscious of her danger as is Marcela herself, and
indeed, have heard her in a previous scene caution Lisardo to say
nothing to Félix of their relationship and gravely warn him: "if your
indiscretion should arouse / suspicion then my life, at very least, /
Would surely be endangered, and what is more, / My honor would be,
too" (". . . me van en rigor, / a una sospecha creída, / hoy por lo menos
la vida, / y por lo más el honor"). Calderón skillfully increases both
Marcela's fear and our fears for her by allowing both her and us to witness
the steadily intensifying pressure exerted upon Laura by Félix's questions, and her progressively diminishing resistance. Thus her initial firm
denial that she knows anything about the man seen by Félix in her room
gives way under his rigorous inquisition to her reluctant admission,
"although I can tell you, / You must not learn it" ("aunque lo puedo
decir, / tú no lo puedes saber"), a response that provokes him to still
more insistent probing and her eventually to complete capitulation. But
with tension at its height and the audience in keenest expectation of
Marcela's downfall, at the very moment when Laura begins to tell all ("sí
diré"), Marcela takes direct action to prevent Laura's revelations and
provides a diversion by emerging from behind the tapestry, her veil of
course in place to conceal her identity, crossing the stage with an angry
gesture toward Félix as she passes. This last-minute intervention—
another example, if one were needed, of Calderón's impeccable sense of
dramatic timing—allows Laura to turn the tables upon Félix and to
counter his accusation "I saw a man there in your room" ("vi en tu
aposento un hombre") with a counter-charge of her own: "And in yours I
saw a woman" ("Yo en el tuyo una mujer"). With Marcela out of immediate danger, tension slackens, but not enough for us to relax more than a
little. The second act ends with Félix and Laura still engaged in stormy
disagreement, and we can anticipate from Félix's angrily sceptical retorts
that he intends to probe the matter further. Under Calderón's guidance
we therefore move on to Act III in a register of excited misgiving
precisely calculated to ensure our maximum enjoyment of further predicaments and additional confrontations.

    Another stage technique in which Calderón excels is in the manip-
ulation of dramatic irony. His cloak-and-sword plays are loaded with
instances of irony, but we shall restrict ourselves to mentioning two
examples. In the second act of *No hay burlas con el amor* Beatriz is
visited by Alonso, who makes eloquent protestation of his love for her, a
common enough occurrence in Golden-Age comedy, but made extraordinarily hilarious for the audience on this occasion by the fact that the
chaste Beatriz, though horrified by his intrusion, accepts unques-

tioningly the sincerity of his declaration. Beatriz prides herself upon her indifference to men, while believing, in her vanity, that no man could fail to be infatuated by her beauty. We know, however, that Alonso is only pretending to be in love with Beatriz. We have heard, after all, in a previous scene between Alonso and his friend Don Juan, what is Alonso's true attitude to Beatriz. He would "rather fight with ten plain men at once" (con diez hombres legos") than woo so pedantic a woman. It is clearly only with great difficulty that Juan manages to persuade Alonso to pretend to be in love with Beatriz, a ploy devised by Leonor to distract her elder sister's attention from her own love affair with Juan. With our memories of this recent scene still fresh, we can relish the contrast between Alonso's seemingly eager pronouncements of devotion and his authentic feelings of reluctance. But it is not until later in the play, in the course of a second disagreement between the two friends, on which occasion it is Juan who is reluctant and Alonso who is the gallant eager to return to Beatriz's house, that we experience the full charge of irony laid by Calderón in the scene of Alonso's first encounter with Beatriz. For as Alonso strives to persuade his friend to accompany him on a second visit to Beatriz, it becomes clear that on that first visit, even as Alonso regaled Beatriz with manufactured compliments, conscious all the while of his lack of genuine feelings for her, below the level of his own awareness he was beginning to be drawn to her beauty and attracted by her personality.

We take our second illustration of Calderón's handling of dramatic irony from the encounter between Don Juan and the veiled Doña Clara in the park in Act III of *Mañanas de abril y mayo*. Irony here is generated in the first place by our knowledge of Clara's true identity while Juan suffers under the wrong assumption that he is addressing Doña Ana. Ironies of misunderstanding soon proliferate, however, when Juan hurls insults at the woman he believes to be his mistress. For if these insults had been applied to Ana they would have been entirely inappropriate. Despite all Juan's jealous suspicions, Ana is a woman of exemplary conduct, as the audience is well aware. The audience is equally conscious that the scheming Clara in fact deserves the insults heaped upon her: "False siren, harpy, lying sphinx, you serpent / That lurks beneath your beauty's snow and roses" ("falsa sirena y engañosa arpía, / esfinge mentirosa, / áspid de nieve y rosa"). Yet a further ironical dimension is added when Clara reacts with outraged indignation to the charges, and Don Juan withdraws them with the sincere, but, as we appreciate, mistaken apology: "Forgive me, madam, / My words were not for you" ("Perdonad, mi señora, / que no hablaba con vos").

We hope that the observations so far made regarding *Casa con dos puertas*, *Mañanas de abril y mayo*, and *No hay burlas con el amor* have established their value as excellent examples of the cloak-and-sword genre. But some further comments might now be offered on each play separately to demonstrate its individual merits.

Casa con dos puertas mala es de guardar

The critic Valbuena Briones has described *Casa con dos puertas* as simply a "copy with variations" ("copia con variantes") of *La dama duende,* an opinion we do not share.[26] It is true that *Casa con dos puertas* derives the basis of its plot from *La dama duende.* Both comedies introduce us to a heroine whose brother has brought a male guest to the house, but who, out of concern for his honor, insists that she keep herself hidden away from his guest in a concealed room. In both cases the brother's prohibition only serves to stimulate the sister's curiosity about the guest and to provoke her into devising ways of meeting him. As Marcela amusingly puts it in Act II, scene I: "when one finds a book with lines erased, / One's curiosity is roused to read them" ("y es como el que halla en un libro / borradas algunas letras, / que por sólo estar borradas, / le da más gana de leerlas"). Nevertheless, comparison of the two plays reveals significant differences in both plot development and characterization, sufficient differences indeed to justify our view that *Casa con dos puertas* is a play of outstandingly individual merit.

It should be noted, for instance, that whereas in *La dama duende* most of the action centers upon one house, that of Ángela and her brothers, in *Casa con dos puertas* Calderón chooses to diversify rather than centralize, and two different houses are made into places of equal importance for the progress of the plot. Moreover, both these houses are designed by the dramatic architect with special features that facilitate deceptions, cause complications, and increase confusions. The house of Félix and Marcela has a hidden room, its entrance concealed by a screen or tapestry, which therefore fulfills the same function as the famous fake cupboard in *La dama duende.* There is, however, no equivalent in the earlier play to the special feature which characterizes Laura's house. Hers is the "House with Two Doors" mentioned in the title, and the two doors are used for a frenzy of exits and arrivals which conspire with the excited comings and goings within Félix's house to perpetrate a hilarious complexity of intrigue, outdoing even that created by the tricky maneuvers and the flurried exits and entrances of *The Phantom Lady.*

Also noteworthy is the fact that Calderón furnishes his "House with Two Doors" with two heroines. In *La dama duende* Ángela dominates the action, her friend Beatriz being assigned to a decidedly subsidiary role. But Marcela's friend Laura in *Casa con dos puertas* is given a part equal in importance to that of Marcela herself. Laura is even supplied, like Marcela, with an overprotective guardian: her father,

Fabio, behaves like an older version of Marcela's watchful brother, Félix. The female protagonists are both well characterized and what is more, given interestingly different personalities, the contrast in their moods, attitudes, and conduct representing one of the play's most salient qualities. Marcela is sister to the phantom lady. An adventuresome and inquisitive spirit, she breaks out of the confinement imposed by her brother and zestfully sets about bringing novelty, mystery, and romance into her life. Yet she is not simply a copy of Ángela. The latter was a widow, experienced in love and sensuous by nature. Marcela is much more innocently mischievous, far more youthfully impetuous and opportunist. When she tries to prevent Lisardo from departing from her brother's house in Act II, she blurts out her love for him with unashamedly youthful directness: "My lord Lisardo, / It seems to me that it is not gallant / To leave Ocaña thus, without your saying / Goodbye to one who loves you" ("Señor Lisardo, no se / que sea acción cortesana / el iros sin despediros / hoy de una mujer que os ama"). And near the end of Act III, when she prefers to lie to save herself rather than protect Laura's reputation by telling the truth (namely, that Laura is not the veiled lady brought by Félix from Laura's house), there is a youthful ring to the selfishness of her whispered response to the enraged aside of Laura:

| **Laura:** You do me wrong, Marcela. | Pues, tú, Marcela, me agravias. |
| **Marcela:** Yes; but every man
Is for himself. | Sí, que soy primero yo. |

Marcela's inexperience of life also manifests itself in her unfailing optimism. When she seeks to persuade Laura to let her use her house for a meeting with Lisardo, she blithely assures her doubtful friend that nothing can go wrong because surely they'll not get "caught the first time we transgress" ("luego han de cogernos en el primer hurto?"). This optimistic view is soon proved to be mistaken by the return of Fabio, Laura's father, while Lisardo is still in the house, an unhappy occurrence which prompts Laura to scold her friend by sarcastically echoing Marcela's previous words of reassurance: "You see, Marcela, that we have indeed / Been caught red-handed in our first transgression" ("¿Ves, Marcela? En el primero / hurto al fin nos han cogido").

In contrast to the optimistically adventurous Marcela, Laura believes in playing safe, and the predicaments in which she finds herself in *Casa con dos puertas* are generally, like the one just mentioned, created for her by her friend's behavior. Laura takes a decidedly pessimistic view of life, always tending to assume the worst, a characteristic which she shares with Don Juan, the lover of Doña Ana in Calderón's *Mañanas de abril y mayo*. These two characters even tend to express their pessimism in similar terms. Thus, for instance, in Act I, scene 1, Don Juan insists to his friend Don Pedro that "Bad news is more reliable than good" because "the bad news / Invariably turns out to be true, / And the other kind inevitably false" ("Es más honrado / el mal que el bien"; "uno siempre está tratando verdad, y otro está mintiendo"). We might compare these words with Laura's assertion to Félix in Act I, scene 3, that bad events have always spoken the truth ("dijeron verdad siempre"). Laura also reminds us of Juan in that her brooding pessimism, like his, is mostly applied to matters of love. Both persuade themselves that their lovers are unfaithful. There is a difference, however: Juan's jealousy develops from the fact that he had encountered another gentleman in Ana's garden, whereas Laura's jealous obsession that Félix is being unfaithful to her with a woman called Nise is almost entirely founded on her own suspicious imaginings. Jealous women are commonplace in Golden-Age comedy, but women so absurdly and persistently jealous as Laura are rare. Félix's affair with Nise had ended before his relationship with Laura, and the opening scene, began. He never sees Nise in the course of the play; indeed, she makes not one single appearance. Laura, however, imagines that she sees her at every turn. Thus she is convinced that the mysteriously veiled woman who crosses the room during her argument with Félix in Act II (in reality Marcela) must be the hated Nise. Even at the end of Act III, when Félix brings a veiled woman to his house (again Marcela), Laura is still sure that the woman is Nise.

Laura's absurdly unreasonable jealousy lends her character an admirable degree of individuality. It also serves to illustrate Calderón's exceptional ability to loosen and disarrange the tidily established conventions of the cloak-and-sword genre in the interests of dramatic novelty. It makes a refreshing change to discover that the unhappy Félix at the beginning of *Casa con dos puertas* is not one of those innumerable *comedia* gallants jealously laboring under the misapprehension that his mistress has another admirer, but is, on the contrary, a man quite differently aggrieved, having been wrongly accused of infidelity by his jealous lady.

Two more examples of Calderón's ability to make creatively dramatic changes in cloak-and-sword conventions are worthy of mention, both taken from Act III. In this final act Laura takes advantage of her father's absence (he has left to spend some days on his country estate) to move into Marcela's room in Félix's house, for, jealously suspicious as ever, she wishes to spy secretly upon his movements. She has also agreed that Marcela can again use her "house with two doors" for an assignation with Lisardo. An audience knowledgeable of *comedia* conventions might well expect soon to witness a scene within the house in which the lovers' meeting will be interrupted by Fabio's sudden return. Indeed, there has already been such a traditional scene, with just such an interruption in the previous act. But this time Calderón chooses to disturb our complacent expectations by introducing variations to the norm. Unexpectedly, the scene switches to a road near Ocaña where we come upon Laura'a father at the very moment of his decision to return home (after a fall from his horse). The playwright exploits the scene admirably to create a high register of suspense. Fabio's decision puts us into a mood of excited anticipation, which intensifies still further when the old man tells his servant that he intends to use the other door of the house on his return, that is, the door further from his daughter's room, so as to avoid disturbing her at so late an hour. (She of course, is not at home where he imagines her to be.) Fabio's discovery of Marcela and Lisardo now impresses us as unavoidable, and we await with considerably more eagerness and concern than we should have felt, had we not met Fabio on the road to Ocaña, the scene in Laura's house when Fabio enters through that "other" door. But in this case also Calderón proves much too good a dramatist to live entirely up to his audience's expectations. For, instead of bringing us inside to witness Fabio's confrontation with the lovers, he keeps us outside the house on the wrong side of one of its two doors, sharing directly in Félix's angry frustration as the gallant pounds on it in vain for entry. Calderón makes splendid use of offstage resources to tantalize us first with the sounds of Fabio's banging on the other door, then with the clash of swords and other noises of uproar. We strain our ears, with Félix, to interpret them, until at last "our" door opens and Lisardo emerges with the veiled Marcela. Ironically, having rescued her, he now endangers her life by charging Félix with her safety, but fortunately Marcela's brother does not share our knowledge of her identity and is convinced that she is Laura.

The characters of Félix and Lisardo, it should be observed, are almost as well drawn and as well contrasted as are those of Marcela and Laura. Lisardo is the true gentleman of the play: discreet gallant, protective lover, loyal friend, brave rescuer. The pursued, not the pursuer, in his relationship with Marcela, he is not the type of man to brag about his sexual appeal. Modestly, in Act I, scene 2, he declares that he cannot understand "how any men / Can be so vain, so arrogant, that they can / Boast that women have made advances to them" ("cómo hay hombres / tan vanos, tan arrogantes, / que de que ha habido mujeres / que los buscaron, se alaben"). Increasingly attracted to Marcela, he decides nevertheless to put friendship before love and leave the district when he is led to believe that his friend Félix is his rival for her affections. Félix, on the other hand, displays a strikingly less admirable, though perhaps for that reason more interesting, personality, dominated by two almost pathologically insistent impulses: his obsessive urge to safeguard his honor, evidenced by his unreasonable confinement of his sister; and his abnormally jealous nature, which drives him to a disturbingly physical outburst when he thunders upon the door of Laura's house at nightfall and bellows his grievances in a fury of selfish disregard for his lady's reputation. As we have seen, Laura also is possessed by an extraordinarily jealous disposition, so that we may strongly suspect that their stormy courtship will be followed by an extremely turbulent marriage, which could well end in tragic death if ever Félix's devilish suspicions should cause him to imagine that his wife has brought dishonor upon his name. But we can feel much more optimistic about the future married life of Lisardo with Marcela. His stable principles should steady her wilder urges, while her spirited zest for novelty should save him from the dullness of a too-worthy existence.

The dramatic quality of *Casa con dos puertas* is such that it displays only one feature that might seriously be criticized. We refer to Félix's extremely lengthy monologue in Act III, describing the hunting activities of Philip IV. As we have mentioned, this monologue, though present in the only surviving seventeenth-century manuscript, is not found in any of the early printed versions of the comedy. Several critics, notably Northup, have defended its inclusion. Northup argues that "Félix's description of the king's hunt finds its exact counterpart in Laura's account of the queen's boating party. . . . To restore Félix's parallel narrative is to restore to the play the one element necessary to make it completely symmetrical from start to finish."[27] J.E. Varey goes further. He reminds us that the play contains yet another speech in which the court is eulogized: Félix's monologue in Act I describing his first encounter with Laura in the gardens of the royal palace at Aranjuez. According to Varey, Calderón intended us to draw a contrast between the harmony and serenity of court life, as portrayed in these three speeches, and the predicaments, both comic and more serious, of his confused protagonists.[28] It is possible to go further still and to defend the inclusion in Act III of Félix's description of the hunt on the grounds that it throws additional light on his character. The obsessive way in which he dwells upon the gory details of the kill, upon the stage-by-stage destruction of the beautiful heron's delicate life by two ruthless birds of prey, suggests a man with a cruel fondness for displays of violence, an impression confirmed by his behavior later in this final act. Nevertheless, the fact remains, as Northup himself concedes, that Félix's wordy monologue clogs the progress of the action. Moreover, it seriously reduces the dramatic effectiveness of the scene in which it is pronounced, which offers an otherwise highly entertaining conversation between brother and sister in which Félix gravely explains to Marcela how a mysterious lady had appeared in his house and aroused the jealousy of Laura, while his sister (the veiled lady in question) stifles her laughter and gives fake exclamations of astonishment and sympathy. Remove from this scene Félix's lengthy description of the hunt, as seventeenth-century theatre producers evidently did, with or without the permission of the playwright, and *A House with Two Doors Is Difficult to Guard* becomes extremely difficult to fault.

Mañanas de abril y mayo

Calderón often used popular proverbs and sayings for the titles of his comedies, as both *Casa con dos puertas* and *No hay burlas con el amor* clearly demonstrate. In *Mañanas de abril y mayo* he again evidently exploits a proverb, but is influenced in addition by a popular song. The proverb which he had in mind was "Mañanas de abril, dulces son de dormir, las de mayo mejor, si no despierta el amor" ("April mornings are good for sleeping, May mornings even better, unless love awakens"). As for the popular song, which is also used by Lope in a number of plays, notably *El acero de Madrid*,[29] Calderón includes a version of it near the beginning of Act I:

Mornings of April and May,	Mañanicas floridas
Fresh-scented and joyful with song	de abril y mayo,
Rouse up my maiden today:	despertad a mi niña,
Let her not slumber so long.	no duerma tanto.

This is one of several glosses, echoes, and repetitions of the title inserted to remind us to associate the stirrings and upheavals of love with the awakening of spring. It is noteworthy that both proverb and song specify not simply the season but the time of day, a reference that it suited Calderón to retain, since his protagonists are presented as upper-class members of seventeenth-century Madrid society, and the ladies and gentlemen of that society were in the habit of rising early to meet their lovers discreetly, before too many people were abroad. It would appear that such a custom was not restricted to Golden-Age Spain. A character in Shakespeare's *Twelfth Night* alludes to love as "matter for a May morning," a phrase which at first we thought of borrowing for the title of our translation of Calderón's comedy.

Calderón adopts many methods to place his characters in a setting and atmosphere redolent of "Mornings of April and May," and so successfully that those aspects of his play are among its most memorable features. In particular, he situates several key scenes in the gardens of the Buen Retiro at dawn, notably the first encounter between Clara and Hipólito and the final scene of Act III. We have already conjectured that the first performance of *Mañanas de abril y mayo* took place in the real gardens of the Retiro. But audiences at subsequent performances in the public theatres (the *corrales*, or courtyards) would have to rely almost entirely on their imagination to distinguish between these morning scenes in gardens and, for instance, the night scenes in the houses of Doña Ana and Don Pedro, because stage effects were few, and in any case both day and night scenes were invariably performed in broad daylight.[30] Calderón, however, amply assisted them to sense the morning freshness and to visualize the flowering of spring. In a modern

theatre, equipped with suitable backdrops and sets, such assistance is of
course less necessary. Even so, Clara's enthusiastic declaration, as she
walks through the Park in Act I, that ". . . in all my life I've never
seen / So beautiful a morning" ("Mejor mañana no vi / en mi vida"), and
Hipólito's lyrical comments in Act III as he talks to the disguised Clara in
the Flower Garden, "Here on the margin of this flowery arbor / Which
spring embellishes with so much art" ("En aqueste hermoso mar-
gen, / en este florido albergue, / que la hermosa primavera / a tanto
estudio guarnece") still add to our appreciation of the scene. Even when
Calderón moves us away from the gardens into streets and houses, he
manages to ensure that we take with us the scent of morning and the
breath of spring. In Pedro's house, for instance, when Hipólito in a long
speech refers back to his morning meeting in the Park with a mysterious
lady, he begins his lyrical description:

I went this morning	Esta mañana salí
To that green loveliness, that brake divine,	a ese verde hermoso sitio, a esa divina maleza,
That pleasing paradise, the royal Park	a ese ameno paraíso,
[Act I, sc. 5]	a ese parque. . . .

The same character also stimulates our memories of gardens on spring
mornings in Act II (none of which actually takes place in the Park), as he
lingers in the street outside Doña Ana's house. He pronounces a eulogy
in which he associates Ana with Flora, mother of spring (to his delight,
and our amusement, he discovers that the house of "Flora" is situated,
appropriately, on Garden Street), then delivers this lavishly meta-
phorical bouquet:

Here is	
The balcony where Dawn may well appear	Este es el balcón por donde, en tornasoles envuelta,
At any hour, appareled in sunflowers,	sale el alba a todas horas,
And garlanded with jessamine and lilies,	de jazmines y azucenas coronada, pues el día
For surely it is here, behind her por-tals,	en sus umbrales despierta.
Where Dayspring rises.	

It must be said that the type of imagery used by Hipólito here is
commonplace in the *comedia:* lovesick gallants regularly compare their
ladies to spring, describe their beauty in terms of flowers or sunlight,
associate their arrival with the coming of dawn. But the number of such
comparisons and associations in this play is extraordinary. Hipólito
meets Clara in the royal Park and exclaims regarding the veil that
conceals her face:

your cloudy veil
Conceals the morning in its folds, and
you
Control the sunrise. At whatever hour
You deign to manifest your fiery bril-
liance,
At that precise moment dawn would
break,
Day would have light, the breath of
dawn would blow [Act I, sc. 3]

esa negra sutil nube
trae consigo la mañana;
y a cualquier hora que vos
descubriérades la llama,
amaneciera, y tuviera
luz el día, aliento el aura.

He pursues Clara from the Park into Ana's house and begs her forgiveness that he:

should dare to tread the sphere,
This porch that's canopied with flowers
of spring,
And you resplendent in your love-
liness,
The sweetest flower of all [Act I, sc. 4]

la esfera,
dosel florido de la primavera,
donde son vuestros bellos
resplandores
la primera oficina de las flores,
pisar mi pie presuma.

Later he will follow Ana into the Flower Garden in the Retiro, with the
words:

since I go with you, O lovely
goddess
Of these green meadows, any place
will be
the Flower Garden; for the green and
purple hues
Are dim beside the sparkle of your
eyes,
And fountain's pearl and crystal far surpassed
By your foot's snowy whiteness.
[Act III, sc. 2]

que yendo con vos, hermosa
deidad de estos campos verdes,
cualquier sitio será
la Florida; que le deben
a vuestros ojos de fuego
y a vuestra planta de nieve
púrpura y verde las flores,
cristal y aljófar las fuentes.

And we could mention other allusions of this kind.[31] There can be
no doubt that their accumulated profusion results from the playwright's
deliberate intention to create an atmosphere appropriate to his comedy.
Neither is there any question that the familiar images of dawn and the
conventional comparisons with spring, drooping from general seventeenth-century use, are brightened and revived by their contact with
the freshness of Calderón's *Mornings of April and May*.

The freshness in the air of *Mañanas de abril y mayo* is matched by
the freshness assumed by several of its main characters, notably Clara, to
whom, indeed, the very adjective "airosa" (breezy, zestful, jaunty) is

applied on several occasions. Clara is different from the usual cloak-and-sword heroine in that her way of life is unhindered by overprotective male relations. She appears to be happily fatherless and brotherless, and consequently exhibits herself on her balcony and parades about the Park at will. Her maid sums up for her exactly the sort of woman she is in Act I, scene 2: "You are a woman, if I may be frank, / Who likes her freedom—doing what she will, / Whether right, or wrong" (". . . en justo o injusto / muy amiga de tu gusto / de tu libertad amiga"). When we first meet her, for instance, she is on her way to the Park, determined to go there that particular morning simply because her lover, Don Hipólito, has ordered her to stay at home. In this case we must admire her independence of mind and applaud her action as "right." On the other hand, we are soon to see her "doing what she will" in a way that is morally "wrong" when she takes refuge from Hipólito in Ana's house. Not only does she tell Ana (a stranger to her) an entirely untrue story about fleeing from an irate husband, but, as she takes refuge in an inner room, she deliberately leaves her distinctively jaunty white hat in Ana's hands, so that Hipólito will assume that the innocent Ana was the veiled lady who teased him in the Park. Not that we can dislike or condemn Clara for her behavior: we derive too much amused enjoyment from her clever impulsiveness. And she continues to engage our affectionate good humor through the rest of the play.

The fond pleasure which we take in her reaches its height at the end of Act II, when she takes her revenge upon Hipólito for being a "false-hearted lover" by revealing in an eloquently abusive speech that she, and not Ana, was the lady whom he courted in the Park. Much of Clara's attractiveness as a heroine derives from her lack of that solemn respectability embodied by the other female protagonist.[32] Ana keeps to her own house as much as possible and does her best to safeguard her reputation. Yet, ironically, she finds not just her identity but also her moral character confused with that of the flighty Clara. But in the course of the play Clara at least pursues only one man. And her love for him is genuine, as her jealous reaction to his interest in Ana reveals. Moreover, her flighty extremes of conduct are provoked to a considerable degree by her eagerness to retain her lover's attentions; for, as she clearly recognizes, Hipólito is irresistibly drawn to a woman who keeps him guessing. The man himself admits as much in conversation with his friend Luis in Act I, scene 3: ". . . I'm much attracted / By a designing woman. That is the [only] reason / That I love Doña Clara" (". . . ya veis cuanto me arrastra / una mujer tramoyera, / pues el serlo sólo es causa / de que a doña Clara ame").

Unlike Doña Clara, Hipólito, the other most strongly individualized character in the play, is portrayed as an incorrigible rake. Valbuena Briones suggests that Hipólito is based on a real individual known to the playwright.[33] More probably, Calderón was concerned to satirize not a person but a social type that he despised, the "every lady's man" or "señor para-todas" (to borrow Clara's scornful description of her faithless lover), who spoils the happiness and mars the reputation of every woman toward whom he directs his dishonorable intentions, yet who, if he happens to contemplate marriage, looks about, as rakes usually do, for a lady "noble, virtuous, / And well-reputed" ("de buena opinión y honesta") (Act II, scene 1). Hipólito describes Doña Ana approvingly in those terms when he tells his friend Don Luis that he hopes to marry her within the month. Not that we can take Hipólito seriously as a man with marriage genuinely in mind. We remember too well his cynical advice to Luis: "love a host of women, / All for your pleasure, none to your regret" ("querer por tu gusto a todas, / por tu pesar a ninguna") (Act III, scene 2). We might recall especially the manner in which he recoils horror-struck when Ana expresses the belief that he is a married man: "I will not be encumbered with a wife, / For that's a shock I won't recover from" ("pero no me acumuléis / que soy casado, que es susto / de que jamás sanaré") (Act II, scene 3).

Hipólito continues unrepentantly on his philandering way, despite Clara's efforts to teach him a lesson. Even after Clara has made it bluntly clear that Ana never has been interested in him, that it is she, not Ana, who has been flirting with him, Hipólito persists in attempting to woo Ana, while at the same time still pretending devotion to Clara. Deceiver to the last, when he discovers in the Flower Garden at the end of Act III that once again he has been wooing Clara in the mistaken belief that she was Doña Ana, he attempts to retrieve the situation by persuading Clara that he has been aware of her true identity throughout their conversation. Fortunately she is unconvinced and prefers to retain her independence, claiming that she loves him no longer, rather than accept marriage to him, an attitude which Hipólito, behaving in character, accepts with relief rather than disappointment.[34] Their failure to marry should be applauded as an admirable departure by the playwright from the conventional ending in the interests of psychological truth.

The outcome of the relationship of the other couple in the play, Juan and Ana, is less certain, though the ambiguity is possibly cause by a defective text rather than by any deliberate intention on the part of the playwright to end on a note of mystery. As the play stands, a director may choose either to show Juan accepting Ana's hand or to show him rejecting her. In the first instance, Juan's ambiguous observation to Luis: "And if my gratitude seems less than heartfelt / She [Ana] may express it for me by the warmth / Of her embrace" ("ella os pague con los brazos / lo que con alma no puedo") might be made clear for the audience by Juan's taking Ana in his arms. In the second case, Juan instead would turn away from Ana and push her into the arms of Luis to emphasize his continuing misapprehension that she is a woman of loose morals, unworthy to be his wife. One is reminded of the different interpretations that can be given

to the end of Shakespeare's *Measure for Measure*, in which Isabella
makes no response in words to the Duke's proposal of marriage, so that
when the play is staged she may either be shown to take his hand, or, as
in some recent productions, to turn away from him in disgust.

For our part, we are convinced that Juan and Ana are meant to
marry at the end of *Mañanas de abril y mayo*. Moreover, it seems
probable that their marriage figured unmistakably in the original text of
the comedy. Hartzenbusch draws attention to the speech in which Luis
declares that his grievance against Juan for the death of his cousin is
removed. The critic believes that this speech is defective, and leads us to
suppose that its missing lines contained an explanation for the presence
of Luis's cousin in Ana's garden, an explanation that demonstrated Ana's
innocence in the matter.[35] Hartzenbusch's opinion appears plausible,
not least because Ana's predicament reminds us forcefully of that of
several other wrongly accused Calderonian heroines whose innocence is
established by means of a last-minute speech of revelation. We are
reminded particularly of Leonor in *No siempre lo peor es cierto*. She,
like Ana, is a virtuous woman made to seem guilty by misleadingly
circumstantial evidence. Like Ana she is driven to a state of desperate
melancholy by her undeserved misfortunes. Like Ana she is in love with
a man of abnormally suspicious inclination, pessimistically disposed to
accept that "the worst is always certain." Leonor's predicament ends
when Diego finally confesses that he had invaded Leonor's room without
ever having received anything but the harshest discouragement from
her, and when Carlos, persuaded at last that "no siempre lo peor es
cierto," offers her his hand. Of course, no last-minute confession is
possible from the intruder in this play, since the violently jealous Juan
had killed him before the action began. It seems, however, reasonable to
assume that Luis was in his cousin's confidence and would therefore be
in a position to testify at the end that the key used by his cousin to enter
Ana's garden, that key which persuaded Juan of her complicity, was in
reality obtained by guile and without her knowledge.[36]

No hay burlas con el amor

In the 1630s the cloak-and-sword genre in Spain produced a new
subgenre, a grotesquely comic derivative known as the *comedia de
figurón*. Some of the best comedies of the Golden Age belong to this
subgenre, notably Rojas Zorrilla's *Entre bobos anda el juego* and Moreto's *El lindo Don Diego*. We have already alluded to the presence of
parody in cloak-and-sword comedies. The extravagantly extreme attitudes of the honorable gallant, the jealous lover, the virtuous lady are
mimicked for our entertainment by lackeys and ladies' maids. In the
comedia de figurón, parody of such attitudes is not simply present but

predominant, elaborated and exaggerated to the extent that it characterizes the entire action of the play. In *Mañanas de abril y mayo* there is, it will be recalled, one scene in which the *gracioso*, Arceo, is discovered by Doña Ana in her bedroom. In the darkness she mistakes him for a gallant and he then plays the part, to our profound amusement, of the solemn man of honor, concerned to safeguard a lady's reputation. In Rojas Zorrilla's *Donde hay agravios no hay celos, y amo criado*, the *gracioso*, Sancho, engages in a much more prolonged impersonation of a nobleman, in this case his master, while his master pretends to be the lackey, a hilarious reversal of roles which is maintained for more than two acts. Not even this grotesquely comic play, however, is a true example of the subgenre. The genuine *comedia de figurón* takes parody to still further reaches of grotesque absurdity. Sancho is a typical lackey who masquerades as a nobleman. The *figurón*-protagonist is not an impersonator but simply plays the fool by being himself. He is not a low-born lackey but an authentic nobleman, endowed by nature with an absurdly silly disposition. Don Diego in *El lindo Don Diego* is just such a *figurón*, a notably born *gracioso* figure, grotesquely unable to display the attitudes and maintain the standards of conduct demanded by his social class. Calderón never composed a pure *comedia de figurón*, but a number of his comedies display the influence of the subgenre. In *No hay burlas con el amor* he probably moves further away from the "straight" cloak-and-sword traditions and further toward the hilarious distortions of the *comedia de figurón* than he does in any of his other comedies.

What serves to distinguish *No hay burlas con el amor* from more typically cloak-and-sword plays is, above all, the manner in which two of its main characters, Alonso and Beatriz, are represented. Alonso displays an almost *figurón* personality, behaving for much of the play in a fashion much more characteristic of lackey-*gracioso* than of noble gallant. As for the real *gracioso* of the play, Alonso's servant, Moscatel, while not devoid of certain typically *gracioso* traits (when he is caught by Don Pedro in the latter's house he blurts out his master's name in predictably comic fear for his skin), he conducts himself generally in a fashion more appropriate to a nobleman than to a lackey. Calderón exploits the untypical traits of the man to throw into exaggerated relief the absurdly untraditional behavior of the master. In particular, the servant's behavior in love forms a grotesquely comic contrast to that of Alonso. For Moscatel appears in the first scene of Act I as a man genuinely in love ("de veras enamorado"). He sighs and describes his sighs as sighs from the soul ("suspiros que el alma debe"). He refers to the nobility of his passion. The *gracioso* speaks and suffers, in fact, in a manner strikingly reminiscent of any number of Golden-Age gallants, who express their grave sickness of love in the opening scenes of innumerable cloak-and-sword plays. Later Moscatel endures the other emotional afflictions that most commonly attack the Golden-Age dramatic hero. He experiences the anguish of jealousy when his beloved Inés attracts the attentions of his master, Alonso. And he even suffers a torment of worry about his honor, his lady's virtue, and her reputation. Moscatel's seriously felt passion, a source, needless to say, of much amusement for the audience, is strikingly different from the hearty disrespect displayed by his master toward the emotion of love. Alonso, indeed, displays an attitude to love directly contrary to that normally manifested by a cloak-and-sword nobleman. In the play's first scene he threatens to dismiss Moscatel from his service for daring to fall in love, which he considers to be:

The worst of rogueries, the basest deed,	la mayor bellaquería, bajeza y alevosía
The blackest perfidy that was ever found	que cupo en humano pecho, la más enorme traición,
In the heart of man, the greatest treachery	que haber pudo imaginado.
That could be imagined.	

Subsequently, he puts his feelings more bluntly in a down-to-earth comment that might have been made by any *comedia gracioso* when he declares that he "wouldn't give two figs for any love" the world had in it ("No daré por cuanto amor / hay en el mundo dos higas") (Act II, scene 4). But if Alonso is opposed to true love, he is certainly not against lust, and pursues a Celia here and a Clara there for purely sensual purposes. *Gracioso*-like, he will even make a lascivious grab for a buxom maidservant, as his treatment of Inés demonstrates. Also, he likes to take his erotic pleasures quickly. Accordingly, as he reveals in an entertaining monologue in Act II, he avoids respectable women, who would expect him to linger for hours in the street outside their balconies. In any case, he displays the *gracioso*'s aversion to physical discomfort, and would therefore always avoid the risk of being soaked by a bucket of slops thrown from a window on a cold night. He prefers, consequently, to consort with the other kind of women, those whose doors he can bang on for entry without bothering about their reputations; those who admit him on his first visit, even give him a seat, and doubtless more besides.[37]

Alonso's extraordinarily ungallant behavior continues well into the play. In the last scene of Act II, when the father of Beatriz and Leonor returns unexpectedly, he is discourteously reluctant to hide to protect the ladies' honor. Significantly, when he does hide it is not in the dignified refuge of an inner room; he has to squeeze, together with Moscatel, and in truly *gracioso* fashion, into the absurdly inadequate space provided by a well-stocked china cupboard. Then when the coast is clear he is told, like many a gallant before him, to make his escape by jumping from a balcony window. Diego, wooer of another Doña Beatriz, is invited to do exactly that at the end of Act I of *No siempre lo peor es cierto*. But Alonso does not respond to the invitation as Diego does. Instead, he reacts like Diego's lackey companion, Ginés: he hesitates in cowardly fashion and worries about the possibility of breaking a leg in the descent.[38]

If Alonso may therefore be regarded as almost a *figurón*, then Beatriz is just as nearly a *figurona*. She strikes us, indeed, as blood relation to Moreto's famous dandy, "el lindo Don Diego." Certainly she shares his extraordinary preoccupation with dress and appearance and his absurd vanity. Before we meet her in person, we are warned by Juan's description that

As for her dressing, she is so affected,
She tries all fashions but discards not
    any.
She curls her hair at least three times a
    day,
And she is never satisfied with it.
                [Act I, sc. 1]
	Tan afectada en vestirse,
	que en todos los usos nuevos
	    entra, y de ninguno sale.
	Cada día, por lo menos,
	    se riza dos a tres veces,
	y ninguna en su contento.

Moreover, like Diego, she believes absolutely in the "deadly" effects of her beauty upon the opposite sex. In her view, one glimpse of her is enough to make a man die of love for her on the spot. Such vanity makes her, as it makes Diego, credulous beyond belief. Like Moreto's fop, she will accept unquestioningly any ridiculous tale that others devise to deceive her, so long as it conforms to her conceit of herself. Thus Beatriz has as little difficulty in believing Alonso is madly enamored of her as Diego has in accepting that a countess is obsessed by his person. But vanity and credulity are not, all the same, Beatriz's principal defects, as they are in the case of Diego. Nor is her extraordinary prudery her most notable fault, though that characteristic is sufficiently dominant to make her recoil in horror from her sister's amorous activities and to make her resolve to tell tales to their father at the first opportunity. What characterizes Beatriz above all is her absurdly affected speech. She is, as Wilson puts it, "a pedantically Gongoristic lady."[39] She has devoted so much of her time to reading poets such as Góngora and his followers, instead of pursuing a normal womanly occupation like needlework, that she now speaks in the way her favorite poets write, with circumlocutions, in parentheses, with violent distortions of word order, and in particular by means of a vocabulary that persistently avoids ordinary words in favor of erudite or recondite terminology. Thus her mirror is her "magic glass" ("hechizo de crystal"), her gloves are her "gantes" ("quirotecas"), Leonor is her "libidinous sister" ("hermana libidinosa"); and when she alludes to her virtuous self it is to "the gleaming whiteness of my chaste *persona*" ("el candor / de mi castísimo bulto") (Act I, scene

2). An excellent example of her Gongoristic style is provided by her disapproving description of the love letter received by Leonor:

That sullied sheet on which a goose's quill	Ese manchado papel en quien cifró líneas breves
Has traced a few brief lines in Ethiop liquid	cálamo ansariano, dando cornerino vaso débil
From vessel of chalcedony	et etíope licor.
[Act I, sc. 2]	

As a comic character, Calderón's affected heroine surpasses her French descendants, Moliére's *Les Femmes savantes*, and at least equals her English counterpart in *Marriage á la mode*. As regards her antecedents, Calderón appears to be acknowledging a debt to Lope by his mention of *Los melindres de Belisa* in Juan's speech in the first act. But Beatriz should in no way be considered simply a derivative of Belisa, whose affectations are physical rather than linguistic (she fusses, she swoons, feels fevered, complains of chills) and who is not prudishly averse to men but has been spoiled by too many attentions from them, so that she is overcritical of her suitors and finds it impossible to select one who fits all her requirements for a husband. Lope's *La dama boba* might be another source of inspiration. Finea, far from being an intellectual pedant like Beatriz, is presented as educationally subnormal; but there is a resemblance in that both women are transformed by love. Moreover, the contrast drawn by Lope between Finea and her cultured sister Nise may have made Calderón aware of the amusingly dramatic possibilities offered by sisterly rivalries. If these Lopean works are Calderón's only sources (admittedly, there may be others as yet undiscovered), then he deserves our unqualified admiration for the striking originality of his heroine.

Despite the "figuronish" behavior of both Alonso and Beatriz, *No hay burlas con el amor* is not really a full-blown *comedia de figurón*. An out-and-out *figurón* is impervious to change and to criticism. He may be taught a lesson in the course of the play by other characters who dislike him, but he is incapable of learning that lesson. Don Diego, for instance, is as vain and foppish at the end of *El lindo Don Diego* as he is at its beginning. On the other hand, both Alonso and Beatriz are reformed by the power of love, and leave their outlandish ways to become courtly gallant and conventional lady. Alonso's friend Juan has told him in the play's first scene that "it is love that makes a man courageous, / Generous, prudent, gallant" ("Amor es quien da valor / y hace al hombre liberal, / cuerdo y galán"). Alonso is disbelieving, but events prove Juan right. After falling in love with Beatriz, Alonso rejects silliness for good sense, as his earnest confession of his previous frivolity and his discreet revelation of his new seriousness, contained in his final speech to Beatriz, clearly demonstrate. And the way in which he inter-poses himself between his beloved and her possibly vengeful father at the end of the play shows that he is now capable, as earlier he was not, of acting with courageous gallantry. For her part, Beatriz, from an absurdly prudish critic of love (it should be remembered that the play's alternative title is *La crítica del amor [Love's Critic]*, is transformed by Alonso's attentions into a normal *comedia* lady, who sends a ribbon to her admirer, worries about his well-being, and indulges in intrigue to fur-ther their relationship. Significantly, her pedantic habits of speech, which, dutiful daughter though she is she finds impossible to drop, even to obey her father's angry order, disappear completely as her love reaches its full expression—in the impassioned tirade which she delivers when she discovers the truth about Alonso's courtship of her.[40]

Though not without its more serious side, namely, that occupied by the disgruntled father of Beatriz and Leonor, *No hay burlas con el amor*, probably because of its *figurón* elements, impresses us as a more lighthearted comedy than *Casa con dos puertas* or *Mañanas de abril y mayo*, for its ending does not give us much cause for unease or misgiv-ings. There is no reason to doubt that Leonor and Juan will be happy in their married life together. As regards the other pair, Moscatel describes Alonso at the end as suffering the "worst of all misfortunes, bound in wedlock" (". . . casado, / que es el mayor de sus males"), while Inés alludes to her mistress as a woman made to love against her will and left "worst of all, subjected" (". . . rendida que es lo peor"). But we are disinclined to take the servants' cynicism seriously. Beatriz, we suspect, had always wanted in her deepest self to be "subjected," her pedantic prudery being camouflage for her sexual frustration. And Alonso, while he may not make Beatriz an entirely faithful husband, is certainly not the type to threaten her life because of suspicions about her virtue. Besides, it is difficult to imagine that Beatriz, with her steadfastly "chaste *per-sona*," would ever give her wayward husband cause to doubt her devo-tion.

---

1. Both *Casa con dos puertas* and *La dama duende* were published in Calderón's *Primera parte de comedias* (Madrid, 1636).

2. See Ángel Valbuena Briones, "Nota preliminar" in Calderón de la Barca, *Obras completas*, 2nd ed., vol. 2, *Comedias* (Madrid: Aguilar, 1973), p. 273.

3. See A.L. Stiefel, "Calderóns Lustspiel *La dama duende* und seine Quelle," *Zeitschrift für Romanische Philologie* 19 (1895): 262-64.

4. See Frederick A. De Armas, *The Invisible Mistress: Aspects of Femi-nism and Fantasy in the Golden Age* (Charlottesville, Va.: Biblioteca Siglo de Oro, 1976), pp. 123-29.

5. It is noteworthy that this allusion to the prince's baptism is made in the very first lines of the comedy.

6. Calabazas' remark is made in Act I, sc. 1. The description of Ángela is that offered by Don Manuel himself in Act II of *La dama duende*.

7. According to Jonathan Brown and J.H. Elliott, *A Palace for a King: The Buen Retiro and the Court of Philip IV* (New Haven/London: Yale University Press, 1980), the gardens and park "underwent continual expansion and refinement from 1634 to the end of the decade" (p. 74).

8. See Emilio Cotarelo y Mori, *Ensayo sobre la vida y obras de D. Pedro Calderón de la Barca* (Madrid: Tip. de la *Revista de Archivos, Bibliotecas y Museos*, 1924), p. 156.

9. The dance has also been attributed to Moreto. A manuscript of it survives in the Biblioteca Nacional, Madrid.

10. See Cotarelo, *Ensayo*, p. 157. The magnificent Coliseo theatre of the Buen Retiro palace was not built until 1638-1640.

11. See Richard W. Tyler and Sergio D. Elizondo, *The Characters, Plots and Settings of Calderón's Comedias* (Lincoln, Neb.: Society of Spanish and Spanish-American Studies, 1981), p. 349.

12. See Calderón de la Barca, *No hay burlas con el amor*, ed. Ignacio Arellano (Pamplona: EUNSA, 1981), pp. 141-43.

13. See Kurt and Roswitha Reichenberger, *Bibliographisches Handbuch der Calderón-Forschung* 1 (Kassel: Thiele and Schwarz, 1979): 166.

14. See N.D. Shergold and J.E. Varey, *Representaciones palaciegas, 1603-1699: Estudio y documentos* (London: Tamesis, 1982), pp. 242, 246; and idem, *Teatros y comedias en Madrid, 1687-99: Estudio y documentos* (London: Tamesis, 1979), pp. 294, 297, 304. As regards *No hay burlas con el amor*, Arellano (p. 143) observes that the play was still in the repertoire of the company of Antonio de Prado in 1651, sixteen years after that company first staged the comedy.

15. See Ada M. Coe, *Catálogo bibliográfico y crítico de las comedias anunciadas en los periódicos de Madrid desde 1661 hasta 1819* (Baltimore: Johns Hopkins Press:/London: Oxford Univ. Press, 1935), pp. 38, 140-41; Nicholson B. Adams, "Siglo de Oro Plays in Madrid, 1820-1850," *Hispanic Review* 4 (1936): 342-57; E. Juliá, "Preferencias teatrales del público valenciano en el siglo XVIII," *Revista de Filología Española* 20 (1933): 113-59.

16. We are indebted for most of this information to Henry W. Sullivan, *Calderón in the German Lands and the Low Countries: His Reception and Influence, 1654-1980* (Cambridge: Cambridge Univ. Press, 1983).

17. It should be noted that the word *comedia* did not mean "comedy" in the Golden Age, but simply "play." We use *comedia* in this sense.

18. See Act III, sc. 2, and note 44 to that play.

19. See Bruce W. Wardropper, "Calderón's Comedy and His Serious Sense of Life," *Hispanic Studies in Honor of Nicholson B. Adams*, ed. John E. Keller and Karl-Ludwig Selig (Chapel Hill: Univ. of North Carolina Press: 1966), pp. 179-93.

20. "In these plays Calderón, a most consistent thinker, expresses the same attitudes to the world as in his serious plays: in both kinds he conveys its confusing reality, the disastrous effects of human frailty and sinfulness, problems of cognition and identification, the deceptive appearances of both truth and falsehood" (Wardropper, "Calderón's Comedy," p. 180).

21. See *A secreto agravio, secreta venganza*, Act III, in *Obras completas*

1, *Dramas*, ed. A. Valbuena Briones (Madrid: Aguilar, 1969), p. 445.

22. Textual uncertainties, however, make possible different interpretations of the ending of this comedy. (See our comments, pp. xxxv-xxxvi, and our note 36 below.)

23. Wardropper observes that "amusing as the comedy is, it is forever teetering on the brink of tragedy" ("Calderón's Comedies," p. 182).

24. Cf. Wardropper's comment that "*El médico de su honra*, in which the catastrophe is caused initially by pre-marital errors, is, so to speak, the sequel of a never-written cloak-and-sword play" (ibid., p. 186).

25. We quote, of course, from Lope de Vega's famous *Arte nuevo de hacer comedias*.

26. See his "Nota preliminar," *Obras completas*, 2: 273.

27. See George T. Northup, "Some Recovered Lines from Calderón," in *Homenaje ofrecido a Menéndez Pidal* 2 (Madrid: Editorial Hernando, 1925), p. 498.

28. See J.E. Varey, "*Casa con dos puertas:* Towards a Definition of Calderón's View of Comedy," *Modern Language Review* 67 (1972): 83-94.

29. The version of the song used by Lope in *El acero de Madrid*, Act I (1610), is almost identical to that employed by Calderón. Compare Lope: "Mañanicas floridas / del mes de mayo, / recordad a mi niña / no duerma tanto."

30. See John Varey, "The Staging of Night Scenes in the 'Comedia,' " *American Hispanist* 2, no. 15 (1977): 14-16.

31. That most of these allusions are made by Hipólito is hardly surprising. Juan broods upon his lady's imagined disloyalty throughout the play and is therefore disinclined to admire her in poetic flights of eloquence.

32. It is significant, however, that both heroines are in revolt against the double standard for men and women. Clara's protest is more vocal: her devastating attack on Hipólito's male chauvinism is heartwarming. But Ana, too, implicitly rejects the right assumed by gallants of Golden-Age drama to nourish suspicions of the ladies they claim to love (for example, in Act II, when she tells Juan that a man who really loved her would believe her), suspicions that are the inevitable result of the way in which women are both idealized and enslaved, and in which men are predators and jailors as well as worshipers.

33. See his "Nota preliminar," *Obras completas*, 2: 568.

34. Robert ter Horst takes a different view of this couple's failure to marry, suggesting that they "desist for the pleasure of continuing their affectionate rivalry" (see *Calderón: The Secular Plays* [Lexington: Univ. Press of Kentucky, 1982], p. 139).

35. See *Comedias de D. Pedro Calderón de la Barca*, 2: 294, Biblioteca de Autores Españoles, vol. 9.

36. It is possible, of course, to base one's interpretation of the ending on the text as it stands, rather than as it could be reconstructed. Kenneth Muir gives such an interpretation in his *Shakespeare: Contrasts and Controversies* (Brighton: Harvester Press, 1985). He points out that Ana has continually stressed that if Juan loves her he ought to trust her, and that, once Clara proves that Ana is innocent of flirting with Hipólito, Juan does not again raise the question of the man with the key. Juan realizes now that he has unjustly suspected Ana in one case, and tacitly admits that he has been wrong in the other. In marrying Ana he demonstrates at last that he can trust her *without proof.* Kenneth Muir believes further that, though in retrospect members of the audience may be sceptical

about the success of this marriage in view of Juan's jealous temperament, we should not pursue characters beyond the fall of the curtain. Kenneth Muir's interpretation reflects his attitudes as a specialist of English literary criticism.

In contrast, Ann Mackenzie, as a Golden-Age Hispanist, perceives in Calderonian drama an instructive power which involves us in the idea of a future for the characters after the drama ends. In her view, Calderón's ability to suggest to us such a future is an indication of his genius. As regards the ending of *Mañanas de abril y mayo*, she believes that Calderón gives us cause "to doubt if indeed all's well that ends well" (the words are borrowed from J.E. Varey's comments on "*Casa con dos puertas*; Towards a Definition of Calderón's View of Comedy," p. 92). She contemplates the marriage of Juan and Ana with misgivings, since Juan impresses her persistently as a man incapable of bestowing complete trust on any woman. Markedly different from the rake Hipólito, in that he devotes himself exclusively to one woman, he nevertheless shares Hipólito's cynical view of womankind. Moreover, Ann Mackenzie regards Juan's behavior at the end as that of a man still troubled by doubts. She believes, in fact, that Calderón intended his public to feel profound sympathy for Ana, and to question seriously whether the inherently suspicious Juan can bring her anything but unhappiness. Both Kenneth Muir and Ann Mackenzie wish to record the scholarly stimulus and enjoyment they have received from observing the differences between English and Hispanic critical conceptions of the theatre.

37. See his speech in Act II, sc. 4.

38. See our *Four Comedies*, p. 161.

39. See Edward M. Wilson and Duncan Moir, *The Golden Age: Drama, 1492-1700* (London: Benn/New York: Barnes and Noble, 1971), p. 106.

40. See Act III, sc. 4.

THREE
COMEDIES

by Pedro Calderón de la Barca

Casa con
dos puertas
mala es de
guardar

A House with Two Doors Is Difficult to Guard

DRAMATIS PERSONAE

Don Félix
Lisardo, his friend
Marcela, Don Félix's sister
Fabio, an old man
Laura, his daughter
Celia, her maid

Calabazas, Lisardo's lackey
Herrera, Don Félix's attendant
Silvia, Marcela's maid
Lelio, Fabio's servant
Other servants

The scene is set in Ocaña

ACT I

Scene 1: A country place, not far from the town

[*Enter Marcela and Silvia, mantled.
After them Lisardo and Calabazas*]

Marcela: They're following us, Silvia, are they not?
Silvia: Yes, madam.
Marcela: Well, wait. [*To the men*] Gentlemen,
Come no further; no, go back, for if
You try to find out who I am, you'll find
I'll never come again where we have met:
And if that's not enough, go back because
I beg you now to do so.
Lisardo: Madam, the sun
Could hardly stop the heliotrope from turning
Toward its light; the bright pole star could hardly
Prevent the magnet from admiring it,
Nor would it be less difficult for the magnet

To stop the steel from being attracted by it.
Then if your brightness equals that of the sun,
My happiness is like the heliotrope:
If your resolve is like the polar star,
Then my regret will make me like the magnet;
And if you're harsh, even as the magnet is,
My eagerness will be as strong as steel.
Then how can I decide to stay behind
When I behold my sun, my polar star,
My magnet leave me—I who am
The heliotrope, the magnet, and the steel?[1]

Marcela: But, sir, the sun each evening disappears
And leaves the heliotrope; and every morning
The northern star departs and leaves the magnet;
Then if the sun and northern star may go,
You have no better reason to complain
At my departure. Tell your stubborn self—
Sir Lodestone, Sir Magnet, or Sir Heliotrope—
That night has come, and so the sun departs,
Or that the day has now eclipsed the star.
And now stay here; for I must warn you, if
You should attempt to penetrate my secret
And find out who I am, I'll not return
To see you in this place, which is the field
Of our love-tournament. Since I've been led
By foolish whims that robbed me of my sleep
To see you here, have confidence in me,
Trust what I say, for much depends on it.

Lisardo: Then, madam, since you are recalcitrant,
I must perforce fall back on my desire.
Even supposing it were courteous
Not to come after you, it would be also
Stupidity. Which would offend you more,
Discourtesy or foolishness? Confess
It would be foolishness, for the simple reason
There is no cure for it. So let me choose
To be discourteous rather than a fool.
For six successive dawns blind Love ordained
That on this road you'd act the highwayman.
Six times I've met you, coy sun of your sphere,
Veiled nymph of the meadow, and the mystery goddess
Of its spring. 'Twas you who first invited me
To speak with you; for I myself, a stranger,
A passing traveler, would not have presumed.
From that day forth, you were no longer goddess,

Offering delights, but with dissembling ways
A serpent in the grass—for it's a serpent,
Not a goddess, which lurks amid the flowers,
Waiting to kill. You ordered me to come
Back to this meadow on another morning,
And so indeed my love has brought me back,
As to my own particular sphere. I made
No progress, for despite my urgent prayers,
You still refused to draw aside the veil
Through which I've worshipped what I have not seen.
I have consented up till now; but since
Each day my peril here is born again
Without your favor, I'm resolved to owe
To my own obstinacy what you refuse me.
And so I dare to follow you. Either I see you
Today, or else know who you are.

Marcela: Today
Is quite impossible. Leave me today,
And in return I promise you shall know
Within a little while where I reside,
And you'll be able soon to see me there.

Calabazas: [*To Silvia*] And what of you, this maiden's serving-maid,
Let's have the truth. I do not want my soul
To risk damnation. Is there any motive
Which forces you to mantle up yourself?

Silvia: I've nothing to say about that, and if you follow me, you can be well assured that—

Calabazas: That—what, prithee?

Silvia: That you'll annoy me; for, as the proverb says, "Who pursues, persecutes."[2]

Calabazas: By the Lord, I know what this is all about.

Silvia: What is it all about then?

Calabazas: You must both have horribly ugly faces.

Silvia: Not as ugly as yours, my fine friend.

Calabazas: That's a barefaced exaggeration.[3] I'm a regular Cupid.

Silvia: A stupid, rather! It would take the two of us together to make Cupid in my opinion.

Calabazas: How so?

Silvia: Well, I'm the P-I-D part of the word (Pretty If Demanding). As for you, you're the C-U part, which is the beginning of a certain four-letter word.[4]

Calabazas: The part you've left me with is rightly yours, I think.

Marcela: [*To Lisardo*] Give me your trust. I promise you afresh.

Lisadro: What pledge do you give me that my hope of winning
What you have promised me will be fulfilled?

Marcela: [*Unveiling*]   Here is my pledge—to let you see my face.
Lisardo: Oh! Madam, it is perfidy to seek
To foil my daring by such treachery!
How can I let you, after this, depart,
Who followed you before I saw your face?
Marcela: Goodbye.
You can be sure of me. You soon will know
My house, and learn how much I'll try to serve you.
Again I assure you.
Lisardo: Reluctantly, I obey.
Marcela: And I—I leave you confident I owe you
A debt of gratitude. This is my way.
Lisardo: Then God be with you.
Marcela: Heaven keep you, sir.
[*Exeunt Marcela and Silvia*]
Calabazas: That's clever, sir. Let's follow her and find out who she is
with all her tricks.
Lisardo: It would be wrong of us, Calabazas, if she thinks that these
precautions are necessary.
Calabazas: Is it really you who are talking like this?
Lisardo: Certainly it is.
Calabazas: Heavens! If I were you, I'd follow her, even if she were
descending into hell.
Lisardo: Idiot! Would it be fair for me to cause her just such annoyance
as she has sought to avoid, and after she has talked with me several
days running?
Calabazas: It would be a fitting penalty for having got us up so early
these last few days.
Lisardo: Now we're alone, and must wait here a while, let's discuss
who this secretive woman can be.
Calabazas: Yes, let's. Tell me, sir, what's your opinion of what you've
seen and noted.
Lisardo: Upon my word, from the distinction of her language and from
the elegance of her dress, I could believe that she is some noble
lady who likes to meet, and talk secretly, with people who don't
know her, and who has chosen me because I'm a stranger here.
Calabazas: I have a better idea than that.
Lisardo: Tell me quickly.
Calabazas: Well, I say—you can kill me if I'm wrong—I say that a
woman who chooses to flaunt herself and chatter so brazenly with a
man whom she does not wish to see her face is without doubt an
ugly wit who tries to trap people with her trap.
Lisardo: And if I should tell you that I have seen her face and that she's
as beautiful as an angel.

Calabazas: You've got me there! In that case she must be the Phantom Lady who wishes to begin life afresh.[5]
Lisardo: After all, it doesn't matter. I'll know tomorrow who she is.
Calabazas: Then you think she'll come back tomorrow?
Lisardo: Of course—and besides, if she does not come, with the little hope she has left me, I shall have lost nothing, or almost nothing.
Calabazas: But haven't you lost something, seeing that we've got to get up again at crack of dawn?
Lisardo: I'm compelled by my affairs to rise at daybreak like this, quite apart from my feelings of love.

[*Exeunt*]

Scene 2: A room in Don Félix's House

[*Enter Lisardo and Calabazas*]

Calabazas: She must live near us. By the time we reached our house, there was no sign of her anywhere.
Lisardo: It must be getting late.
Calabazas: Yes, it must; for here comes our host, who provides for us as royally as the king might pay for some splendid tournament.[6] He's dressing.

[*Enter Don Félix, finishing his toilet, and Herrera*]

Lisardo: I kiss your hands, Don Félix.
Félix: May heaven guard you, Lisardo.
Lisardo: You're dressed so early.
Félix: Yes, I have
Worries that hardly let me stay in bed,
Where I found no repose. But why should you
Express surprise that I am out of bed?
For did you not inform me yesterday
That you must carry some petitions early
To Aranjuez? How comes it that you have returned
To Ocaña?
Lisardo: We play a game of "Questions
And Answers"; and, if I recall the rules aright,
Answers should never vary. Then since you gave me
The easiest of replies—your cares—my cares
Provide my answer, for it is my cares
That bring me back to Ocaña.
Félix: Arrived but yesterday, and cares today?

Lisardo: Yes, alas!
Félix: To force you to confide in me,
    I will confide in you, Lisardo.
Calabazas: [*To Herrera*] As they are going to bombard each other
    with two enormous speeches, Herrera, have you got something for
    breakfast capable of satisfying the likes of me?[7]
Herrera: Come along to my room, Calabazas. Once you've stepped
    over the threshold, there's bound to be at least one cold joint
    within
                                    [*Exeunt Herrera and Calabazas*]
Félix: I know, Lisardo, you have not forgotten
    That happy time when we were fellow-students
    At Salamanca; and you will recall
    How, glorying in my freedom, I insulted
    Vain deities of love, and triumphed over
    Beautiful Venus and Cupid with his arrows,
    So that I crowned my freedom with her sunbeams,
    His feathers being spoils of victory.
    Ah! Lisardo, had I never entered
    Such an unequal combat, those two immortals
    Could not have taken the revenge they did.
    Had they but shot me in the usual way,
    By means of a shaft that had been loosed at random,
    Which might have pierced another, not by an arrow
    Shot in revenge, and dipped in such a poison,
    That like a bird it hurtled through the air,
    Struck like a thunderbolt this heart of mine,
    And feeds there like a serpent. The first time
    I felt that blow which wounds but does not kill—
    (What can be worse than power to do just that?)
    Was in the springtime, on an April evening—
    But I am wrong—it surely was at dawn.
    Be not amazed that it should be the evening,
    And yet be dawn, for as I do remember
    Clearly, that day by means of borrowed splendor
    Dawned in the afternoon.[8] Upon that day
    I went, as many times before, to hunt;
    And reached at length the royal pleasure-house
    Of Aranjuez, which is not far from here,
    And always served us as our park and gardens.
    I burned to enter there, not comprehending
    What drove me then to see what I had seen
    So many times before. Entrance is easy
    If their majesties are not in residence.
    I walked toward the garden of the isle.

How easily, Lisardo, do we run
Into misfortune, engineer our doom!
Even as the moth delights to flutter round
The candle-flame from which it meets its death,
Agitating its transparent wings,
Which quickly turn to flaming red, so we,
We wretched mortals feel impelled to probe
Misfortune, circle round a deadly peril,
Ignorant of what draws us. I'll continue.
Near the first fountain there's a rocky place
In which all animals seem to congregate
To shelter from the spraying of the fountain.
There was a woman leaning on the fringe
Of myrtle, seeming like an emerald ring
In which the waters sparkled even like diamonds
As foils to her beauty. She gazed upon her image
In the fountain's basin, so still and so absorbed,
That for a moment I was left in doubt
Whether she was a woman or a statue.
The nymphs of burnished silver standing there
Around the fountain look so much alive
That anyone might wait for them to speak,
While she looked so inanimate that none
Would think that she was capable of motion.
It seemed to me that Nature addressed Art
After this fashion: "Do not pride yourself
That here you make dead marble seem alive
With more effect than I can make the living
Seem dead. For we are equal. I can make
A statue from a woman, while you create
A woman from a statue. Behold a lifeless being
Beside a piece of living marble!"[9] Then
I parted the foliage to look on her
With greater ease—impudent that I was.
The sound awaked her from her ecstasy—
I hoped this ecstasy was not from love.
Somewhat disturbed, she turned to look at me.
I am not sure, but think that I exclaimed
She should not gaze upon her beauteous image,
Lest she should be enamored of herself;
For since both nymph and fountain there were present,
I could not help referring to Narcissus.
Serious and chaste, she did not answer me,
But turned her back and hurried in pursuit
Of a group of women walking on ahead.

She traversed flower beds, or went down paths,
Which made no difference, because the earth,
Touched with her foot, put forth so many flowers
That it became impossible to tell
Where flower beds ended and where paths began,
Since what were paths before were roses now.
The dress she wore was neither court nor country,
But it was half and half: trimmed like a lady's,
But simply graceful like a village girl's;
She had a jaunty hat with curled feathers
(About which Earth and Air would later quarrel
Whether their hue betokened flower or bird).
I followed her until she joined the throng,
That wandering choir of nymphs, who interweaved
In sonorous harmony with the muted rhythms
Of leaves and birds and fountains; so each step
Was like a celebration, each hesitation
Part of a dance. I knew them all. They lived
Here at Ocaña. But I did not know
The one who caused my pain. From the first instant
I felt in my very soul what now I feel:
From the first instant I loved her. (Let no one say
That he could fall in love a second time.
Though he may look here, talk there, and court,
And write a billet-doux, win some, lose some,
He'll fall in love but once, for same effects
Must have a single cause.) I inquired of her
From some of her companions; I learned her birth
More than matched her beauty. The reason why
I had not seen her until then, I found,
Was that her father brought her up in court,
Until they came to Ocaña, that she might live
Where she could slay. I will not tell you now
How happily I wooed her, for lost happiness
Is but a greater woe; but you must learn
That, touched at last by constant courtesies,
By kind and loving services, she allowed me
To talk with her sometimes through the garden lattice,
When night and garden were sole witnesses
Of our sweet converse. For I wished to trust
In them alone. It would have been wrong of me
To deny the stars and flowers—the splendid pride
Of night and garden—the former's influence,
The latter's knowledge, because stars and flowers
Have always worked harmoniously together

As lovers' confidants. Thus for a time,
Favored by Fortune with a following wind,
I sped through the uncertain seas of love,
Until the wind changed to a hurricane,
Created by a storm of jealousy,
Which stirred up mountainous seas.[10] I tell you
If ever you should fall in love, *you'd* find
How little can the pilot then be trusted,
And how unsafe the boat. Doubtless you think,
In hearing me complain of jealousy
That *I* was jealous? But you are mistaken,
It is not I who feel it; but it is I
Who am the cause. And such are the effects
Of jealousy that it can kill as surely
When it's occasioned as when it is felt.
If not to kill one, what could be its purpose?
This is the way of it. Here at Ocaña
There is a lady I once used to court.
To avenge herself on me, she told my new love
About my former feelings, and pretended
She had received great favors from me then.
Oh! Lisardo, how easily can lies
Appear as truths where jealousy's concerned.
Forthwith my lady, in a jealous fit,
Cut herself off from me, and will not even
Permit me to see her, so that I may speak
In my own defense. And now, my friend, it is
For you to judge whether these cares of mine
Can let me sleep or rest. I'm so besieged
By countless evils, vexed by dire distresses,
That I am near to death. I have offended,
Unwittingly, the loveliest of angels.
And is it not the worst of all misfortunes
To have to suffer so for an offense
Of which one is not guilty?

Lisardo: Be comforted, Félix.
Although the jealousy of someone else,
Of which you complain may cause you some distress,
So long as you yourself are free of it,
It brings with it a kind of consolation.
There is as great a gulf between the pain
Of causing jealousy and suffering it,
As between one who suffers pangs of love,
And one who inspires them. When you spoke the word
"Jealousy," I pitied you; but when

You said the lady's jealousy was based
On misconceptions, not upon the truth,
My pity turned to envy, for I know
No keener pleasure for gallants and ladies—
So long as the grievance can be quickly settled—
Than when they make their peace to quarrel, or
Quarrel to make their peace. So, Félix, go
And see your *belle*. I'll wager that this instant,
However much she tries to hide the fact,
She, in spite of her jealousy, desires
More even than you do to be undeceived.

[*Enter Marcela and Silvia. They open the door, which is
screened by a tapestry, and stand between the tapestry and
the door.*]

Marcela: [*Aside to Silvia*] I'm going to see my brother by this door
which leads from my apartment to his. Although he doesn't know
that I left the house this morning, by visiting him so I shall prevent
him from entertaining any suspicion.

Silvia: Keep back, madam, for he is talking with that guest of his, and
you know that my master does not wish him to talk to you, or get so
much as a glimpse of you.

Lisardo: While you await that pleasurable hour
When you will call upon your lady, will you
Let me distract you by telling you my troubles
As you have told me yours. Listen to me.

Marcela: Let's listen to him, Silvia.

Lisardo: After I had exchanged my scholar's dress
For that of a soldier, and my pen for a sword,
My quiet studies, attending on Minerva
At Salamanca University,
For blood and horror as I followed Mars
In the campaign in Flanders, although I had
No patron, I obtained a company.
The campaign over—it would not have occurred
To me, to quit before—I took my leave,
And so returned to Spain. I hoped to merit
The signal honor of wearing on my breast
One of the crosses of the martial orders,
Which with the luster of nobility
Enhance a soldier's courage.[11] That was the aim
Of my journey to Madrid. His Majesty—
May Heaven protect him and prolong his days,
And my he be the Phoenix of our age!—
The King postponed the reading of my suit

Till a more peaceful time, free from vexations.
He came to Aranjuez, the Spring's Pavilion.
How could it not be worthy of this title,
Seeing the Queen of Flowers, the Fleur-de-lis,
The loveliest, purest, sweetest of all flowers,
Comes there and brings with her so many bright
And dazzling blooms, enough to make the sun
Envious of their brilliance.[12] So I followed
The Court there, and I must confess
More for the pleasure than necessity;
For now the King is served by ministers
Who know how to attend to everything,
So that one's presence is unnecessary
For one's deserts to meet a fit reward,
Thanks to the watchfulness of him who shares
The weight of such an edifice of power,
As Atlas had the help of Hercules.[13]
So I arrived at Aranjuez. You came
To visit me at my inn; and when you found
That I was badly lodged—as badly indeed
As those petitioners camping in the woods—
You urged me to return with you to Ocaña.
The town, you said to me, is but two leagues
From Aranjuez, and it will be easy
To go there when an audience is held,
Returning in the evening. I agreed,
Rather to please you than for my convenience.
You know all this, my friend; but I have need
Of this preamble to a tale of love,
More wonderful, perhaps, than all of those
Cervantes told.[14]

Marcela: [*Aside to Silvia*]   This is where I come on the scene.

Félix: I am impatient, Lisardo, to hear your story.

Lisardo: One day when I arose extremely early,
So that I could reach my destination
Before the sun came over the horizon,
Arriving at the convent just outside
The gates of Ocaña, I beheld a woman
Among some poplar trees. I liked her figure.
I bowed to her politely. Before I had taken
A dozen steps, she called me by my name.
I stopped, dismounted, gave my horse's bridle
To Calabazas, and went toward her, saying,
"Happy the stranger who is known by name
To such a noble lady!" She, forthwith,

Hastened to mantle up her face, and answered
In a low voice: "A gentleman of such parts
Is not a stranger in any part of the realm."
To that she added other compliments,
So flattering, that I shall not repeat them.
I do not know, indeed, how any men
Can be so vain, so arrogant, that they can
Boast that women have made advances to them.[15]

Silvia: [*To Marcela*]   He's telling of our adventure.

Marcela: [*To Silvia, aside*]   How can I prevent him from telling the rest? I'm afraid that he'll provide information that will awaken the suspicions of Don Félix.

Félix: Continue.

Lisardo: When in this manner we had talked awhile,
Her face still hidden, she took her leave of me,
Forbidding me to seek to know her name
Or where she dwelt. So long as I obeyed,
She promised she'd return another day
To the same place. Six times since then
Dawn has drawn back the curtains of the East
To reveal the sun, and six times I have met
This veiled woman by some willow-trees.
At last I determined, vexed by her precautions,
To follow her today when she returned
To Ocaña. It was not possible
To carry out my plan. She had hardly left me
Than she looked back repeatedly and saw me,
And so refused to go a step beyond
The corner of this street.

Félix: This street, you say?

Lisardo: Yes, and the odds are that she lives nearby,
For I lost sight of her immediately.
It was here she told me I must let her go
Because my curiosity endangered
Her very life.

Félix: What a strange woman!

Marcela: [*Aside*]   Now
I'm bound to be found out.

Félix: Go on.

Lisardo: Well, I—

[*Enter Celia, wearing a cloak*]

Celia: Don Félix, a woman wants to speak with you
In secret.

Félix: Certainly she may.
Marcela: [*Aside*]   Whoever you are, woman or angel,
        You have arrived just in the nick of time
        To save me.
Félix: Soon you can complete your story.
        But for the moment let me, I beseech you,
        Talk with this woman, for she is the servant
        Of the lady I have mentioned.
Lisardo: My life upon it,
        If it does not turn out as I predicted.
        Go to, find out what her message is.
        Goodbye for now. It's of no consequence
        That there's no time at present to hear me out.

                                                    [*Exit*]

Félix: What motive brings you, Celia?
Celia: Don't be surprised
        That I have not come sooner. It required
        A lot of courage to come at all; and if
        My mistress knew of it, she'd surely kill me.
Félix: So she is very much annoyed with me?
Celia: Yes, but she sent me this way on an errand.
        I couldn't refrain from coming in to see you,
        And speak a moment with you.
Félix: How is your lady?
Celia: She does complain about your perfidy
        And your ingratitude.
Félix: May God abandon me
        If I have ever wronged her!
Celia: Why did you not
        Explain yourself to her?
Félix: She will not hear me.
Celia: If you would be discreet and promise me
        Not to betray me, I would dare to lead you
        To a place where you would find her.
Félix: Ah! Celia,
        I would be dumb as marble.
Celia: Well, follow me; and if my master
        Is not at home, I'll sign to you and leave
        The door ajar. You will be able to enter
        And go to her room.
Félix: You've given me back my courage—
        My life indeed.
Celia: Now is the time. Don't wait,
        But follow me.

Félix: I will be close behind you.
Celia: [*Aside*]   What fools men are! How easy to conduct
A lover to his mistress's house!

                                  [*Exeunt Félix and Celia*]
Marcela: I breathe again. I've had a lucky escape, Silvia.
Silvia: How can you say you've escaped? These gentlemen will soon
resume their chat, and the tale will be completed.
Marcela: No, I will prevent it.
Silvia: How?
Marcela: By writing to him to keep my secret until he has seen me, and
that will be no later than this evening.
Silvia: What? You'll tell him who you are?
Marcela: Lord! Lord! May Heaven preserve me from that!
Silvia: What will you do then?
Marcela: I have an idea. Laura's my brother's mistress;
Laura's my friend; Laura knows what love is.
I will confide in her this very day.
And, Silvia, on this day you shall behold
A wondrous scene that's acted in Love's name.
For I'll pretend—but no, I do not wish
To tell you yet, because a scene like that
Never gives so much pleasure when performed
If it has been explained before the show.[16]

                                                    [*Exeunt*]

Scene 3: A room in Fabio's house

[*Enter Fabio, an old man, and Laura, his daughter*]

Fabio: What is the matter? Your grief is very strange,
Since it has marred your beauty's roseate hue.
What is the trouble that for several days
Has gripped you with such melancholy, that
You do nought but sigh and weep?
Laura: If I knew, my lord,
The cause of my distress—[*Aside*]   I would to God
I knew it less well—my grief would then be less
And consolation more: for knowing it
Would be a first step to a cure. My grief
Is but a natural melancholy, sir,
And so it is impossible to know
Whence it arises. Nature herself created
The gulf between an ordinary sadness
And melancholia.

Fabio: I know not what to say,
Save that your grief has such effect on me
That while you suffer thus, I suffer death;
Since, when I see you in so sad a humor,
I don't expect to live.

                                                    [*Exit*]

Laura: O Heavens! What shall I do,
Being so racked with grief that my life's threatened?
What can this be? Alas! It is too plain
That it is jealousy. For a raging fury
Which wounds the feelings and astounds the reason,
A poison in the breast, a settled anger
Which damages the heart, what can this mean?
What serpent, what wild beast, what hideous monster
Could be responsible, but the many-headed
Hydra of jealousy—for only this
Could cause the rage, the venom, and the wound.
If only, Félix, I had sooner known
About your earlier love, I would not then
Have plunged so deep myself, till I was doomed.
For though I then was ignorant of love,
And lived a carefree life—How things have changed!—
I knew at least that love is slow to die—
Perhaps it never does. So let him love
His precious Nise then: he's welcome to her;
And just leave me to die.

[*Enter Celia, who removes her cloak, and folds it hurriedly*]

Celia: Madam!
Laura: What is it, Celia?
Celia: Live, madam, live!
I played my role, madam;
And, as I think, I did it pretty well.
I gained admittance to his house, and told him
That, passing down the street on other business,
I had not wished to go so near, without
Seeing him, if only for a moment.
Then with a sigh that would, I swear, have melted
A bronze or marble statue, blindly shaken,
He asked about you. So I said you were angry,
Adding that if you learned that I had been
To visit him, you'd kill me. Then, as if
The idea were mine alone, I asked him why
He did not come at once to explain himself
And pacify you. He replied he dared not,

And that you would not hear him. So I said
That I would bring him to your room, despite
The great risk to myself, if he would promise
That he would not reveal I brought him there.
He swore to keep the secret and was grateful.
I've brought him with me and he's waiting now
For the signal to come in; and since my lord
Your father's out, I'll call him. Now you know
What's happened up till now

Laura: Call him then,
For though I think that I am justified
In being jealous, I want so much to see
What excuses he will try to make,
That I'm prepared to pocket up his guilt.

                                                    [*Exit Celia*]

The more jealous and angry a woman is,
The more she wants to hear the man's excuses,
Notwithstanding she does not believe them.
For jealousy is such a strange disease,
Lies bring it some relief. I may not manage
To be convinced by his excuses, but
At least I'll hear *him* speak them.

[*Enter Celia, with Don Félix*]

Celia: [*Aside to Félix*]   Lord Fabio
Is out, and so you have an opportunity
To talk with my mistress.
Félix: You give me the chance
To rescue now my life and happiness.
Celia: [*Aside to Félix*]   Do not let on that you have dared to enter
Because I asked you. [*Aloud*]   What is this, Don Félix?
How do you come to enter—
Félix: Hush, Celia!
Celia: —this room?
Félix: For goodness' sake, be quiet.
Laura: What noise is this?
Celia: The noise, madam, comes from Don Félix,
Who has burst in, without considering
That if my Lord Fabio returned, you'd be—
Laura: This is amazing impudence, sir. You dare
To come into my house, my very room?
Félix: Alas, madam, he who desires to die
Fears nothing more; and if my death is able
To avenge me for your scorn, I willingly

Will die before your eyes, and so be happy
At least by dying.

Laura: The fault is yours, Celia.

Celia: Mine, madam?

Laura: If you had shut the door.

Celia: Madam, I did.

Felix: Yes, madam, it is not with Celia now
That you should quarrel; why should she be blamed
For my transgression. It is me alone
That you should scold and punish. But no, you wish
To scold her, since it has become your custom
To persecute the innocent.

Laura: Indeed,
You are quite right. I take a natural pleasure
In being monstrously unjust. For you,
My lord, of course, have never corresponded
With Nise; you have never called on her,
And she has never been to visit you.
Is it not so? Yes, I'm a cruel woman,
Impatient and incensed. I persecute you,
Though you are innocent—for you're innocent,
Are you not, sir? But if that's so, and I
Am such a fickle, faithless, unjust woman,
Why do you seek me? What do you want from me?

Felix: I merely wish to show you that you're wrong,
Your jealousy ill-founded.

Laura: My jealousy,
Don Félix?

Félix: Yes, Laura, and—

Laura: Who told you I was jealous?

Félix: Your conduct toward me makes it plain enough.

Laura: How so?

Félix: This is how. Either you're jealous,
Or else you're not. If not, why do you feign
An anger which you do not feel? And if
You are, why don't you want me to explain?
No jealous person ever would refuse
To hear an explanation; so, if you're jealous—
Whether to let me exculpate myself,
Or else to satisfy you, deign to hear me.
Or, if you are not jealous, speak to me.

Laura: Your arguments might carry more conviction,
If, when a woman was annoyed, it followed
That she was jealous; but it is not so.

For I can be annoyed and not be jealous,
And therefore I have nothing more to hear from you,
Nor you to say to me.
Félix: By heavens above,
Whether you are annoyed, or jealous too,
You have to hear me now, before I leave
This house.
Laura: You'll go at once, if I do listen?
Félix: I will.
Laura: Well, speak, and then be off.
Félix: Should I attempt to deny that I loved Nise . . .
Laura: Kindly stop there. Is this how you propose
To persuade and satisfy me? I was expecting
A thousand courteous protestations, true
Or false—for sorrows are consoled by lies—
Enough to say, I thought you'd give a thousand
Assurances of amorous fidelity,
And then you throw the confession in my face
That you have loved her. Have a care, sir!
For while you think to appease me, you are still
Insulting me.
Félix: Why won't you let me finish?
Laura: What! Sir, do you imagine after this
You can excuse yourself?
Félix: Without a doubt.
Laura: [*Aside*]   May Love permit it!
Félix: Hear me.
Laura: And afterwards
You'll go?
Félix: Yes.
Laura: Very well. Speak, sir,
And then be off.
Félix: It would be foolish of me
To say I did not love her once; more foolish
For you to imagine that my love for her
Had any likeness to my love for you.
No, it was not a genuine love, but merely
A kind of apprenticeship. I learned with her
How to love you.
Laura: But sir, the science of love
Cannot be learnt; and love does not require
A course of study at the university.
It gets enough instruction on its own.
Such, indeed, is the nature of the subject

That study teaches only how to blunder
In love; so those who do the most research
Into love's science, know least about its practice.
Félix: Let me endeavor to explain myself
By another example. Suppose a man's born blind.
He tries to imagine the splendor of the sun,
That supreme planet as it rolls and follows
Its azure course: admires it for the picture
Formed in his mind. Then one fine night
He sees for the first time, looks at the sky,
And the first object that his eyes behold
Is a bright star. In wonder, he exclaims:
"There, doubtless, is the sun! It is exactly
As I imagined it! How magnificent!"
But as he stands there, lost in wonderment,
The actual sun above the horizon peers,
And quite obscures the brightness of the star
With its much greater glory. So I ask you
How can that star offend the glorious sun?
It fades to nothing when the sun comes forth.
I used to be like that blind man. I lived
In a blind ignorance of love, before
I loved you. In that state I tried to imagine
What love would be. I found what I thought was love,
Adoring what I saw. Alas! It was not
The sun, but a star. I was enchanted by it
Until I saw the very sun of love.
Laura: I don't accept that: the way I understand it,
It's Nise who is sun unto my star,
And I'm a star beside her. The proof of it
Is that you only come at night, beneath
My casement, while you visit her by day.
Which of us then must be the sun, and which
The star? Does not one see a star at night,
The sun but in the day?
Félix: Good heavens, Laura,
I tell you, you're mistaken. May a thunderbolt
Strike me if I have had a meeting with her
Since you have come to live here in Ocaña!
And is it not enough to give the lie
To what she says of me, that it is she
Who says it? For where women are competing
The keenest blow that one can give her rival
Is to confess to her her jealous fears,

When she who listens is herself as jealous.
Laura: I know for certain that she told the truth.
Félix: How do you know it?
Laura: By the pain I felt—
For what is bad is certain to be true.
Ill fortune, as 'tis said, has always been
An excellent astrologer, because
It has invariably foretold the truth.
Félix: And so you do admit that you are jealous?
Laura: Is it surprising that, upon the rack,
I should confess?
Félix: If causeless jealousy
Tortures you now so much, how could you bear it
If you had real cause for—
Celia: My Lord is here!
Laura: Go through this door; it leads into a room
With another door which opens on the street.
Félix: I'm going—but first tell me how we part.
Laura: As you wish.
Félix: On your part without anger?
Laura: Come again tonight. I wish to see you,
Although the thought of Nise troubles me.
Félix: Ah! How you deceive yourself!
Laura: Ah! Don Félix.
How you hurt me!
Celia: Ah! how convenient
It is to have a house which has two doors!

                                   [*Exeunt*]

ACT II

Scene 1: A room in Laura's house.

[*Enter from one side Laura and Celia, and from the other Marcela, wearing a cape, and her attendant, Herrera*]

Laura: Welcome, Marcela.
Marcela: How happy I am, my dear,
To find you at home.
Laura: It's I who am happy, since
I receive a visit from you.
Marcela: I suspect rather
You'll be put out, since I am going to cause you
A bit of bother.

Laura: I'll be bothered only
Till I learn how to serve you. Celia,
Bring some chairs. We shall be better here.
It's quieter here than in the drawing-room.[17]
Herrera: When shall I return to fetch you, madam?
Marcela: At dusk, Herrera. That will be soon enough.
Herrera: The dew is dangerous then—but as you wish.

                                    [*Exit*]

Marcela: You're my friend, lovely Laura; more than that
You're noble and full of sense. I cannot find
A better confidante than such a woman
Who's fond of me, intelligent and noble.
Laura: These are extraordinary preliminaries.
I'm now so curious that I am more eager
To know about it, then you are to tell me.
Marcela: Are we alone?
Laura: Yes. Leave us, Celia.
Marcela: Oh!
I don't mind her. She may stay.
Laura: Begin.
Marcela: Listen carefully, Laura. My brother Félix
These last few days has brought a gentleman
To stay with him—a friend since they were boys—
Who wishes to remain near Aranjuez
For that at present is the sacred sphere
Of our King Philip: there is focused now
The light of the fourth planet.[18] This offer
Of hospitality was most ill-advised:
So much so, that before his guest arrived
He had to make me give up my apartment
And banish me to a small room at the back.
Where I should live and so discreetly too,
And so well hidden, that his guest had not
The faintest inkling I was in the house.
Doubtless my brother hoped to circumvent
The gossips of Ocaña by this method—
But what a foolish method!—lest they should blame him
For having lodged a young guest in his house
In which he has a maiden sister living.
And such was his circumspection, that apart
From keeping me in isolation, he even
Concealed with a tapestry the door between
His room and mine, so that his friend would never
Suspect the house had any other quarters.
That door is used by Silvia alone

In going back and forth to tidy up.
Well, so much for Lisardo, who lives at home
Without the slightest notion that a woman
Is in it, too. And that's enough of Félix,
Who fondly thinks that by such means alone
He's found an effective remedy against
His friend's beholding me, or talking to me.
That's enough of them. Now for myself. When I
Saw how my brother tried to shut me in,
I found offensive such absurd precautions;
For there is nothing drives a woman wild,
However sane, more than such lack of trust.
How ignorant and misguided is a man
Of honor who behaves in such a way!
For it is when one's eager to forget
That one remembers; or when one tries to sleep
By hook or crook, the very efforts one makes
To sleep drive sleep still further off;
Or when one finds a book with lines erased,
One's curiosity is roused to read them.
So, Laura, this precaution of my brother,
Together with my natural curiosity,
Or else my fate, awakened in my heart
A keen desire to find out if our guest
Possessed a mind as noble as his face.
Without my brother's prohibition, I
Would not have dreamed of this.
Eve's curiosity (that original sin)
We women have inherited, and so
That I could speak with him, without his knowing
Who had conversed with him, I went one morning
To the gardens on the road to Aranjuez,
Where he would have to pass. He came indeed.
I called to him, Laura, imagining that to talk
With him was no great matter, since it was
Mere curiosity or willfulness.
Alas! how easy is it to embark
Upon a tempting peril, but how hard
To extricate oneself. The sea, for instance,
Beckons invitingly and seems quite calm
To all who see it. Its waves are frolicking.
But even the most confident of men
Ever to wander through that wavering waste
Of waters went astray, and he bewailed

The fury of its onslaughts. So with me:
I judged the sea of love was calm and tranquil,
But scarcely was I aware of its caress
Before I felt its violence instead.
You will be thinking, Laura, that I'm worried
Simply because I am in love; but no,
The matter is more serious than that,
For I am buffeted by a storm of honor,
As well as love. This is what worries me.
This morning, while I stood between the door
And the tapestry (of which I have just told you)
I overheard our guest relate to Félix
The tale of our adventure. Happily
Celia—I can say it before her—
Arrived to interrupt them. But the danger
Is not yet over. Our guest may any moment
Complete his story, and I am afraid
That his description of me—for he saw
My face uncovered—or the cautious way
In which I talked with him, or even the fact
He followed me to a point so near the house—
That these will cause my brother to suspect.
So, Laura, it is vital that I talk
With this Lisardo, before their heart-to-heart
Can be resumed. And so I've sent a note
By Silvia, asking him to come and see me
Here in this house, where I shall stay, until—

Laura: Stop there a moment! You've abused the rights
Of friendship; and before you wrote to this gallant
To make an assignation at my house
You ought to have reflected at *your* house
That there were serious drawbacks to your plan.

Marcela: I did reflect, Laura, and I know
How to manage everything, without
Your getting involved.

Laura: How can you manage that
Seeing that I—

Marcela: Listen, I'll tell you how.
Your house has two doors. I've instructed Silvia
To introduce him by the door that gives
Upon the other street; and in this way
This young man who's a stranger to Ocaña
Will never know that he is in your house,
And so you run no risk.

Laura: I run the risk
That he will make inquiries, and that tomorrow
He'll learn what he is ignorant of today,
And think the veiled lady he has seen
Is I.
Marcela: Be calm. I will take off my mantle
And welcome him as though this were my house.
Laura: That's all very well. But if my father returned
And found a man here?
Marcela: It's hardly likely, is it
That he'll return so soon, or we be caught
The first time we transgress. You'll render me
This service surely. It's fitting that a lady
Should so oblige a friend.
Laura: [*Aside*]   I cannot tell her
The inconvenience that I fear the most.
It is that Félix should arrive and find them
Together, and think I favor a liaison
Between his sister and his friend.

[*Enter Silvia*]

Silvia: [*To Marcela*] I've run all round Ocaña twenty times
Before I found him.
Marcela: And you've found him now?
Silvia: Yes, madam. I have given him your note.
No sooner had he read it than he followed
Close at my heels, and at this very moment
He's waiting at the door—the one you mentioned.
Marcela: So, as you see, you can't get out of it.
Laura: I serve you against my will.
Marcela: Take off this mantle,
Celia; and, Silvia, bring Lisardo here.

[*Exit Silvia*]

Laura, he must not see you. You're too lovely
To pass for a servant.
Laura: Marcela, you are now
The mistress of my house. Look after it well.
[*Aside*] Oh, the things that one is forced to do,
Whose friend is but a fool!

[*Exeunt Laura and Celia*]

[*Enter Lisardo, conducted by Silvia*]

Silvia: You're here, my lord, in the veiled lady's house,
And see her face.

Lisardo: What happiness is mine!
Marcela: Your memory is defective, Lord Lisardo,
    If you imagine I'm the kind of woman
    Who would pursue a man for love.
Lisardo: I feared
    As much, I must confess, and so lost hope
    Of my good fortune; for, in my experience,
    Lack of confidence accompanies ill-luck.
Marcela: Although I might have sent for you today
    Just for the pleasure of your conversation,
    Yet I would not, my lord, have taken this freedom
    If I had not to make, without delay,
    Complaint against you.
Lisardo: Complaint against me, madam?
Marcela: Yes, and it is of some importance to me
    To tell you what it is.
Lisardo: Since you imply
    That my offense was done in ignorance,
    And not intentionally, you seem to excuse it.
    But it's important that you tell me now
    What I have done, lest I commit again,
    While I'm still ignorant, the same offense.
Marcela: Did you not start this morning, to recount
    The tale of our adventure to some man?
    And were you not prevented from concluding
    Your tale, by the arrival of a maid?
Lisardo: Madam, I will not try to excuse myself,
    Although that would be easy. Before a woman
    So well informed about me—in a country
    Of which I am a stranger—before a woman
    Who is concerned to stand well with my friend,
    Who keeps a servant stationed in his house
    To tell her of my discourse—I have no course
    But to be silent and withdraw; for, madam,
    Before being your gallant, I was his friend.
Marcela: My lord, I now perceive that from the details
    Which I have given you, you suspect that I
    Am she with whom Don Félix is in love.
    You are mistaken. And you must believe me—
    If indeed a man in love is capable
    Of believing anything—not only am I not
    Don Félix's lady, but for me to be so
    Is utterly impossible.
Lisardo: You will not

Convince me by your argument, if you start
By a denial of its premises.
Who could have told you of my name, and kept you
So well informed about me? Who could have told you
Of what we said in private—there's no time
To tell you of it—in Don Félix's room?
Marcela: To clear your doubts, let it suffice to answer
That I'm the friend of a noble, lovely lady
Don Félix loves. Just now she spoke of him
And mentioned you in passing, telling me
Some things about you, since you are his friend.
For though he is a perfect gentle knight,
Secrets are best kept when they are not known.
And now I beg you not to tell him more
Of my appearance, or that you have seen me
And know my house. For I must tell you, sir,
That if your indiscretion should arouse
Suspicion, then my life, at very least,
Would surely be endangered and, what is more,
My honor would be, too.
Lisardo: You doubtless think,
Madam, that I no longer have a reason
To doubt you, but in fact you've left me now
Still more confused than ever. For if you're not—

[*Enter Celia*]

Celia: Madam, my master's coming down the passage.
Marcela: [*Aside to Celia*]   That's the last straw. Can we get *him* away?
Celia: [*Aside to Marcela*]   No, madam; my master has come through
            the door
Through which this gentleman entered. It would not do
For him to discover that we have a house
With another door.   [*Aloud*]   He's coming in.
Lisardo: What shall I do?
Celia: Hide in the neighboring room.
Lisardo: I don't know what to do.
Marcela: Quick, quick! For if you're seen—
Lisardo: God! What a mess I'm in!   [*He hides in a neighboring room*]

[*Enter Laura*]

Marcela: I am beset now with appalling problems!
Laura: You see, Marcela, that we have indeed
           Been caught red-handed in our first transgression.
           You've put me in a pretty situation!

Marcela: Who could have predicted that your father
Would have returned so soon?

[*Enter Fabio*]

Fabio: How now, Celia?
Since when have you acquired the careless habit
Of leaving this door open?
Laura: The reason's simple.
Marcela's come to see me. As this door
Was nearer to a house she had to visit,
I ordered that it should be opened, sir.
She used it to come in, and left it open.
These things happen.
Fabio: Pardon me, dear Marcela.
As it is dark, I did not see you there.
Laura: [*Aside*]   I fear the worst!
Celia: [*Aside*]   What an awful mess!

[*Exit*]

Silvia: [*Aside*]   What a shock!
Marcela: I heard of Laura's trouble, and my fondness
For her caused me to visit her, and see
If I could ease her pain, comfort her sadness.
Laura: My trouble's such, that what you meant to be
A remedy but adds to my distress.
I do believe, indeed, that you have come
To make my trouble worse. For this attack
Gets more acute with your intended cure.
Fabio: I don't know what to say to you, nor know
How to discover means to cure your sickness.
Hullo there! Lights!

[*Enter Celia with the lamps, which she places on the desk.
Herrera enters after her*]

Celia: Here they are, my lord.
Herrera: Is it not time,
Madam, for us to leave, now night has fallen?
Is it not time for us to go?
Marcela: [*Aside to Laura*]   My dear,
It pains me that I leave you in the midst
Of these vexations.
Laura: [*Aside to Marcela*]   I am left to pay
For another's fault.
Marcela: [*Aside to Laura*]   What else can I do, alas?
Forgive me. I must go.

Fabio: Allow me, madam,
    To escort you home.
Marcela: There is no need, my lord,
    For you to take the trouble. God be with you.
Laura: [*Aside to Marcela*]   It would be better to allow my father
    To go with you, so that the gentleman
    Who's trapped here can escape.
Fabio: I insist on going with you.
Marcela: Since you do me such honor, it would be churlish
    To refuse your courteous offer.
Fabio: Give me your hand.
Marcela: You're so gallant, I can't refuse that favor.
                    [*Exeunt Fabio, Marcela, Herrera, and Silvia*]
Laura: Ah! Celia, tell me, tell me if there was
    Ever a situation worse than mine.
    For no one will believe that this man here
    Is quite unknown to me. And if he sees me,
    Will he not realize the truth, and know
    Marcela's not the mistress of this house?
Celia: It's easy to avert the consequences,
    Thanks to the absence of my master. Quick!
    Retire a moment. I'll get this gentleman
    To make his exit, and he'll go away
    Still in the dark, without a glimpse of you,
    Nor of Marcela.
Laura: It just remains for us
    To carry out your plan. Let's do it then.
    Open the door. But stay! I hear a noise
    In the next room.
Celia: Here is another problem!

    [*Enter Félix*]

Félix: Night had already spread its somber mantle
    (That evening cloak the sky dons for disguise)
    When the stars, Laura, found me at your door.
    My yearning so forestalled the promised hour
    That I came early, waiting in the street,
    Lest I should miss one jot of time with you.
    I saw my sister come out of your house,
    Escorted by your father, and so I dared
    To enter, for our reconciliation
    Has filled me with such joy, I won't delay
    One moment before seeing you again
    Softened toward me.
Laura: You have acted wrongly.

For I observe that you have scarcely freed me
From one distress before you bring another.
[*Aside*]   I'm so upset that I can hardly speak
A word to him.   [*Aloud*]   Did the household take so long
To retire for the night, that you had to enter brashly
Without considering that at any moment
My father may return.

Felix: I only wished
To tell you, Laura, that I'll wait in the street
Till the hour to speak with you. If I do that,
You can't maintain I've come from another tryst
When I come to you. So I'll return to my post.

Laura: Yes, go at once. When my father has retired
For the night, we can talk together without haste.
Please go, and do not keep me in this state
Of panic. I am worried, for I think
That he suspects our love. He's very restless,
Coming and going, and he's even taken
The key to the other door.   [*Aside*]   I have to lie
To guarantee that gentleman's escape.

Félix: To dissipate your fears, I'll go at once.
I'll be in the street.

Fabio: [*Offstage*]   Ho! there! Lights!

Laura: Heavens! There's my father.

Celia: You're right.

Félix: Since your father has the key
To the other door, I cannot get away;
And so I'll hide in this room.

Laura: No, wait! please wait.
You must not enter.

Félix: Why?

Laura: Because my father
Uses that room for writing; and he spends
A good part of the night there.

Félix: Good heavens, Laura,
You have another motive for refusing
To let me enter, and I know what it is.
I saw within when I began to open
The door, a man in the dark.

Laura: Look here—

Félix: And what is there to look at here?

Laura: Have a care—

Félix: Nothing can prevent me.

Laura: My father's coming.

Félix: Unhappy that I am!

What a dilemma! If I make a noise,
Fabio will learn his wrong; and, if I'm silent,
I suffer mine.

[*Enter Fabio*]

Fabio: You here, Félix? What does this mean?
Laura: [*Aside to Félix*] For God's sake, think what you are doing?
You are a gentleman, and you should protect
A lady's honor before everything.
Félix: [*Aside*] What she says is true. I think it best
For me to dissemble—if indeed one can
Where jealousy's concerned.
[*Aloud*] I came to fetch my sister. I was told
That she was at your house.
Fabio: I have just left her
At her own door. I acted as her escort.
Laura: So I've been telling him.
Félix: God keep you, sir,
For the signal honor you have shown my sister.
Fabio: She's now at home, awaiting your return.
Félix: [*Aside*] I know not what to do. To stay here, madness.
To retire at once, leaving a man here, shameful;
To disturb the house for this man, most injurious;
To wait for him in the street, impossible.
This house has two doors and I am alone.
I wish that I had brought Lisardo with me,
That trusty friend. But I have found a way
To reach the truth. [*Aloud*] God be with you, sir.
Fabio: May He preserve you equally.
Félix: [*Aside*]   By heaven,
We'll see today if fortune favors boldness.
          [*Exit hurriedly; Fabio sees him to the door and lingers there*]
Fabio: Lights for Don Félix, Celia.
                              [*Exit Celia, with torch*]
[*Taking another torch*] Come with me, Laura;
I must speak with you in private.
Laura: [*Aside*]   Another shock!
What has he to say to me? And how
Will all this finish?
                              [*Exeunt Laura and Fabio*]

[*Enter Celia with torch, which she carries like one afraid*]

Celia: Don Félix vanished without waiting for me to go down to light
him to the door. It's obvious what he intends to do—it is to come
back here as quickly as possible. But the other fellow will have left

before he gets back, for my master is in his room with Laura.
There's no time to lose. [*Opening the door*]   Sir—My lord!

[*Enter Lisardo*]

We're in a dreadful mess because of you.
Lisardo: I know how much I owe you; for although
I've not heard clearly, at least I know the house
Is not without its problems.
Celia: Come, let us go.
Lisardo: Let us.
Celia: [*aside*] Once he's out of the house, who cares
What happens, or how many killings there are
In the street outside.
                          [*She extinguishes the torch. Exeunt*]

[*Enter Don Felix*]

Félix: Before she came to light me to the door
I hid me in a corner of the staircase,
Enveloped in my cloak; and I was dying
Of jealous misery. There was no time
To send this man away; and, in any case,
I doubt if they would risk it, as they thought
That I was in the street. I will pretend
That I'm a servant who is in the secret,
Conduct him to the street, for that's the reason
I have remained, inspired by misery.
That is the door, and it is open now.
[*Calling softly*]   Hola! My lord! Follow me. Have no fear, Sir! You
        won't reply. Then, by heaven
Your silence makes me seek you out within.
                                              [*Exit*]

[*Enter Laura, with a torch*]

Laura: In fact my father had nothing of importance
To say to me—just that he has to go
To a nearby village where he has an estate—
So I've come back to my unhappy plight.
What's become of Celia? Where are you, Celia?
They have all gone, and left me here alone,
Beset by dangers. I'm sure it must be so,
For no one comes. Alas! What shall I do
In this predicament? Félix, no doubt,
Is lingering in the street, while the other man
Is still in hiding here. There's nothing for it:
No matter what the risk, my honor's paramount.

Marcela, pardon me on this occasion.
Hsst, sir.
Placed in such danger by a woman's folly,
Do not be startled now at sight of me.

[*She opens the door, and Don Félix enters, muffled in his cloak*]

Félix: How could I be otherwise than startled
    To see you Laura—
Laura: Oh! dear Lord, what's this?
Félix: —So inconstant—
Laura: Unhappy that I am!
Félix: —And so false?
Laura: Dear God, what does this mean?
Félix: It means—if I can manage to explain—
    It means the greatest disillusionment
    That ever man was brought by jealousy—
    But no, I lie—
    For what I feel now is not jealousy,
    But outrage!
        [*He paces up and down, and she follows him*]
Laura: [*aside*] I'm dying. [*aloud*] Félix, my love, my lord, my
    master.
Félix: Laura, my ill, my death, and my dishonor,
    What do you want of me?
Laura: I want to love you;
    That's all.
Félix: And I, of course, believe you, since you say so.
    Well, let's suppose you never had a man
    Hidden in that room, and let us suppose
    That was not the reason why you barred
    My entry there; suppose you did not come
    To speak with me, believing I was he;
    Suppose I did not see—then what did happen?
    What did I really see? The devil take me
    For being so considerate of your honor
    Till now. I'll say no more. I understand
    Nothing of this. Adieu, Laura; farewell.
Laura: One moment; stay; for you must listen to me
    Before you go.
Félix: What, madam? Could my eyes
    Be deceiving me?
Laura: Yes, they might well do so.
Félix: They deceive me, you say?
Laura: What did you see?
Félix: The figure of a man there in that room.

Laura: Perhaps it was a servant.

[*Enter Celia, in cheerful mood*]

Celia: My lady, at least
Nothing now will happen in the house,
Since both of them are outside in the street
          [*She notices Don Félix and is visibly perturbed*]
Félix: A servant indeed! Think again.
Celia: [*aside*]   What next?
How can he be here? I'm at a loss.
Laura: Don Félix, don't you see how my misfortunes
Are tightly linked together to condemn me?
Yet I am innocent.
Félix: So doubtless I'm the guilty one.
Laura: Don Félix,
Since I esteem and love you, I won't tell you
What would absolve me, for it would not be
In your best interests.[19]
Félix: That's the stale excuse
To which a guilty person has recourse
When he has no defense against a charge.
All's over, Laura; what is done is done.
And so farewell.
Laura: Consider, I beseech you
Félix: Let me go.
Laura: You shall not leave me thus.
Félix: If you detain me, I'll cry out, and so
Rouse up your father and proclaim to the world
Just what you are.
Laura: Félix!
Félix: Do not compel me
To be oblivious now of the respect
I owe your loveliness—for jealousy
Murders respect. Farewell.

                                                        [*Exit*]

Laura: Stop him, Celia.
Celia: How on earth can I?
Laura: Though you flee from me,
Félix, I'll seek you out. Ah, Marcela,
In what a quandary you've landed me!

                                                        [*Exeunt*]

Scene 2: Lisardo's room in Don Félix's house

[*Enter Lisardo and Calabazas*]

Calabazas: What's the matter, my lord? Where have you been
At this hour?
Lisardo: I don't know, Calabazas, where I've been,
Nor what is wrong with me.
Calabazas: After leaving without me—
Which isn't done with a respected lackey—[20]
You come home like a thunderbolt at crack
Of dawn, and what is more, livid and wild,
Furious, dismayed, angered—
Lisardo: Don't pester me;
And don't start uttering a pack of nonsense.
Pack our bags instead. I must get away from here.
But before I do, go into the next room
And ask Don Félix if I can have a word.
Calabazas: He's not at home. In spite of the late hour
I think he has not yet come home to bed.
Lisardo: Lucky man! He will have gone to celebrate
His reconciliation with his lady. But I—
How unfortunate am I; so many things
Have happened to me!
Calabazas: What things?
Lisardo: Listen, and I'll tell you,
But only if you spare me your advice.
As the veiled lady had sent me a note,
Inviting me to visit her, I went.
Her maid conducted me across the garden
And upstairs to a drawing-room, and there
I found the lady I had met before
Among the trees. Suffice to say, she was
As sensible as she was beauteous. At once
She started to reproach me on a matter—
Heaven knows what! And then her father came
And knocked upon the door. She hustled me
Into a neighboring room. While I was there,
I heard some conversations taking place
In the next room, but since I was listening
Behind a closed door, I could understand
Little or nothing. I could not distinguish
The words, but only heard a murmur of voices;
And then a man half entered. I threw back
My cloak and grasped my sword; but at that moment

The door was shut again from the other side,
So that I could not then distinctly see
The stranger's face or form. After a while,
Another servant came, looking distressed,
To lead me secretly into the street,
And as we went she begged me not to tell
Don Félix. Now I am besieged by doubts—
Warring suspicions—and I'm so perplexed,
I don't know what to do. For if I say
Nothing to Félix, and it should transpire
That I am justified in my suspicions—
That she's his mistress—then I would be acting
Like an enemy, ungratefully,
A poor return for friendship, when he took me
A guest into his house. On the other hand,
If I confide in him, and if this lady
Is not his mistress—as she may not be—
Then I betray a woman's trust in me,
Dishonoring my noble lineage.
Then since it is not right to speak, nor yet
To remain silent, and since two misfortunes
Beset me thus, then my best plan must be
To turn my back on both of them and go.
That is the only way not to offend
Against Don Félix by my silence, or
Against the lady if I did speak out.
Therefore prepare our luggage for the journey.
I want to set off before break of day.
I'll give as reason why I leave Ocaña
That my suit's nearly settled,[21] though I leave
With an intelligent and lovely woman
My life and soul.

Calabazas: Upon my word, sir, it's a resolution which does you credit.

Lisardo: Since you approve, Calabazas—and if you refrain from boring me with your chatter—you may have that traveling-coat I've recently had made.

Calabazas: I kiss your hands, sir, in token of my obeisance—not so much for the cloth, though that in itself would be a fine present, but because you've given it to me all made up. And while the servant who is responsible for looking out your things is getting herself out of bed, listen while I tell you in a word how much can be saved by getting ready-made clothes. [*He plays both parts, using different voices*]

> "Master tailor, how many yards do you require?"
> "Seven and three quarters."

"Quiñones does it with six and a half."

"Good luck to him then; but if he keeps his word, I'll shave off my beard."

"How much of taffeta?"

"Eight."

"Make it seven."

"Seven and a half would be the absolute minimum."

"And how much Rouen linen?"

"Four yards."

"Surely not."

"If it's an inch less, I can't manage."

"And how much silk?"

"Only a foot or so, but you'll need five yards of wool."

"What about buckram for the facings?"

"Half a yard."

"Cloth of Anjou?"

"Same again."

"Buttons?"

"Thirty Dozen."

"What! Thirty dozen?"

"Just count them for yourself. Ribbons, pockets, thread, and that's the lot; well, let's get all this to your house, sir. Now then, sir, put your feet together, head up, arm out."

"Master tailor, you're making a clown of me."

"What smart breeches you're going to have!"

"Listen: I want the doublet with wide sloping shoulders, and full at the bottom."

"Oh, I didn't bring any frieze for the coat-tails."

"Well, you can see to that; I don't mind."

"Oh! I was forgetting the linings."

"Make them out of this old cloak."

"I'll go now and see to the cutting out right away."

"When will it be ready?"

"Nine o'clock, tomorrow."

"It's one o'clock. How late the tailor is!. . . Master tailor, I've had to stay in all day waiting for you."

"I couldn't help it, for I've been trying to finish a petticoat, which consisted of so much cloth, I couldn't get it finished."
[*He changes to a different tone of voice*]   "Sir, this is a poor piece of work, as dry as dust."

"Try soaking it then."

"The breeches are tight."

"No matter; the cloth will stretch."

"This doublet is too loose."

"No matter; the cloth will shrink" (and that has to be that, as

though cloth stretches or shrinks according to the tailor's orders).
"The cloak is short."
"Long cloaks are out of fashion this year, and it reaches
almost to your garters."
"What do I owe you?"
"A mere trifle. Twenty for the breeches and twenty for the
doublet and sleeves; ten for the cloak; thirty for the but-
tonholes."—In fact, there is so much fuss and bother that, look at it
how you will, whoever gives me a ready-made coat gives me a jewel
without price.[22] I'm going to see about your things. I'm in my
glory, as well as in your grace—so all's well.[23]

                                                            [*Exit*]

Lisardo: What a fool he is! But I would to God I had his gaiety, instead
of feeling all these vexations, suspicions, and perplexities so keen-
ly. Devil take the woman, the mystery woman, with her mantle,
and her precautions, from which I can't disentangle the truth.

[*Enter Calabazas*]

Calabazas: I've just told a maid to lay out our things because we're
leaving today for God-knows-where.[24]
Lisardo: You should have added that I'm banished from Ocaña by a
woman's tricks.

[*Enter Marcela, wearing a cloak, and Silvia without one. They
stay at the door*]

Silvia: [*whispering to Marcela*].   Think what you're exposing your-
self to, madam.
Marcela: [*To Silvia*]   Don't say anything, for I am not disposed
To listen to you. He leaves today, you say?
Silvia: Yes, madam.
Marcela: Why are you so astonished, Silvia,
That Love inspires me to such wild behavior?
Laura has doubtless told him who I am,
And he is fleeing from me.
Silvia: What do you propose to do?
Marcela: Speak frankly with him.
Since my brother has not yet returned
At this late hour, it is unlikely that
He'll come back before nightfall, for he's wearing
Evening dress. Wait at this door, Silvia.

                                                      [*Exit Silvia*]

Lisardo: [*To Calabazas*]   Go and see if Don Félix is returning.
Calabazas: Don Félix? No. But here's the mystery lady.
Lisardo: What do you say?

Calabazas: *Ecce quam amas!* Behold her whom you love.
Marcela: My Lord Lisardo,
It seems to me that it is not gallant
To leave Ocaña thus, without your saying
Goodbye to one who loves you.
Lisardo: What! you have
Already learned of my departure?
Marcela: Bad news is swift.
Calabazas: [*Aside*] Good heavens! She must have commerce with
Old Nick! I wonder if this mysterious lady is none other than
Catalina de Acosta, searching for the whereabouts of her statue.[25]
Marcela: So you're leaving?
Lisardo: Yes, I'm leaving—fleeing
From you. You are the cause.
Marcela: [*Aside*] What shall I say to him? [*Aloud*] I presume
from that
You now know who I am. If that's the cause
That makes you go away, may God go with you!
But you must also know that I could not
Be frank with you, since you could not have kept
My secret once you knew it.
Lisardo: I do not understand you.
I know of you—I swear it—only what I've learned
From you yourself, and that is why I'm going.
It is your lack of confidence in me
That chases me away.
Calabazas: [*At door*] Tst! Tst! Don Félix is coming to this room.
Marcela: How unfortunate I am!
Lisardo: Why are you worried? Why are you upset?
You are with me.
Marcela: That's true.
But now that my misfortunes come in crowds,
Dogging my heels, know this—that I am—No,
I cannot, I cannot speak another word,
For he is coming. My life is in your hands.
Protect it.[26] I must hide in here. [*She hides*]
Lisardo: O Heavens!
Deliver me from mortal doubts. For she
Must be his mistress, since she is so anxious
To stop him seeing her.

[*Enter Don Félix*]

Félix: Lisardo.
Lisardo: What is it, Félix?

Félix: I've had a frightful blow, and come to seek
  Advice and consolation.
Lisardo: Leave us, Calabazas.

                                        [*Exit Calabazas*]

  Hearing that you had not returned all night,
  I thought indeed that you were celebrating
  Your reconciliation with your lady;
  And do you now come back at break of day
  And tell me you have suffered a bad blow?
Félix: Yes, one misfortune always brings another.
  Lisardo, you were right when yesterday
  You spoke of jealousy, assuring me
  Its dire anxieties and sad effects
  Were very different for the victim of it
  Than for the causer of it. There is a gulf
  Between the one who suffers and the one
  Who causes it. For now today I suffer
  The anguish which I formerly inspired.
  How much I would prefer for a hundred years
  To be the cause of jealousy than suffer it
  For a mere moment.
Lisardo: But how, or by what cause,
  Was your jealousy provoked? [*Aside*] Good Heavens! He
  Followed the lady, and his jealousy
  Has been provoked by us, by me and her.
Marcela: [*Aside*] May heaven grant a respite to my pain!
Félix: Yesterday, then, I went in humbleness
  To the house of my beauteous enemy, and through
  My prayers and tears I made her recognize
  That her suspicions were unjustified.
  So in the evening I returned to her,
  Joyful and hopeful, since her cruelty's seeds
  Had all been sown, to reap her favor's fruits.
  I was compelled by various circumstances
  To open the door of an adjoining room—
  Cursed be my forbearance!—when I saw—
  What foolish keenness!—in the darkness there
  The figure of a man.
Lisardo: [*Aside*]   Heavens! He must mean
  What happened to me last night.
Félix: A curse on me!
  For even if it meant her father came,
  And that his honor then was compromised,
  I should have entered then and killed the man,

But I did not. I managed to remain
Concealed nearby, determined to return
To seek the man, and find out who he was.
Lisardo: And did you?
Félix: No, by God! A maid already
Had got him out. I went immediately
In search of him, but I could find no trace.
I have been waiting all the morning there,
Thinking he would return. A foolish notion!
Tell me, my friend, is there in all the world
A man in greater agony today
Than I? I'm jealous, but I do not know
Of whom I'm jealous.
Lisardo: [*Aside*]   I'm brought against the truth
Of my worse imaginings. The lady here
Was the one in question, I the man in hiding.
The facts are all too clear. But yet, so long
As he does not realize that it was I,
Nor that she's hiding here, my swift departure
Will end the episode. When I'm far away,
Silence will set its seal on everything:
He will not learn the extent of her offenses,
Nor will he have a grievance against me.
Félix: What are you thinking that you do not answer?
You seem dumbfounded.
Lisardo: I am more dumbfounded
Than you imagine.
Félix: Tell me what I should do.
Lisardo: I see one remedy—to forget.
Félix: Ah! Can I?
That is the question.

[*Enter Calabazas, who remains at the door*]

Calabazas: My lord, there is a lady here, who says
She wants to speak with you.
Félix: It's her, no doubt.
She's come to see me, but I do not want
To see her.
Lisardo: First make certain it is she indeed.

[*Enter Laura, with her face concealed*]

Félix: How could I fail to recognize her? It's she.
And what she's after now is, in a word,
To make me think I'm totally misled.
Lisardo: Now I'm more confused than ever. If she's

His mistress, and he found me in her house,
Who on earth's the other woman?
Laura: I appeal to you,
My Lord Lisardo, as a gentleman,
To leave me with Don Félix, as I wish
To speak with him in private.
Félix: Who told you, madam
Don Félix will consent to speak with you?
Laura: Please leave us.
Lisardo: I'm your obedient servant, madam.
[*Aside*]   I'm forced to leave the other woman here,
Shut up, till later. I'll keep a close lookout,
Though I've no longer anything to fear,
Since my veiled lady is not after all
His mistress.
                              [*Exeunt Lisardo and Calabazas*]
Laura: Now we're alone, Don Félix, I can tell you
Without reserve what brings me here. Please listen. . .
Félix: What is the use? I know what you will say—
That it was but a dream, a mere illusion,
That I have been deceived in all I've seen
And heard. If that's the purpose of your visit,
There's nothing which you have to say to me,
And there is nothing which I wish to hear.
Laura: And if that weren't at all my purpose, but
Something quite contrary: What then?
Felix: How so?
Laura: Hear me out. I will explain it to you.
Félix: After I've heard you, you will go away?
Laura: Yes.
Félix: Speak then.[27]
[*Marcela peeps through the door*]
Laura: I'll not attempt to deny
There was a man in the room—
Félix: Stop there. Is that
The way to persuade me? Can that be the fashion
By which to appease me? When I was expecting
Tender submission, loving protestations,
Do you instead confess to the offense?
Do you not see how in repeating it
Over and over again, you hurt me by it
Over again?
Laura: If you won't hear me to the end—
Marcela: [*Aside*]   Was there ever such a cruel plight?
Félix: What else is there for me to hear?

Laura: A lot.
Félix: Will you go after I have heard you?
Laura: Yes.
Félix: Speak then.
Laura: It would be wrong for me to deny
There was a man in my room, whom Celia
Admitted to the house: for to face a man
And deny something he has seen and heard
Is like one's offering a desperate man
A noose by way of comfort. But, equally,
For you to think that I myself have acted
Dishonorably to your love or my firm faith,
That would be like imagining a blemish
Could ever mar the dawn's pure roseate sunlight,
Because the brilliance of the sun is full
Of darkness in comparison with my honor.
Félix: Who was this man then?
Laura: That I cannot tell you.
Marcela: [Aside] Was there ever such confusion?
Félix: Why?
Laura: I do not know him.
Félix: What was he doing
In hiding there?
Laura: That too I do not know.
Félix: Where then is your excuse?
Laura: My ignorance.
Félix: That's fine! Your ignorance is your excuse,
While I'm to blame because I want to know.
How indeed can you possibly expect me
To stifle what I know by dint of what
I do not know? Laura, Laura, you have no excuse.
Laura: Don't press me, Félix; for, although I can tell you,
You must not learn it.
Félix: So you said before,
And I found it hurtful and insulting then.[28]
By God, I will not stand the repetition.
You must tell me the truth of the matter, here and now.
Marcela: [Aside] What shall I do? Alas! to excuse herself
She'll ruin me.
Félix: Tell me the truth, for I would rather know it
Than to go on imagining the worst.
Laura: I'll tell it then.[29]
Marcela: [Aside] No she will not. I will prevent her. Love,
Who gives me boldness, grant me too success.
[She crosses the stage with her face covered, making a

threatening gesture to Don Félix; he tries to follow her and
Laura detains him]
Marcela: That's what I wanted to see.
Félix: Who is this woman?
Laura: You're playing to perfection
A man surprised.
Félix: Let me follow her,
To see if I recognize her.
Laura: Yes, I see!
You want to appease her, telling her that you
Have left me to run after her. You shall not.
Félix: Laura, my dearest one, may heaven forsake me
If I know who she is.
Laura: But I know, sir,
And I will tell you. It was Nise. Yes,
I recognized her by her mien and gait.
Félix: I tell you it was not; nor do I know
How the woman happens to be here.
Laura: "That's fine! Your ignorance is your excuse,
While I'm to blame because I want to know.
How indeed can you possibly expect me
To stifle what I know by dint of what
I do not know?" Good-bye, Félix.
Félix: If
The explanation I have given you
Is not enough, how do you expect me, Laura,
To believe you when you will not credit me?
Laura: Because I tell the truth; and furthermore
I am who I am.[30]
Félix: And so am I.
And I have seen a man within your room.
Laura: And I a woman in yours.
Félix: I do not know
Who she was.
Laura: Nor did I him.
Félix: Oh yes, you did, Laura,
And you were about to tell me.
Laura: I'm going away,
And shall not tell you now. I would prefer
Not to give explanations to a man
As rude as you.
Félix: Look here, Laura.
Laura: Let me go,
Félix.
Félix: Well, go! For it's a bitter thing

To have to beg while knowing that one has
Cause for complaint.
Laura: Stay where you are. It fills me
With rage to think I have to suffer now
Such disloyalty, when I came with love.
Félix: I have no reason to reproach myself.
Laura: And if it comes to that, neither have I.
Félix: Because I saw a man there in your room.
Laura: And in yours I saw a woman.
Félix: O God! If this
Is love—
Laura: If this is love, for goodness sake—
Félix: ⎫
         ⎬ May fire from heaven consume such love! Amen! Amen!
Laura: ⎭

ACT III

Scene 1: Marcela's room in Don Félix's house

[*Enter Marcela and Silvia*]

Silvia: You were audacious, madam.
Marcela: When I perceived,
In listening to Laura, she was going
To tell him what had happened at her house,
And that I should be lost, I took a sudden
Resolution to cut short her tale—
Hence my rash action. When disaster looms,
One's bound to take a risk.
Silvia: That's very true.
Marcela: What gave me courage
Was seeing Lisardo and assuming he
Was waiting to discover what would happen
To his imprisoned lady. Thus aware,
I was not frightened of the undertaking;
For, if things should go badly, in Lisardo
I had at least a man who would defend me.
As it happened, I was more successful
By far than I could possibly have hoped:
For I was able safely to return
To my own room; and through the jealousy
I left behind me, things got so confused
Lisardo had no need to get involved

On my behalf; neither did Laura finish
Her tale, nor Félix recognize me; so
The worst is over.
Silvia: That was a queer business,
I do declare, and if you've learned your lesson,
So much the better.
Marcela: Has it ever happened,
Silvia, that a peril one's escaped
Served for a warning for the future? No,
Quite the contrary! That I have come so well
Out of this danger has encouraged me
To think how best to arrange for Don Lisardo
To see me again.
Silvia: Listen! I hear a noise.

[*Enter Don Félix by the concealed door*]
Félix: Marcela!
Marcela: What on earth's the reason, Félix,
For this intrusion?
Félix: I come here in the hope
Of being enlightened by your common sense
And calmed by your compassion.* When you left,
After your visit to Laura, I went there,
Entered her house, I found there, I saw there—Oh!
Marcela: Tell me, what did you find? What did you see?
Félix: A man.
Marcela: How could that be?
Félix: She came to see me here
To excuse herself, but while she was about it,
A woman came out of my bedroom, and
Prevented it.
Marcela: How infamous!
Félix: This woman
Must have been here with Lisardo, but
He, being a discreet and prudent man,
And fearing he had damaged the respect
He owed my house, insists that he knows nothing
About the affair. Be that as it may—
For nobody admits to anything—
Laura is jealous, and declines to hear
Either my explanation or excuses.
As for me, not wishing to augment

---

*The lengthy speech by Félix describing Philip IV's hunting activities begins at this point in the Osuna manuscript and continues for 149 lines. See Appendix following the play (pp. 68-70) and our comments in the Preface and Introduction, pp. x-xi, xxx.

My suffering, I neither wish to see
Nor talk with her. Yet I would like to learn
What she is thinking. I've puzzled about this
And now I think I've hit upon a ruse
To accomplish it.

Marcela: Are you going to tell me what it is?

Félix: It's this, Marcela: that you should pretend
That we have quarreled, so much so that now
We're still at loggerheads; and while you're waiting
For things to improve, you want to stay with her.
And in that way I'll have a spy in the camp,
And thus relieve the fire which now consumes me.
For you'll be on the watch and quickly find,
No doubt, the identity of the muffled man,
Then in secrecy tell me all about it.

Marcela: There are some strong objections could be raised
Against this plan. However, I shall go
To her house this very day.

Félix: Today? You can't do that.
Whether she wished to demonstrate how little
She was affected by my misery,
Or simply to increase it, she left home
Early this morning to visit Lake Antigola.[31]

Marcela: Well, then depend on it, I'll go tomorrow.

Félix: You bring me back to life. From this day forth,
Marcela, I shall owe my life to you.

                                                    [*Exit*]

Marcela: Is not this a wonderful piece of luck,
That he should ask me for the very thing
I could have wished for? But see who has come in
Unannounced.

Sylvia: It's Laura, madam, accompanied by Celia.

[*Enter Laura and Celia, wearing hats and capes*]

Marcela: What! My dear Laura, calling at this hour?

Laura: Don't be surprised, my dear, for I have had
A terrible experience.

Marcela: Who could doubt it?

Laura: Yes,
And just as you came yesterday to me,
So now today I come to beg your help.

Celia: "Learn then, ladies, that today
Can change indeed from yesterday."[32]

Laura: You do not know, my dear Marcela, that

Don Félix saw the man whom you concealed
Within my house.
Marcela: Good gracious!
Laura: It matters little
To tell you when or how. No sooner was
Disaster merely possibility
It turned into reality. I was impatient
To explain myself to him, and, careless of
My reputation, I came here to see him.
I entered his room; but at the very moment
When I was telling a convincing tale
Which would not compromise myself or you,
A woman who was hidden in his closet,
And who was doubtless Nise—
Marcela: Who could doubt it?[33]
Laura: Emerged from her hiding place, to fill my heart
With as much jealousy as his.
Marcela: My dear,
What shocking conduct! What did Félix do?
Laura: He wished to follow her—I would not let him.
Then both of us repeated our complaints.
I would not listen to him, nor was he
Prepared to learn of mine. Then afterwards,
In order to pretend that I was happy
And free from care—How hard it is, Marcela,
Upon the soul, to struggle to be happy
When one is sad!—I went with friends of ours
To Lake Antigola. There that tranquil vista
Ought to have made me happy, but for me
All happiness is dead. So there was nothing
Could bring relief. Neither seeing the queen
(May she reign forever, so that the blossom
From France may yield in time fruit in Castile!)[34]
In her green carriage drawn by splendid horses
As golden as the sun, a ship to sail
Upon the land, she reached the water's edge
In order to embark; nor yet beholding
How that brief stretch of water, whose waves were ruffled
By the soft breezes, seemed to imitate
Those of the ocean, upon recognizing
Who the traveler was, were made as still
As silver ornaments, their ripples glass;
Nor yet the sight of the barque, like a sea-coach,
With oars for horses and the helm for bridle,

Letting the railing down that formed its steps
Giving access to the deck, so that it might
Admit within its sphere the sun in person,
Guarded by Dawn herself; nor yet the sight
Of lovely ladies like the lesser flowers
Attending on the rose, reminding one
Of a legendary choir of nymphs,
Weaving their dances through Diana's groves;
Nor even the sight
Of the ship traversing that expanse of crystal,
A sight so lovely as it neared the isle
Where the pavilion is, and bearing flowers
So that it was impossible to tell
Which was the barque and which was the pavilion,
So many flowers in both, it seemed they fought
A naval battle of blossoms for their lives,
And to their deaths, not even that sight, Marcela,
Could bring me ease. For all that lovely splendor—
The water's merriment, the joy of flowers,
The gentleness of the breezes, the leaves' music,
The ladies' beauty, laughter in the meadows—
For me was misery, misery to my eye,
Made jealous as I was because of Félix.
If even that cannot distract one's mind,
One's on the danger list. I don't intend
To talk to Félix, for it would be wrong
And quite unworthy of me to give him
The opportunity to augment my pain.
So I would like to use a stratagem,
And if you prize my friendship you will aid me.
In order to discover whether Nise
Frequents his room, I'll spy on him tonight,
Using that door there which you told me of,
Leading to his room, and which he keeps concealed
Behind a tapestry. You're bound to ask
How I can thus absent myself from home.
I will tell you. My father has departed
To a village where he has some property,
And he will not be back till four days hence;
So I can be your guest now for some nights,
If friendship can persuade you to this favor
Worthy a friend so well-born, so discreet,
So noble and intelligent.

Marcela: How can I,

Laura, refuse to grant what you request,
Since you are using the same argument
I used with you before, and your distress
Persuades me, as it is the same as mine.
There is one drawback, though. If you remove it,
Come when you will, my dear, this house is yours.
Laura: What is this obstacle?
Marcela: It is my brother,
Who suffers the same anguish as you do,
And for the self-same reason. It is no matter
That I betray him:
For women always should combine together
Against these men. My brother has just asked me
To feign that I have fallen out with him,
And, on this pretext, that I should request you
To grant me some days' hospitality,
So I can serve him as his spy-in-chief,
If, then, I stayed to be your hostess here,
He would complain—
Laura: Listen! that is better still.
Of course you shall pretend to quarrel with him,
And go off to my house. That will ensure
He won't suspect that I am in his house.
Marcela: You're right: my absence will prevent his having
Any suspicion of it.
Laura: How shall we manage?
Marcela: Nothing is easier. Give me my mantle, Silvia.
You'll tell Don Félix that I've gone to Laura's
And that, to make our quarrel plausible,
I've chosen to go at night.
[*Aside to Silvia, while she dons her mantle*]   Go find Lisardo.
Tell him from me to come and find me there
This evening without fail. And then return
And act as Laura's maid.
[*Aloud*]   Come with me, Celia, for our plan depends
On changing maids as well as houses.
Laura: So soon?
Marcela: In matters such as these, the less one thinks
About them, the more likely is success.
Laura: Marcela, you are going to my house.
Be careful of it, and of my honor too.
Marcella: Since you remain in mine, be careful likewise,
And of my honor. I wonder where this ruse
Will end?

Celia: Shall I tell you? There will be a scene
Ending in marriage for us all—or worse.

[Exeunt Marcela and Celia by one door,
Laura and Silvia by another]

Scene 2: A garden

[Enter Lisardo and Calabazas]

Lisardo: What's that paper you've got there?

Calabazas: What it should be: an exact and reasonable account of what you owe me since I've been in your service.

Lisardo: Why give it to me at this moment?

Calabazas: Because at this moment I wish to leave your service.

Lisardo: For what reason?

Calabazas: Isn't it obvious? Because you've not taken me into your confidence these last few days.

Lisardo: What do you mean by that?

Calabazas: I mean that you have been very distracted.

Lisardo: My unhappiness is the cause.

Calabazas: It isn't right that a master of mine should be so secretive, as if to imply that I cannot keep his secrets. You walk about all on your own; you come and go all on your own, and always without me. It seems, sir, we are as far apart as love and money. Take just one example. If some veiled lady comes to see you, it's "Clear out!" If you're going to visit her, it's "Wait for me; it won't do for you to accompany me." This can't go on. What grief for the mother who bore me! What use am I to you now? That's why I want to find without delay a more humane master; because, as far as I'm concerned, no one could be worse than you. Even a pedantic would-be wit, who's really a nit-wit, couldn't be worse; nor a man with a sound wit and an unsound fortune; nor a busybody with no wit at all, nor a poet who writes plays—even ones presenting masters and men alike as pumpkin-pates; nor a painted fop who talks all la-di-da; nor even the sort—and that's the worst of all— who does his wooing in the palace.[35]

Lisardo: Alas! my dear Calabazas, the adventures
Which have befallen me these last few days
Have happened publicly, so you must know them,
Without the need for me to tell them to you—
The talk with that veiled woman in the country,
The secret meeting with her in her house,
The adventure that I had while I was hiding—
Like the one that Félix later had—
And then her visit to me, and my being put right

By the other woman on Félix's lady-love;
And then her going off in the way she did.
Well it all speaks, is indeed *seen* for itself,
And there's no need for me to explain it now.
So, even if I wanted to, I could not
Inform you more than you can see yourself.

Calabazas: She's a wonderful schemer at least.

Lisardo: That's true; and therefore I am baffled still
By what has happened, and I am dismayed
That I'm still wondering who in fact she is.
When I supposed she was Don Félix's lady,
I didn't speculate at all; but after
I'd talked with her, and since Don Félix's lady
Entered, and categorically denied
That she was the other lady, I've acquired
A great desire to find out who she is;
For I no longer need have any fear
About her honor, as I did before
On account of Félix.

Calabazas: I might well be able
To tell you who she is.

Lisardo: You?

Calabazas: Me.

Lisardo: Tell me then.

Calabazas: Heavens! yes, I know who she must be.

Lisardo: Don't keep me in suspense.

Calabazas: Well, she's a schemer,
Isn't she? So I know who she must be.
She's an intriguer, isn't she? So I know
Who she must be. She's a know-all, isn't she?
Oh! I know who she must be. She's a chatter-box,
Isn't she? That all goes to show
Who she is. I swear it does.

Lisardo: Then tell me.

Calabazas: Strictly between outselves—

Lisardo: Get on with it.

Calabazas: She's a duenna, that's what she is.[36]

Lisardo: What nonsense!

[*Enter Silvia*]

Silvia: Lord Lisardo, I would like a word with you.

Calabazas: Where did this girl spring from?

Lisardo: What do you want with me?

Silvia: A lady whose house you know begs you to call on her this
evening. Knock at her window. Farewell.   [*Exit*]

Calabazas: Hi! Most veiled of all veiled ladies!
Lisardo: Stop! Where are you going?
Calabazas: Let me go. I merely want to give her two or three slaps to carry to her mistress.
Lisardo: Who could take seriously your foolish chatter?
Calabazas: I want to teach her not to be an interfering duenna from this time forth.
Lisardo: Listen. Now that cold night comes on apace
Amid the reddened haze of dusk that bids
The sun depart together with the day,
And I'm expected elsewhere, find me a buckler,
And wait for me here.
Calabazas: I wait for you?
Lisardo: Yes.
Calabazas: No sir. I should have to be a double-dyed Jew to do that.[37] You can't go alone to a house where you were locked up and frustrated, and where, as we know, there's a father for sure, and possibly a lover in the offing as well.
Lisardo: I must go alone, I tell you.

 [*Enter Don Félix*]

Félix: Where are you going, Lisardo?
Lisardo: I don't know how
To keep things from you any longer, nor
How I will manage to recount to you
All that has happened since I came to stay
Here at Ocaña. Are you busy now?
Félix: I? I have nothing at all to do tonight.
Lisardo: Nothing at all?
Félix: No, the flame consuming me
In order to intensify the heat
Has called a truce.
Lisardo: Then I would like to tell you
Without misgiving what my problem is.
For if till now I have refrained from telling
The end of the story I began this morning,
It was because of you and the esteem
In which I hold you. But since I have found
That none of this affects you after all,
And you're the man you are,
I am determined to confide in you
The secret of my love. Come, let us go.
Not to lose time, I'll tell you on the way
A strange adventure.
Félix: Let us go. You do me

A signal favor in distracting me
From the pain that fills my heart; and so your love
May serve as antidote to cure that love
Which poisons me.
Calabazas: What about me, sir?
Lisardo: Wait here for our return.

[Exeunt Lisardo and Félix]

Calabazas: Well, that's a fine test of my patience! To stay here, keeping
mum, with nothing to see or hear, when there's no other pleasure
or entertainment when a man's in service than to hear, so as to
know, and to know, so as to tell! And he would deprive me of even
that pleasure by leaving me in the dark. But upon my word that
shall not be. Calabazas will have his day. Simply because he has
kept me out of it, I'm determined to follow him. I'll dog their
footsteps muffled in my cloak; or if I should fail—as I won't,
methinks—to spy on him and gossip about him, I ask you, what's
the good of being his servant?[38]

[Exit]

Scene 3: A road on the outskirts of Ocaña

[Enter Fabio, stumbling with fatigue, and a servant, Lelio]

Lelio: Take heart, my lord, for we are near Ocaña.
Fabio: The pain is so acute, I can't go further.
I thought, dismounting from my horse and walking
A while, to overcome by exercise
The pain I suffered from my fall, but yet
I must confess that never in my life
Have I been so exhausted.
Lelio: It was lucky
That the mare fell when we had scarcely traveled
A league from home, so that you could return
More easily—and there you'll get the care
To effect your cure.
Fabio: It's in this leg I feel
The pain. It bore the whole weight of the mare.
Lelio: You should remount: then you'll arrive the sooner.
Fabio: It's better, Lelio, that I should walk
A little more, and so prevent my leg
From stiffening up.
Lelio: You're right, sir. But I think
As night is closing in, that though you might
Improve your leg by walking for a bit,
You would get home at an unseemly hour,

Perhaps when everyone has gone to bed,
And no one to attend your injuries.

Fabio: You're right.
Get the mare ready, it's tethered to that tree,
And let's be on our way, since that is best
For my condition, Lelio. And yet
I have a presentiment which says to me
That I should not be hasty to return,
In order to avoid upsetting Laura.
She loves me so much that I am afraid,
If I return home in this dreadful state,
Today might prove to be her last.[39]

Lelio: No doubt
She will be grieved, as a daughter ought to be.

Fabio: I'll wager she already has retired.

Lelio: No doubt she has.

Fabio: I shall be sorry to awaken her.
We can't do otherwise—but what I'll do
To save her from disturbance is to knock
On the main door—it's furthest from her room—
And so she may not hear me.

Lelio: Your health's the main concern; for that is what
My mistress thinks of most.

Fabio: Don't be surprised
To see me act with such consideration,
For at my age I'm lover of her virtue,
As much as others love her loveliness.   [*Exeunt*]

Scene 4: A street near Fabio's house. Night.

[*Enter Lisardo and Félix*]

Félix: Your story has delighted me, Lisardo.
I have never heard a stranger one.

Lisardo: That's most of it.
I have omitted many little details,
For fear of boring you. And now, farewell.
Now is the hour—she is awaiting me.

Félix: One moment. You say you're going to see a lady
At the same house where you have been in danger,
And yet ask me to leave you. Those two things
Don't hang together. I'm not the sort of friend
Who is contented with the passive role
Of confidant. I set more store by action
Than upon words. By all means meet your lady,

But I intend to act as sentinel
Outside the house till dawn.

Lisardo: It would be wrong
Of me, Don Félix, to refuse such proof
Of friendship.

[*Enter Calabazas, looking as though trying to see, without being
seen*]

Calabazas: If I could make out what they say, as I can make out where
they're going, then I'd make out indeed, knowing both where
they're going and what they're saying. Let me get closer.

Lisardo: But what is this?

Félix: It is a man, if I
Am not mistaken, who is following us.

Lisardo: Let's draw our swords.

Félix: Who goes there?

Calabazas: No one, now;
For I'm not going since I stopped.

Félix: Who are you?

Calabazas: An honest man.

Lisardo: In that case, pass; if pass
You can.

Calabazas: I'd rather not pass, but play instead
A court card.

Félix: Then I'll lead my ace of spades,
Which is my sword.⁴⁰

Lisardo: Let's kill him.

Calabazas: Stop!
My goodness, sir, you're killing me, and me
Is Calabazas.

Félix: Who did you say?

Calabazas: Calabazas.

Lisardo: What does this mean?

Calabazas: I only wished to see
Where you were going, as you wouldn't tell me.

Félix: By God, let's beat him black and blue.
            [*The two noblemen set about Calabazas*]

Calabazas: Enough, enough, sirs!

Lisardo: Let him go, we do not wish to cause
Any disturbance when the house we're after
Is near at hand.

Félix: What! Lisardo! The lady
Whom you are meeting lives at hand?

Lisardo: Yes, Félix.

Félix: And she is beautiful, you say?

Lisardo: Yes—very.
Félix: Her father lives with her?
Lisardo: Yes.
Félix: And it was there
  In this house, you had to shut yourself
  In a chamber?
Lisardo: Yes.
Félix: And you and she were there
  Together when that other lady came
  Upon the scene—the one who later came
  In search of me.
Lisardo: Yes.
Félix: Look here! the night is filled
  With gloomy shadows, darker than before,
  For even the moon is absent. It may be
  That you're mistaken.
Lisardo: Not at all, I assure you.
  This is the window on which I must knock.
  That is the door which they will open for me.
Calabazas: [*Aside*]   I know the house now. Good!
Félix: [*Aside*]   This very window? And this very door?
  Heaven preserve me! This is Laura's house.
  Its double exit has been utilized
  For double-dealing.
Lisardo: Retire a little while I give the signal.   [*He taps at the grating*]
Félix: [*Aside*]   Alas! Alas!   [*Aloud*]   If I am not mistaken,
  When you told me your tale just now, you said
  The woman who's waiting now to talk with you
  Was the same one who hid within my closet?
Lisardo: Yes.
Félix: And that the other woman, she who came—

  [*Celia appears at the window*]

Celia: Tst!
Lisardo: I'm being called.
Celia: Is it you,
  Lisardo:?
Lisardo: Yes, it's I.
Félix: [*Aside*]   The voice of Celia.
Celia: One moment. I will open for you.
Lisardo: It is her maid who spoke to me. She said
  She'd open for me.
Félix: Before she does so,
  Just tell me this—
          [*Celia opens the door*]

Lisardo: Too late. She's done it.
Félix: If it should be—
Lisardo: Farewell. She's waiting for me.
Félix: —The lady who—
Celia: Enter quickly.
Lisardo: We will talk later.
                    [*Exit Lisardo. When Félix tries to follow him inside,
                              Celia shuts the door in his face*]
Félix: And to crown all, Celia has banged the door
        Upon my face.
Calabazas: If one receives a blow on the face from a door, one isn't
    dishonoured, provided it has a lock to make a show of steel, for a
    flourish of cold steel is enough to temper any affront.[41]
Félix: [*Aside*]   What's happening to me? Was there ever such
        Uncertainty as this? Dear Heavens! He's come—
        Has he not—to meet in Laura's house
        The lady who departed from my chamber
        When Laura entered? So Laura can't be she.
        But in that case, who on earth can it be,
        Since it's *her* house? O fool! Why did I tell
        Marcela not to come here till the morning?
        She'd have found out the truth. But while I loiter,
        Reasoning thus, I give an opportunity
        For my dishonor. So then, Jealousy,
        Let's cease to reason and press forward quickly
        To see the obvious truth. Either the woman
        Is Laura, or not Laura. If she is not,
        What have I to lose by clearing up
        My worrying doubts? And if it's she,
        What do I lose, because in losing her
        I lose my life, my soul? I'll break this door down.
        But how can I presume to do this, when
        To Lisardo's service I have pledged myself?
        But what do friendship, trust, consideration,
        Propriety matter? When Jealousy commands,
        The heart of man has room for nothing else.
        Not friendship, no, nor honor can prevail.
                [*He bangs hard on the door, as if trying to bring it down, and
                at the same time more hard knocking is heard from within
                some distance away*]
Calabazas: What are you doing sir?
Félix: I'm going to kill you.
Calabazas: Oh, don't do it, sir, if at all possible.
Félix: What is that knocking at the other door?
Calabazas: Nothing surprising. Another gentleman

In front of another door, who's filled with rage,
And pounding there, as you are pounding here.
Fabio: [*Off*]   Open the door, Celia. Open, Laura.
Celia: [*Within*]   O heavens! It is my master.
Félix: It is Lord Fabio.
                    [*The clash of swords is heard within*]
Fabio: [*Within*]   What! Have I come home to be a witness
Of my dishonor?
Calabazas: Good God! They're fighting in there with swords.
Félix: Curse on this door!   [*He moves away*]

[*Enter Lisardo, with his arms around Marcela, as if feeling his
way in the dark*]

Lisardo: Fear nothing, madam, I know
The man who's knocking. He's a man of trust.
Marcela: Lead me, Lisardo. Once we reach your house,
Protected by it, I'll have nought to fear.
Lisardo: Come, madam. Do not be mistrustful of
The man who's with me.
Marcela: Is it Félix?
Lisardo: Yes.
Marcela: But have a care, Lisardo; Félix is—
Lisardo: Why
Do you hesitate? This is no time for coyness.
Felix?
Félix: Who is it?
Lisardo: Myself and my misfortune.
Félix: What has happened then?
Lisardo: While I was conversing with this lady,
Her father came and knocked.[42] And then, impatient
At the delay in opening, he burst the lock.
Drawing his sword, he entered in the chamber.
But we put out the light, so I was able
To get the lady out. Lead her to safety,
For I'll remain to cover your retreat,
And prevent anyone from following you.
Calabazas will stay with me.
Calabazas: Not if he can help it, he won't.
Félix: It might be better if he went with her,
And both of us stayed here.
Lisardo: Are we to leave her
So much alone? It is not right, because
In such a predicament the primary duty
Is to the lady. So you had better take her
Without me; bear her to safety.

Félix: You are right.

[*Aside to Marcela*]   So, Laura, are you in my power at last?

Marcela: [*Aside*]   Alas! that I should be so unfortunate.

Félix: [*Aside*]   Alas! I'm dying.

Marcela: [*Aside*]   How I tremble!

Félix: Come with me, madam; though you don't deserve

Any consideration, I am who I am,

And therefore I must act to save you.

Marcela: [*Aside*]   Was ever woman so unfortunate?

Félix: [*Aside*]   Was ever man so horribly unlucky?

[*Exeunt Félix and Marcela*]

[*Enter Fabio, a torch in one hand, a sword in the other, Lelio and other servants with drawn swords*]

Fabio: Although I'm old and feeble, yet my honor

Will give me strength for my revenge.

Lisardo: Stop!

You shall not pass.

Fabio: My sword will carve.

A passage through your heart.

[*All fight*]

Calabazas: Ah! Wretched Calabazas!

What put it in your head to play the spy?

Lisardo: [*Aside*]   Now that Félix has got clean away,

I'll quit the field before I'm recognized.

That is not cowardice, but the braver course.

[*Exit*]

Fabio: Wait, coward! Come back!

Calabazas: Who would have supposed

My master would have left me in the lurch?

Lelio: There's one of them still here.

Fabio: Why are you waiting, Lelio? Kill him.

Calabazas: In God's name, stop!

Fabio: Who are you?

Calabazas: I am only,

If fear does not deceive me, "a curious impertinent."[43]

Fabio: Give me your sword.

Calabazas: There it is, my lord.

And if that's not enough, there is my dagger,

And my shield, and if that's not enough,

I'll give you too my cloak, and then my hat,

My doublet, and my breeches.

Fabio: Are you not

The valet of the man who has outraged

My house?

Calabazas: Yes, my lord; my master
Is an intolerable house-outrager.
Fabio: Who is he? What's his name?
Calabazas: He's named Lisardo.
He is a soldier, and he is a friend
Of Don Félix.
Fabio: Not to waste my vengeance
On the insignificant, I'll spare your life.
Calabazas: Thank you, my lord.

                                                    [*Exit*]

Fabio: With this information to throw light
On my misfortune, I'll go to see Don Félix.
My curses on a house that has two doors,
Since in it one's honor is so poorly guarded.

                                                  [*Exeunt*]

Scene 5: A room in Don Félix's house

[*Enter Don Félix with Marcela, as if groping their way in the dark.
They speak the first lines before their entrance. Then a door at the
other side opens, partly hidden by a curtain behind which Laura
and Silvia are seen peeping*]

Félix: [*Within*]   Hullo, there! Bring a torch!
Herrera: [*Within*]   I'll bring one, sir,
If my sleep-blinkered eyes can light upon it.

[*Laura and Silvia appear behind the curtain*]

Laura: [*Aside to Silvia*]   They're in the room now. Let us listen here.
Félix: [*To Marcela*]   And now, ungrateful woman, now at least,
You can't deny
Laura: [*To Silvia*]   He's speaking to a woman.
Félix: You can't deny now in this situation
That you are light, inconstant, fickle, cruel,
Deceitful and perfidious; for no man
Could find the validity of his jealous fears
So blatantly confirmed, as I have now.
Marcela: [*Aside*]   I doubt if I'll survive!
Félix: Was that the reason why you came this morning
To see me?
Laura: [*Aside*] This must be the muffled lady
Who came this morning to his house.
Félix: Now you are in my power with no excuse.
A curse on all the days that I have loved you,

A curse on all the anguish I have suffered,
On all the anxieties, and all the favors
My love has granted you.

Laura: [*To Siliva*]   Do you hear that?
He admits that he has loved her. How can I wait?

Silvia: Where are you going, madam?

Laura: Ah! Silvia,
How perturbed I am! I'm going closer,
To hear them better.

Félix: Dear God! How much longer ere you bring the light?

Herrera: Light is coming, my lord.[44]

Marcela: [*Aside*]   What will become of me, if light is brought?

Félix: You do not speak? But no, for you admit
I speak the truth, and cannot say a word.
The torch there, ho!

> [*At this point Marcela begins to draw away, and Laura comes forward between them, so that when Félix reaches out for Marcela's hand, he seizes Laura's instead, and is still holding it when at last the torch is brought; Marcela by then has just left, closing the door behind her*]

Marcela: [*Aside*]   Oh! If only I could find the door
And get away, my life would then be saved.

Félix: [*Seizing Laura by the hand*]   Stop! Do not fly. Besides, there is no need,
For all the vengeance I desire is only
That you should be aware that I know all.

Laura: [*Aside*]   He takes me for the other. I'll keep quiet
About my grievance till the light is brought,
When he will see it's I to whom he's talking.

Marcela: In spite of my confusion and distress,
At last I've found the door of my apartment.
May it give sanctuary! For it is fortunate
That it was open.

Silvia: Are you Laura?

Marcela: No,
I am not Laura. But you're Silvia?

Silvia: Yes, madam. What has happened?

Marcela: A thousand sorry accidents. Why do you tarry?

> [*Exeunt Silvia and Marcela*]

[*Enter Herrera, bearing a torch*]

Herrera: Here is the torch, sir.

Félix: Leave it here, and go
And wait outside

> [*Exit Herrera. Félix closes the door behind him*]

Laura: [*Aside*]   When he returns and sees me,
That will be that.
Félix: [*Returning*]   Laura, you see before you
That one man in the world who has stood guard
For his rival's rendezvous.
Laura: [*Aside*]   What does this mean?
How comes it that he's not embarrassed, nor
Upset to see me?
Félix: Yes, I'm the only man
Who has brought his lady to another's arms.
And now attempt to argue if you can
That I'm the one who's guilty of offense.
Laura: What fine dissembling! And how bold you are
To feign the actual grievance against me
That I have against you! For, once aware,
On finding me within your arms, that you
Have been addressing me, and not the woman
You've brought into your house, you yet proceed
To make the same complaints, directing them
'Gainst me, instead of her.
Félix: My patience, sorely strained,
Needed but that. You would presume to make me
Imagine I was speaking here just now
With another woman?
Laura: Why so surprised, Don Félix,
When you know it's true?
Félix: Where is the woman then
With whom I spoke?
Laura: If a house with two doors
Is difficult to guard, a room with two doors
Is even worse. She's gone.
Félix: By heaven, Laura,
Depart from me. Leave off. You'll drive me mad,
If you would have me think that I have not
Brought you here, because your father—Words
Fail me—was outside, and Lisardo was—
I cannot finish—
Laura: You are deceived, Don Félix.
I've spent the night concealed in your sister's room,
Merely to see what I indeed have seen,
While she—
Félix: Stop there! I'll see for myself. Marcela,
Come here!

[*Enter Marcela and Silvia*]

Marcela: What do you want? [*Aside*] I now know all,
And so I must dissemble.
Félix: Tell me, has Laura
Passed the night with you?
Marcela: Has Laura passed
The night with me? Why should she? I was to go
Tomorrow to her house, you will remember.
But, heavens! Why should she stay with me?
Laura: One moment!
Did I not come to see you after dinner?
And did I not ask you then to let me stay
Here at your house? Did I not place *my* house—
Marcela: Do not go on—for none of this is true.
Félix: You see your ruse has failed. How can you say
My sister passed the night with you, when she,
Having retired, was resting in her room?
Laura: You do me wrong, Marcela.
Marcela: [*Aside to Laura*]   Yes; but every man
Is for himself.
Laura: Well, since I am compelled,
The truth shall come to light; and you should know
It was Marcela who—
              [*Knocking within*]
Silvia: Someone is knocking.
Lisardo: [*Within*] Open, Félix.
Félix: Now Laura, you will see
The game is up; for here comes your gallant.
Laura: [*Aside*] That gives me grounds for hope.
Marcela: [*Aside*]   All will be ruined.
If only I could give Lisardo warning
Of the peril I am in. [*She moves to one side*]

[*Enter Lisardo*]

Lisardo: I have delayed
To ensure I was not followed. Where is the lady?
Félix: Here before your eyes. But ere I see her
Within your power, and find my hope is ended,
You'll have to kill my soul.
Lisardo: Until this hour
I would not have believed a nobleman
With a knightly code of honor would deceive
Someone who sought his help. Again I ask of you
The lady I confided to your care.
Félix: Is this not she?
Lisardo: No.

Félix: That is all I need
To make me absolutely lose my patience.
Marcela: [*Aside*] Oh! How unfortunate I am!
Lisardo: If you believe her to be so, Don Félix,
Driven by some reason, then you explain.
Laura: I'm going to lead you from the labyrinth.
Tell me, Lisardo, is not this the woman
Whom you are seeking?
Lisardo: Yes, it's she indeed.
Why have you screened her from my eyes?
Laura: [*To Félix*] Now you will see whither she had retired,
And was resting in her room. [*Aside to Marcela*] It's every man
For himself in this, Marcela
Félix: My shame! This dagger
Shall serve to kill now a dishonored sister.
Marcela: Save me, Lisardo!
Lisardo: [*Placing himself in front of Marcela*] Is this the sister of Don
Félix?
Félix: Yes.
And I will take revenge on her.
Lisardo: You know well
Who I am, and therefore know I must
Protect her, since she is a woman.
Félix: You
Know likewise who I am, and that no man
Dare but to look upon her in my house
Unless he were her husband.
Lisardo: If that is all,
I willingly consent to your condition.

[*Enter Fabio, Calabazas, and servants*]

Fabio: This is the house. Go in.
Félix: What brings you here?
Fabio: Honor, Don Félix.
Calabazas: [*Aside*] Oh! they'll be led a pretty dance—a sword-dance
belike.
Fabio: Where is your friend—Lisardo?
Lisardo: That is I,
Who's never been afraid to show his face
To any man.
Calabazas: He has never been afraid to show his face, that's true; but
he once showed his heels.
Fabio: You are a traitor!
Félix: Fabio, stay your hand.
[*He draws Fabio to one side*]

Your anger has deceived you. The rage you feel
Because of Laura is occasioned by
My behavior; and it falls on me
To protect her as my wife.
Fabio: If Laura marries you,
I have no more to say.
Félix: As proof, my lord,
Here, Laura, is my hand. And since it was
Because your house and my room here have both
Two doors, that Lisardo and I have undergone
All these confusions, here ends the comedy—
A HOUSE WITH TWO DOORS IS DIFFICULT TO GUARD.

THE END

Appendix

[Note: Directors wishing to insert this speech in the text (p. 47) for performance should, in the interest of sense and meter, change the line bearing the asterisk ("And calmed by your compassion. When you left") to: "And made more tranquil by your kindliness." Then begin the following.]

Marcela: They told me you had gone to Aranjuez.
Felix: And so I did; but there is no place, none,
Where I can find distraction from my grief.
Marcela: What happened?
Félix: Today, Marcela, to distract my mind
From Laura's cruelty, I took my sadness
Into the country. I came to Aranjuez,
And on the bridge the huntsmen waited for
The King's arrival there, before they started
A heron from the river bank, the bird
A feathery shoot amid the field of flowers,
Beside the Tagus, at the very point
Where the Jarama joins it, and from thence
It is a wandering monster, a crystal centaur
Made of two parts, the Tagus and Jarama,
Thereafter called the Tagus. The sound of a trumpet,
Authentic messenger, cut through the wind,
So that the foam rose up like hair in terror,
The birds believing that the blast had come
From Norway to our Spain.[45] It was the trumpet
Heralding the arrival of Philip IV
(Greater than the planet of that number,
Crowned with still more laurels than great Mars),
Who hurtled madly in his coach across
The meadows, scattering the shades of night.
He mounted then a horse, a mountainous steed
With eyes of fire, who snorts in eagerness
A cataract of foam.
He was a dappled map, in which was seen
At the same time, fire, water, earth, and air,
In eyes, in foam, in body, and in breath,
Beautiful to behold! No proud king now,
But huntsman first and foremost, he forthwith
On his invincible hand with steady skill
A white gerfalcon set, whose enameling
Of black spots made him seem a piebald hawk,
If hawks indeed are piebald. How exquisite

Of subtle Nature to adorn his beauty
With blemishes! He cautiously secured
The jesses on the gauntlet, so caressed
Its feathers with a feather, that the bird
Was unaware of new captivity.
Then near a pool in which the spring is mirrored,
The heron who had been there since the dawn
Climbed in the air so fast, she was entangled
In a cloud's gossamer meshes, to interpose,
Impartial arbiter, 'twixt fire and air!—
O would that I might have her courage now!—
So that she beat her wings in the etheral reaches
Of that diaphanous sphere, so high, her wings
Must either scorch or freeze. Yet when she beats them,
Or stretches them to keep her balance 'twixt
The elements, she moves them equally
To swoop upon the wind, or soaring up
To face the fiery sun. She had become
A minute speck, when with its hood unfastened
The King lets loose his hawk, which ravenous
Was pecking furiously at the brass bell
Making it tinkle, despite the tiny hindrance
Of its little muffler. Then lo! the whole of space
Was the domain of this imperial harpy!
This royal falcon was the first to climb,
Being swift to soar and swoop. The second rose,
In its strong flight seeking to emulate
The other's cunning tactics. They climb and climb,
Combing the wind, violating the air:
In alternation they pursue the prey.
The heron meanwhile, like an ash-gray ship—
Her legs the oars, her wings the sail, her beak
The prow, her tail the rudder—hastes away.
Her swiftness which the wind itself might envy.
Both pirates, seeing thus their prize escaping,
Grapple with her, until her blood pours forth,
Staining her plumage. They swooped alternately,
One towering while the other plummeted,
A pair of scales in which her life was weighed.
At each assault she hovers to recoup
Her failing forces, fluttering her wings,
Until she hides her head beneath one wing,
Surrendering to her fate. And so she falls,
A blood-red comet with the two gerfalcons
Still at her throat. The King set spurs to aid

His falcon; vexed, perhaps, they had not caught
The heron in the air, he galloped fast
As though to finish the unfinished task.
For anyone who saw both horses and falcon
Could not say which was which, could not discern
Which galloped and which flew,
Since the horsed falcon and the falconed horse
So racing in the sky and on the earth,
Misrepresented jointly earth and heaven.[46]
You'll say that all I have been telling you
Has been untimely; but the long digression
Was necessary, so that my desire
Can be fulfilled. For, as I was returning
By way of Antigola, my sadness tempered—
Thanks to the royal cause!—when I beheld
At the green meadow's edge, among some ladies,
Friends of hers, no doubt, beautiful Laura,
All careless of my care, and I have come
To you for consolation, for I've hit
Upon a plan, Marcela. You must help me;
My life depends upon it, if indeed
It's not already lost, for I have seen
How Laura is so carefree.

Marcela: What has happened
Between you?
Félix: Don't you know?
Marcela: How can I know
When I am shut away?
Félix: Well, listen then,
Although, perhaps, it were better left unsaid.
Marcela: [*Aside*] Now I must act as though I didn't know
A thing about it.*

---

*Continue on p. 47 by inserting the line:
     Félix: When you left last night
Then return to the original dialogue beginning with the line "After your visit to Laura,
. . ."

Mañanas
de abril
y mayo

Mornings of April and May

DRAMATIS PERSONAE

Don Juan   Pernía, Doña Ana's old steward
Don Pedro   Doña Clara
Don Hipólito   Doña Ana
Don Luis   Doña Lucía, her duenna
Arceo, Pedro's lackey   Inés, Clara's maid

The scene is set in Madrid

ACT I

Scene 1: Don Pedro's house, late at night

[*Enter Don Juan, muffled up, and Arceo, with a candle*]

Arceo: As I've already told you that my lord is not at home, it's no use your waiting for him—gentleman, ghost, or whatever—because I don't know when he'll be back to go to bed.

Juan: I cannot leave until I've spoken with him.

Arceo: In that case, I think you'd be better off outside.

Juan: No, I'll be better off inside.

Arceo: Spirit with sword and cloak, who insists on following me, so tedious and so foolish, all muffled up as you are, you can thank the Lord I'm so scared of you—otherwise I would thrust you out into the street at the point of my sword.

Juan: I do not doubt it, man. But do not worry.
I come in peace. I am Don Pedro's friend.
So rest assured.

Arceo: Rest assured, indeed!

Juan: And sit down.

Arceo: I'm in my own house, and I'll sit down if and when I please.

Juan: Very well; stay as you like.

Arceo: You're certainly a peace-loving ghost, and your manners are as polished as those of Don Juan Tenorio's ghostly statue.[1]

Juan: Tell me now, what is Don Pedro doing
That he is out so late? Is it love or gambling
That's keeping him amused?

Arceo: One or t'other, no doubt.

Juan: It makes no difference in my opinion;
For both are ruled by Fortune. Is he now
On a winning spree?

Arceo: I think that I am on a losing one.

Juan: Has he been lucky?

Arceo: How should I know?

Juan: You mean he doesn't trust you with his secrets?

Arceo: He gives nothing on trust, but sometimes he lends me his confidence. [*Aside*] Isn't it enough for him to barge in without a by-your-leave? Must he be a nosey parker into the bargain?

[*Enter Don Pedro*]

Pedro: What is this?

Arceo: [*To Juan*] Wait in the street, and good riddance; or, if you won't to hell with you!

Pedro: Tell me, you fool, what has been happening.

Arceo: You've come back just in time. A little later, and I would have thrown this muffled fellow from a window so high that it would have been years before he came down from his flight into space. By which time he would have been like one of the Seven Sleepers, for he would have found everyone wearing different clothes, using different coins, and speaking different languages.[2]

Pedro: Who is he?

Arceo: I don't know, but I suspect that he's somebody's husband, who comes to see you in discreet disguise, for he refuses to show his face.

Pedro: Well, good sir, whom do you seek here?

Juan: You.

Pedro: Tell me, what do you want?

Juan: I'll tell you when
We are alone.

Arceo: There you see! Wasn't I right?

Pedro: Be off, you idiot!

Arceo: With pleasure. [*Aside*] I'm supposed to go and chat with Doña Lucía, the duenna of the lady next door, but today I'd rather act the servant than the lover, so I'll stay and eavesdrop on their private chat.[3]

[*Exit*]

Pedro: Now we're alone, I wait for you to speak.
What do you want?
Juan: Please close the door.
Pedro: Well, sir,
You keep me in suspense. It is closed now.
Juan: [*Revealing himself*] Now that I kneel before your feet, Don
Pedro,
Let me embrace you.
Pedro: Don Juan, my friend!
How have you dared to come into Madrid
Without considering the risk you run?
Juan: I'm not afraid of death and therefore do not
Protect my life; and since misfortunes long
Companioned me, I now have ceased to fear them.
You know already of my luckless love
Since you're a neighbor of Doña Ana de Lara,
That divine lady with a glorious mind
And crowned with beauty. I was happy then.
I lived exulting in my lofty hopes
Proud of her favor. This is not a boast,
But rather a self-criticism, for you know
The recompense in love is so unfair
That he who least deserves a lady's favors
Enjoys them most. As you already know
My love at first was given a favoring wind
Upon a fortunate sea, until the waves
Grew turbulent, and the barque of all my hope
Met with a storm of jealousy, on tides
Of dire misfortune and unhappiness.
Then in my blind distress—I tell you now
What's known to you already, but let me tell it,
Since grief is mad enough to get some solace
From being recounted often[4]—So, one night,
I left her house, believing that the door
In the garden wall was secret, giving access
To me alone. I went to open it
And heard a key was turning in the lock
On the outside. I stopped what I was doing
And stood aside, to test my jealous fears—
As if one's jealousy would need to search
For evidence beyond its own existence
To be convinced. The door half opened; then
By the dim starlight I beheld a man
Enter with neither light nor lighted soul,
Thus doubly blind. I might have killed him then

Without risk to myself, but wished to know—
O cursed curiosity which imposed
Forbearance on me! That was the evil cause
Of my misfortune; so I stood awhile,
While he edged gradually along the walls,
Less practiced than myself, until he stumbled
Against me, and amazed that near the door
There was another man, he, unafraid,
Exclaimed: "Whoever's here, no matter who,
I will discover him and kill him. None
May enjoy the pleasures I must live without."
What I replied to him, I do not know.
With one accord we moved into the street,
Where we fought hand to hand. As luck would have it,
The duel ended in a kind of draw.
The man who struck me down with jealousy
I struck down dead—as who should say "Our combat
Shall be resolved when one of us is dead,
The other left alive with jealousy."
I had the worse fate; he it was who died
While I, alas, lived on with jealousy.
The officers of justice soon appeared,
Brought by the clash of swords; but I escaped
The arms of the law by taking to my heels.
Not quite escaped, for they had seized my servant
Who waited with my horse not far away.
He told them who I was—for only masters
Who choose good servants master their own fate.
As my identity was now disclosed
I had to absent myself; but being unable
To live with jealousy, absent from its cause,
I have returned in this way to Madrid,
And, trusting to your friendship, I have ventured
To come to your house. Yet, as I've experienced
My servant's blabbing, I have hesitated
From trusting yours. I'll stay a few days here,
Merely to ascertain if I can meet
With Doña Ana, she who has been the cause
Of my misfortunes. I've been wronged by her,
Yet none the less I love and honor her,
So I've returned to the city for one purpose—
To put my grievances to her, and see (alas)
If she by any chance can find excuses
For her behavior. If by talking with her,
With you alone as witness, I obtain

Some satisfaction from her—and before
She makes excuse, I'm ready to accept it—
I'll go to fight in Flanders, comforted
By taking her excuses as the friends
And comrades of my jealousy. For this
Ensures that neither agony nor joy
But both together kill me, as a man
May use a poison as an antidote.
This is a jealous lover's last resort.
All he can do is say: "I come to complain,
Yet ready to believe whate'er you speak;
And since I cannot live, then make me die
From anguish sweetened with a taste of pleasure."

Pedro: The honor you have done me by your choice
Of me, and of my house, now places me
Under two obligations. First to give you
Protection in it. So, Don Juan, I
Willingly put my house at your disposal,
My property, my honor, and my life.
The second obligation is to aid you
In your affair of the heart. You must for this
(Since he is bound to see you) trust my servant;
For though I've had him only a short time
I'm satisfied with him. I will not speak
About your lawsuit now, for you will know
The plaintiff is Don Luis de Medrano
The dead man's relative.

Juan: We know each other.

Pedro: Well, let us leave that now, because today
I do not wish to speak of your misfortunes.
But as regards Doña Ana, all I know
Is that I haven't caught a glimpse of her
Since that eventful night—neither in church,
Nor at her window, nor in Prado Street,
Nor even on Main Street[5]—that's significant
Since I'm her nearest neighbor.

Juan: How kind of you
Don Pedro! But how can I be assured
That all this mourning which now veils her beauty
Is for my sake, and not for the dead man?

Pedro: How quickly you assume the worst!

Juan: Why not?
Bad news is more reliable than good.

Pedro: I understand you not.

Juan: I disbelieve

Anything good that's told me, and believe
The worst imaginable. For consider
Which can be trusted more; since the bad news
Invariably turns out to be true,
And the other kind inevitably false.
By now the night's dark veil has been dispersed
By beauteous sunlight. Go and take your rest,
And make the day be proxy for the night.
Pedro: I cannot; I have business at this hour;
I'm glad I am already dressed for it.
Juan: Your courtship seems a vigil; you come home
So late, and then go out again so early.
Pedro: I go to see if I am justified
In being jealous, to undeceive myself
I'm going to the Park, that charming place
Which is the kingdom ruled by flowers and ladies,
"Mornings of April and May."[6] I go in quest
Of the lady I have mentioned; and meanwhile
You can get some rest.   [*Calls*]   Arceo!

[*Enter Arceo*]

Arceo: Sir?
Pedro: See that a bed is made up in this chamber
Without delay; let it be done discreetly
For it's essential nobody should know
We have Don Juan in the house; and I
Am trusting only you in this affair.
Good-bye.

[*Exit*]

Arceo: You've treated me suspiciously, as people treat their galley
slaves. And it's safe to say that nothing is ever safe from the likes of
them, save what they already have in their safekeeping.[7]
Juan: I was loath to trust in you, Arceo,
Until I knew you.

[*Exeunt*]

Scene 2: A street

[*Enter Clara and Inés*]

Inés: So, Clara, you have quite determined then
On going to the Park.
Clara: Do you want to know

If this can be avoided, Inés? Since
Hipólito forbade it, I believe
That only made me want to do it more;
For if, when yesterday he talked with me,
He'd ordered me to go, I'm pretty sure
I would not then have gone. Since he assumed
That I was bound to obey him, I've been seized
By such an irresistible desire,
That to achieve it I have left my bed
Two hours before the dawn.

Inés: This venial sin
Is nothing new in us; for women all
Inherit from Mother Eve the inclination
To do what is forbidden. What this implies
About your mutual passion, I don't know;
Nor know indeed what motives drive you on.
For Don Hipólito's more often called
Madcap and slanderer than by his name.
You are a woman, if I may be frank,
Who likes her freedom—doing what she will,
Whether right, or wrong. He has bestowed
Affection with an indiscriminate hand
Not wisely but too well, while you prefer
The pleasure of bestowing none at all.
So tell me how a love affair like this,
With partners so ill-matched, can turn out well?

Clara: Doubtless you think you have annoyed me, Inés,
By telling me about his whims and quirks,
And about mine as well; but, on the contrary,
You have delighted me, for there is nothing
That I like more than unconventional men,
And to be judged myself as vain and flighty,
Why! Would you want me to be wholly constant,
Subject to one alone, who might offend me
In countless ways, simply because he knew
My love for him was safe? No, no, not that!
The man that I shall love, will soon discover
That I am wildly unpredictable,
Until the day I take him for a husband.
Therefore to give Hipólito a shock,
I wished to come disguised into the Park,
Where I can walk, and talk, and freely laugh,
Ask questions and engage in repartee,
See and be seen; for even the truest lover

Should not regard his wishes as commands,
Since there is much enjoyment to be had
From—
Inés: What do you mean?
Clara: From the disquiet
I shall occasion him by my behavior.
Inés: You are quite right, no doubt. Well, here we are
In Prado Street, which at one time, they say,
Before the builders used the spade on it,
Was actually a meadow.
Clara: Let's go this way
To Poplar Street; it's like, though not so nice,
As Pajés Avenue.
Inés: People are singing.
Clara: Yes.

                                        [*Exeunt*]

          [*Singing offstage*]
Mornings of April and May,
Fresh-scented and joyful with song,
Rouse up my maiden today:
Let her not slumber so long.[8]

Scene 3: The Park of the Royal Palace

[*Enter Don Luis and Don Hipólito*]

Luis: Merely keeping in your company
May help, Hipólito, to alleviate
The melancholy caused by my bereavement.
Hipólito: It was, indeed, to distract you from the grief
Of your cousin's death, that I have brought you here—
For in the Park the two of us may spend
An entertaining morning.
Luis: The rising sun
Appears more beautiful for being wrapped
In clouds of red and gold.
Hipólito: Here we can see
The promenading people. Over there
How tenderly Don Sancho is attempting
To gain the affections of that lady—wife
Of his friend the lawyer.
Luis: Friendship indeed!
It should be recognized as such, for he
Prevents another from seducing her.

Hipólito: The lawyer's in Madrid about a lawsuit.
You may be sure he knows about that pair,
But has good reason to be friendly with them:
His wife, for appearance's sake; and with his friend
Because he wants to pick his brains.[9]
Luis: You have
A bitter tongue! I wish I could persuade you
To turn over a new leaf.
Hipólito: There is no man
I tell you, Luis, in Madrid today
Who has a sweeter tongue. Is not that Flora?
Luis: Yes.
Hipólito: It's quite a feat for her to come on foot
In search of pleasure.
Luis: Why?
Hipólito: I've never seen her
Come out without her coach. They say she told
Her husband: "With the rent paid for the house
We could buy a coach." "Where are we going to live,"
He asked her, "during the day and night?" She said:
"If I had a coach I'd live in it
By day, and use the coach-house in the night."[10]
Luis: That's quite like Doña Clara; for she spends
Every moment in that part of the house
Which overlooks the street—and all the rest
Is quite superfluous.
Hipólito: Yes, that is true;
And one day when the rent was due, the landlord
Came to collect it. She exclaimed: "What cheek!
I only occupy the balcony
And yet must pay rent for the house as well."[11]
Luis: What would she give, if only she could hear us!
Hipólito: She won't hear anything, because last night
I told her that she must not leave the house.

[*Enter Doña Clara and Inés*]

Clara: Inés, in all my life I've never seen
So beautiful a morning.
Inés: Nor have I.
Cover your face.
Clara: Why?
Inés: Don Hipólito's here.
Luis: Have you ever seen in all your life
A smarter woman?

Hipólito: No, and never before
Has one so stylish come into the Park.
Luis: And her companion is not bad, I vow.
Hipólito: Let us engage, for we are in the field,
Two against two.
Inés: Don Hipólito and Don Luis
Are coming to talk with us.
Clara: Then have a care
Not to reply by so much as a word;
I would not have them recognize me.
Inés: Well,
If we are veiled, and dressed like this—the way
Of all the women here, how can they recognize you?
Clara: If I should answer, just the way I speak.
It's all right in a comedy for a woman,
To think, if she is veiled, she will be safe
From being recognized; but in real life,
It will not do at all.[12]
Hipólito: My veiled lady,
You've come disguised to grace the festival
Which spring is celebrating on these lawns
Where sprightly flowers dance to the tuneful plash
Of water falling on the stones, the sound
Of the wind in the trees. Permit a gentleman
To tell you how superfluous it was
To rise so early, since your cloudy veil
Conceals the morning in its folds, and you
Control the sunrise. At whatever hour
You deign to manifest your fiery brilliance,
At that precise moment dawn would break,
Day would have light, the breath of dawn would blow.
You do not answer. Why! You're speaking to me
In a sign-language? This does not displease me.
Will you not even speak to ask a favor?
No? Then you're the nonpareil of ladies,
The best I've ever met. My very soul
Demands appropriate recompense for proclaiming
The joyful tidings that I've found a woman
Who asks for nothing from me, and says nothing.
Luis: [*To Inés*] And do you, too, observe the rules of silence
Of the Carthusians? What a splendid thing!
I have been looking for a girl like you
For years and years. It matters not at all
Whether you're one-eyed, lame, one armed, left-handed,

Overdemanding, hunchbacked, snub-nosed, bald,
And full of affection, from this moment
I'm desperately in love.
Hipólito: [*To Clara*]   Since you refuse
To talk to me, as though we'd had a quarrel
Show me your face at least. Not even that?
You'll make me think it ugly. Is it so?
I am convinced it must be. Yet a woman
Who's so unique requires no greater attribute
Than speechlessness. But, if I'm not mistaken
That gesture signifies I must be gone.
But look, I do not want to understand
These gestures, for I've never yet been dumb,
And little of your dumb-show gets across.
What are you doing? Turning your back on me!
What dumb talk is that to teach anybody?
Listen to me—Wait!

                                        [*Clara and Inés exeunt*]
Luis: I've never met a more attractive woman.
Hipólito: Let's find out where they live; for heaven knows
I am resolved to see and talk with her
In her own house, this very day, until
I've got to the bottom of this trickery.
Luis: Let's follow them.
Hipólito: Yes, let us follow her,
For as you're well aware, I'm much attracted
By a designing woman. That is the reason
That I love Doña Clara, and this woman,
If I have not mistaken her demeanor,
Surpasses Doña Clara in such arts.

                                                    [*Exeunt*]

Scene 4: A room in Doña Ana's house

[*Enter Lucía and Arceo*]

Lucía: You have nothing you can say to me. You have no possible excuse
for keeping me waiting last night in vain.
Arceo: For heaven's sake, Doña Lucía, I couldn't come.
Lucía: What business kept you?
Arceo: If I could tell you that, you would realize that I am not deceiving
you.
Lucía: What is it I may not know about?

Arceo: Nothing at all.

Lucía: Then I am doubly offended: because you didn't come last night, and because you come today and won't trust me with your secret. That's a horrid insult, Arceo.

Arceo: I don't know what to do. Ah well, no secret should be wholly kept, when you're a duenna, and I'm a lackey. Last night a gentleman came to the house all muffled up, asking for my master—but you are not to breathe a word—this gentleman, then, has been away from Madrid because he killed a man, and he kept me waiting for my master's return—nobody must know about it, remember—and after that they talked till dawn. Then he stayed in the house, where he is to remain hidden, I'm told—mind, you're not to tell a soul—and nobody knows about it but me, and I know how to keep a secret. His name is Don Juan de Guzmán. As he was leaving a lady's house one night—this part of the tale I didn't hear very well—he killed another man. And so he's hidden away like this, and only me and my master know about it. And since I'm trusting you with the secret, don't let it go any further. [*Aside*] Thank the Lord, I've got out of that.

Lucía: In return I'd like to kiss you. [*kisses him*]

Arceo: I'm hoping for more than that.

[*Enter Pernía, a silly old man*]

Pernía: [*Aside*] I've come at a bad moment. Were there ever such shocking goings on?

Arceo: Pernía has seen us.

Lucía: It doesn't much matter. He's not really a jealous type. But you had better go.

Arceo: You bet I will, and show a clean pair of heels.

[*Exit*]

Pernía: Doña Lucía, if it had been anyone but me who had come in, the honor of the house would have been irretrievably damaged. I shall inform my lady of what has occurred, for I hope this day to have my revenge, you ungrateful hussy, for the way you have treated me. I'm mad with rage. Since when, I would ask, has a mere lackey been preferred to a person of my rank, a steward?

Lucía: This man brought me some letters from a brother of mine in the Indies, and, to be quite honest, the kiss was simply payment for delivery—for it's only you I love.

Pernía: Well, let us do a switch, you cruel woman: from this day forth, love him, and give me the kiss.

Lucía: Of course I will [*Embracing him*] [*Aside*] to try to make you hold your tongue, since—but here's my mistress.

[*Enter Doña Ana, in a cloak*]

Ana: What are you doing?

Pernía: It's just that people hereabouts seem to make a habit of kissing.

Lucía: The fact is Pernía brought me news of a brother of mine and my delight led me to behave so uncontrollably.

Pernía: That's so, my lady, and you must believe her.   [*Aside*]   Dona Lucía can produce a brother to serve as an excuse for every embrace!

Ana: Go step outside to see if my coach is there.

[*Pernía begins to exit slowly*]   It's time to go to Mass.

Well, can't you hurry?

Pernía: Isn't this hurrying?

[*Exit*]

Lucía: My lady, must you take so little care
Of your appearance, of your loveliness,
Neglectful of your self, except for grief?

Ana: I cannot be consoled. You'll never see me
Unracked by grief and anguish all my life.

Lucía: What good will it do you?

Ana: Why do you suppose
That I want any good except to grieve?
Although, when I recall that the first step
Toward recovery from calamity
Is to lament, I ought to cease from grieving
That I may grieve the more. My grief is such
I long for death, and have no will to resist it.
Therefore I'd cease from grieving, to ensure
My grief should still continue. Since the day
Don Juan met misfortune in my house—
I know that everybody blames me for it
Though I am innocent—I am lifeless thus,
Less than a shadow of what once I was.[13]

Lucía: If you will promise me to keep it secret,
Perfect in virtue as in loveliness,
As I know you are, I'll tell you that I know
Don Juan's whereabouts.

Ana: How foolishly
With honeyed words you seek to wean my heart
From its despair.

Lucía: I *do* know where he is.
And even if you will not listen to me,
I'll tell you all I know. He came to Madrid—
But keep this secret—and is now in hiding
In our neighbor's house. I heard this from a maid,
But it must go no further. As you can see,
It's a serious matter.

Ana: What are you saying?
Lucía: The truth!
Ana: I don't know whether to believe or not:
It seems too rash to credit such good news.

[*Enter Doña Clara and Inés, with hats and cloaks*]

Inés: [*Aside to Doña Clara on the threshold*]   What are you doing
now?
Clara: I'm carrying on
With the madcap scheme on which I have embarked,
Although it would not matter in the least
Were Don Hipólito to recognize me.
Since he's been charmed by me in my disguise,
And prides himself upon his power to charm,
I am resolved to keep him in the dark
For a time at least.
Inés: Look, there are people here.
Clara: Was woman ever at a loss to find
A lie to extricate her from the web
Of previous lies?—   [*To Ana*]   Fair lady, if the name
Of woman is synonymous with pity,
Although I can but haltingly convey
My agitation, I beg you to allow me
To enter for a while, until a man
Has left the street; and let your house become
Awhile the sanctuary of my distress;
For well I know the dwelling of a goddess
Will always be inviolate.
Ana: I'll be glad
For it to serve, if not as sanctuary,
At least as shelter, for your agitation
Shows that you need to hide.
Lucía: A man has entered!
Clara: Good heavens! It is my husband! I'll withdraw,
Since in compassion you have given me leave,
And prudently allow a maid of yours
To send him packing; for on this depends
My name, my honor, and, indeed, my life.
Ana: But tell me—
Clara: I cannot tarry.
[*Exeunt Clara, leaving her hat with Ana, and Inés*]
Ana: In her haste
And perturbation she has left her hat.
Lucía: I'm going after her, in case she takes the opportunity of stuffing a
sheet or so up her sleeve.

[*Enter Hipólito*]

Hipólito: Forgive me that my feet, weighed down with lead,
Rather than winged, should dare to tread this sphere,
This porch that's canopied with flowers of spring,
And you, resplendent in your loveliness,
The sweetest flower of all.
Ana: [*Aside*]   I will dissemble
And feign displeasure   [*Aloud*]   What makes you so bold
To do such outrage, sir?
Hipólito: 'Tis fortunate
That I am bold, for I could not have rested
Till, Goddess, I had seen you vanquish thus
The cloud which, like a smoky curtain, hid
The flame of your beauty. So, though blinded once
By the smoke, and burned now by your beauty's rays,
I weep and burn. I burn now from the flame
As once I wept from smoke which veiled your beauty.
Ana: I do not understand this flattering style,
Nor do I know, sir, what excuse I've given you
To burst into my house in such a way.
If you describe it as "spring's lovely sphere,"
Mind that you do not spoil its brilliance now
As a flash of lightning dims before the sunrise;
Or, if it's rather smoke that you pursue,
Which takes on divers shapes, do not expect
That you will ever find it, since it never
Assumes the same shape twice. And if you seek
The flame, then come not near it, but return
From whence you came; because the ancient crest
Above the gateway is not used to witness
Behavior such as yours.
Hipólito: You did not let me
Hear you or see you in the Park; and so
It was to see and hear you that I followed,
At risk of your displeasure. Now I know
You were compassionate, to let me hear you
Speak so discreetly at the very moment
I looked upon your beauty. If in the Park
I had heard you without seeing you, my soul
And senses would have been benumbed quite,
Since the harmonious sweetness of your voice
Is poison to the ears; and if I had seen
Your beauty and not heard your words of wisdom
I would have given up my life and soul

As spoils of your resplendent loveliness
That's poison to the eyes. So, hearing you,
Has given me life, for else I should have died
On seeing how beautiful you were; and lest
I died from hearing how discreet you were,
The sight of you revived me. In this way
One poison is the other's antidote.
Good-bye then; since I have been overbold
I do not wish to be ill-mannered too:
The blame for that would obviously be mine;
But for my boldness you must take the blame.

Ana: Whoever saw the like? To come in here
A jealous husband, and go out again
(His former grievances forgotten quite)
Another woman's lover.

[*Enter Lucía, Iñes and Clara*]

Clara: Has he gone?
Ana: Yes.
Clara: Madam, I am deeply grateful to you.
Ana: You have a charming husband.
Clara: God's my witness
How much I'm suffering on that account—
And for his conduct.
Ana: Strangely, he believed
I was the lady he had followed here.
Your hat contributed to this mistake,
And that we both were wearing cloaks, and gowns
So much alike—for just as strokes of wit
Are apt to be repeated, so can dresses
Be duplicated.

[*Enter Pernía*]

Pernía: The coach is here, my lady.
Ana: Lucía, look to see if all is clear.
Lucía: You can leave safely now.
Clara: May God preserve you!
Ana: If you can think of any other way
I can assist you.
Clara: I am much obliged.
[*Aside*] And yet offended, too. I never thought
I could be jealous.
Iñes: Why are you so upset?
Clara: To see him paying court to someone else,
And woo her while I overheard him here.

[*Exeunt Clara and Inés*]

Ana: Everything I see, or hear, or feel
But adds to my distress.
Lucía: What ails you now?
Ana: To see how everybody's luck improves
Save only mine, which withers. That woman now,
Although to blame, has managed to escape;
While I, however innocent, am likely
To lose my life. For it would seem that blame
Has nought to do with guilt, but merely rests
On failure to convince the world at large
That one is blameless.

[*Exeunt*]

Scene 5: Don Pedro's house

[*Enter Don Pedro and Don Juan from opposite sides*]

Pedro: It's good to see you, Juan.
Juan: It is good
To have you back. How did you fare in the Park?
Pedro: Badly.
Juan: How so?
Pedro: Because I did not find
The lady I was seeking. I believe
The reason is she has another lover.
I went to see if I was justified
In my suspicion of a jealous rival,
So that the pains of love might be allayed
By Truth's more painful cure. I fear my rival
Is a friend of mine, who has his own suspicions.
Juan: Is the lady Doña Clara?
Pedro: Yes.
Juan: And her gallant?
Pedro: A man of birth and excellent repute.
He's called Hipólito. But let us leave
This subject for another time; and tell me
What you have been doing.
Juan: I've been suffering,
Despairing, near to death, without a cure.
Tell me what strategem shall we devise
For me to see the woman that I love.
Pedro: I do not know. There is no seeing her.
But let me think if there is any way—

[*Enter Arceo*]

Arceo: Your friend, sir, Don Hipólito is here
      And asks to see you. He's a gossip, sir,
      And he'll tell everybody all he knows.
Juan: Because of what may happen, I will stay
      To be your second.
Pedro: He ought not to see you.
      Withdraw you to your chamber.
Juan: I regret—
Pedro: Do me this favor, Juan.

                                    [*Exit Juan and Arceo*]

      [*Enter Hipólito*]

Hipólito: How are you, Pedro?
Pedro: I'm at your service. And you?
Hipólito: I am at yours.
Pedro: Why do you look about you in this fashion?
Hipólito: To see if we're alone.
Pedro: You see we are.
      What do you want?
Hipólito: That you should lend your ears
      To what I have to say. I went this morning
      To that green loveliness, that brake divine,
      That pleasing paradise, the royal Park,
      Whose greenery surrounds the edifice
      Beneath whose splendid canopy resides
      Our PLANET KING, fourth of that name, and fourth
      Among the planets, MARS, appropriate
      For his heroic qualities, and then
      From CHARLES V, his noble ancestor
      Endowed with sovereign powers, and privileged
      From the fifth planet JUPITER. In this sphere
      Is set the heroic throne from which our suns,
      ISABEL and FELIPE—she beautiful
      Forever, he renowned—send forth the rays
      Of the true Faith, which flash their flowery message
      Across the gardens of the firmament,
      Even to the farthest Indies.[14]
Pedro: [*Aside*]   What does he mean
      To come and tell me what I've seen myself?

      [*Enter Juan and Arceo, who eavesdrop behind the arras*]

Juan: [*Aside*] Doubtless he knows Don Pedro has been there
      To seek his lady, and he comes to complain.
      I'll hear about it now.

Hipólito: Among the women
   So lovely as to make the dawn feel envy,
   Forming and reforming different groups,
   Weaving at random, and unexpectedly
   Changing direction, I saw a veilèd beauty
   Surpassing all the rest, that her mere shadow
   Put in the shadow all the others' beauties.
   I have seen women go into the parkland
   To gather roses from the flower-filled gardens,
   But never till today have I beheld
   A foot that scattered roses on the ground
   With each proud step, turning the jessamine pale
   With envy, leaving all the lilies wilted,
   A woman—how badly I express myself—
   Came down a slope, or rather veiled Charm,
   Call it Enchantment in disguise came down.
   Her filmy mantle with its cloudy folds
   Of various textured hues, sometimes
   Opaque, sometimes transparent, now refuses
   And now concedes a glimpse of the hidden face.
   When is the dawn at its most beautiful?
   When is the sunshine loveliest? Is it not
   When the dawn's shadowed, when the sun through clouds
   Gives coyly of its light, so that one's senses
   Are left uncertain, wagering together
   How much, if anything, they have beheld?
Pedro: [*Aside*]   All this is doubtless leading in the end
   To the revelation it was Doña Clara
   Since he has come to talk of her.
Juan: [*Aside*]   How boring
   Is his affected style, full of conceits,
   Not one original!
Hipólito: A smart white hat,
   Above her cloak, adorned her careless curls,
   And on one side a feather was attached
   By a diamond clasp. This bowed in the breeze
   As though to answer to its blandishments:
   "Since I reply with nods to all who accost me,
   I know far better than my mistress does
   How to submit to the persuasive breath
   Of loving sighs." She had a shapely figure;
   Her dress in good taste, but not splendid—yet
   Is anything more splendid than a dress
   In perfect taste? I will omit—for fear
   Of being tedious—what took place in the Park,

And so proceed to later happenings.
I followed to her house and dared to enter,
And there beheld the dazzling sun of beauty;
And conquered so completely by the sight
That I would then have given not to have seen her
All that I would have given before to see her,
Since like a moth attracted by the flame,
In love with peril, I approached the rays
And went away transported by the danger
Of her transcendent beauty—which I've tried
So feebly to describe. I tell you this
In some embarrassment.

Arceo: [*Aside*]   Here it comes.
Juan: [*Aside*]   Be quiet.
Pedro: [*Aside*] He's going to speak plainly
Hipólito: She is your neighbor.
Only this single wall divides her sphere
From yours. And since you are her neighbor. . .
Juan: [*Aside*] Alas! What's this I hear?
Pedro: [*Aside*]   What shall I do
If Juan hears this?
Hipólito: You must know who she is. Tell me her name.
Since I presume to adore her loveliness,
I must be properly informed; and you,
My good friend, can inform me.
Juan: [*Aside*] I was about to give him my response.
Arceo: [*Aside*]   Stay!
Pedro: [*Aside*] Was ever man in such a quandary?
What shall I do? If I should tell him now
It will encourage him; and not to tell him
Is senseless since he'll simply ask another.
If I reveal to him Don Juan's love
It would be an offense against his honor.
Yet by some tactful phrasing, I can try
To show his love is hopeless, and still keep
Honor untarnished. I can nip in the bud
Their jealousy, and by sticking to the truth
Avoid the dangers that attend on lies.
This would be an achievement! [*Aloud*] Don Hipólito,
Now that I've heard your story, you must listen
To what I have to say. You should be glad
To know the truth before it is too late.
The lady whom you followed to her house
Is Doña Ana de Lara. She's renowned
Not merely for her lineage, but even more

For virtue, and her house is honor's temple.
It would be mad to take this courtship further
For I assure you that you'd be attempting
The impossible.
Hipólito: I asked for information,
Not for advice; and since I have obtained it,
I bid you good day. For if my lofty hopes
Should come to nought—presumptuous as they are—
Failure is glory if the deed is daring:
What nobler prize than punishment like that?

                                                    [*Exit*]

[*Enter Juan*]

Juan: Pray tell me now, Don Pedro, that the sun
Has scarcely glimpsed her while I've been away.
Yet, you are doubtless right: she left her house
Before the sun arose, to flaunt her charms,
The reigning beauty of the royal Park.
Pedro: I don't know what is best to say to you.
Juan: I am not lost for words.
Pedro: What are they then?
Juan: Protection from this peril lies in flight.
I've lost her now twice over. It is vain
To see her or converse with her. So, Pedro,
Order some horses; for this very night,
O unrelenting heavens!
Once and for all I turn my back on her.
Pedro: But realize—
Juan: I realize too well
That when I was here, I found another man
Coming to visit her, and when I'm absent
—I am beside myself—then she goes out—
I have good reason to be so distressed—
To advertise her charms—how cruel she is!—
And so brings back with her—O hideous torture!—
Another lover. Oh that this month of flowers
Could be deleted from the calendar!
And yet the blame is not upon the mouth
But upon me alone, since I pursue
An insubstantial dream; since I adore
A serpent, nay, a basilisk! You mornings
Of May and April, you have proved to be
Not springtime days but winter nights for me!

                                                    [*Exeunt*]

ACT II

Scene 1: A room in Clara's house

[*Enter Clara and Inés*]

Inés: To think of you being melancholy and pensive!
So unable to control yourself!
Where, madam, is your verve, your taste, your beauty,
Your serene self-confidence?

Clara: I do not know.
It matters little, that I, a foolish woman,
Should fail to know the cause of my behavior,
Since I know nothing of my life. Who'd believe
That I could weep, alas, be cut to the quick
By the discourtesy of any man?
I, the proud and self-appointed avenger
Of the female sex, to feel myself brought low
By one man's rudeness!

Inés: Madam, I see no reason
Why you should feel so very much upset.
All things considered, it was you he followed,
And you inspired his compliments to her;
So if you're hurt and gratified at once,
There is some consolation for your pain.
Since you are both rejected and desired,
You are a woman jealous of yourself.
For, after all, you were his real concern,
And for your sake he came into the house
Of another woman. Finding himself involved
He had to pay her easy gallantries.
Consider, if you should reject a man
Simply because he flirts with other women,
You'd have no man to love. For any man
Who does not pay the self-same compliments
To every woman he meets, must be, say I,
A damned strange fellow.

Clara: In spite of all you say—
And I admit I acted like a fool—
I've reached the stage of fully comprehending
His insult, and I am resolved to avenge it.

Inés: By what means?

Clara: Inés, listen carefully.
I'll write him a letter in a feigned hand—
You shall deliver it as from the lady,

Confessing I feel very gratified
By all his compliments, and that I wish
To speak with him alone; that he should have
A sedan chair ready for me, and a house
Where I can meet with him this afternoon.
Vain as he is, convinced of his proud charms,
He'll think he has a love affair in hand;
And so, to underline his disappointment,
I'll go in person, and what he does then
On seeing me, will make a splendid scene.

Inés: But what will you achieve by that?
Clara: Two things.
First, I'll have a jest at his expense.
Second, I'll undeceive him, so he'll know
I was the mystery lady, and henceforth
He won't be able to be puffed with pride
Of his resistless charms, imagining
That other lady had encouraged him
To follow her, and court her.

Inés: Could you not
Accomplish this at home?
Clara: Not in a way
To give me my revenge.
Inés: I'm rather doubtful
Whether you're doing right.
Clara: Why not?
Inés: I'd tell you
Had he not entered with Don Luis now.
Clara: Dissimulate! Let them not realize
Until my plan is carried through, that we
Were the ladies in disguise.

[Enter Hipólito and Luis]

Hipólito: *[Aside to Luis]*   Remember Luis, that it is important
For me to leave her promptly.
Luis: *[Aside]*   Yes, I'll fix it.
Clara: Was it not time to see you before this,
Don Hipólito? So long without you?
I have not seen you since—since yesterday!
Hipólito: That complaint alone might serve to make
My absence from you happy. Love's subtle tactics
Are such that what is matter for complaint
Can be converted to a compliment.
The reason why I did not come this morning

Was I presumed you would be in the Park,
Since you declared last night that—
Clara: Stay your tongue.
For if last night you told me I should not,
How could I leave the house? Heavens! Let me not
Be thought so lacking in propriety,
So frivolous as to disregard obedience.
Luis: I have been telling Don Hipólito
About your loyalty in this respect,
And how he should be much obliged to you
That you defer to him. And he, indeed,
Is well aware of it, and he reciprocates—
Clara: So he, likewise, did not go to the Park?
Hipólito: O heavens, Clara! Is that what you think of me?
When you should know that I can take no joy
In any festival when you're not there.
Clara: And I believe you, as though I had beheld
With my own eyes. For if you had been there
In the Park today, I would have been there too—
That is quite plain, for if I'm in your heart
And you forever bear me next your heart
I would have been there secretly concealed,
Wherever you were.
Hipólito: [*Aside*]   How easy to deceive
Are even the most intelligent of women!
Clara: [*Aside*]   How can this prince of cheaters be so dumb?
Inés: [*Aside*]   Men and women who deceive each other,
Yet think they are in love!
           [*Don Luis makes signs to Don Hipólito*]
Luis: Although in love
It's a prime rule one should not hinder it,
Allow me to inform you that some friends
Are now expecting me and I must take
Don Hipólito with me. I shall be
Your debtor and your most obedient servant
If we may take our leave.
Clara: Come, come, Don Luis,
There is no law-court where you have to play
The advocate. If your client wants to speak,
Then let him speak, and not rely on signs.
Go, Don Hipólito; good-bye. This house
Is always freely yours, to leave or stay.
Just as it's ever open for your entry,
When you want to leave, it's open for your exit.
Inés, show out these men, and shut the doors.

Hipólito: Listen—
Clara: Why should I listen?
Luis: Consider, madam,
That if the blame was mine, the punishment
Should not be his.
Clara: I am not angry with him,
Nor yet with you. I give you the permission
For which you asked.   [*Aside*]   It's hard not to reveal
That I am angry, seeing their secret signs.
                              [*Exeunt Clara and Inés*]
Hipólito: What do you think of Doña Clara's love,
And her submissiveness?
Luis: That you've reduced
A most rebellious woman to obey
Both law and order. Who would have supposed
That Doña Clara ever would become
Submissive, to the extent of staying in
Because you told her not to issue out?
In fact, you've everything in your control.
Hipólito: I have a way with women.
Luis: That is plain,
For you have scored a triumph over this one.
But tell me, for what purpose was the haste
With which we took our leave?
Hipólito: Is my state of mind
Shown so imperfectly by my demeanor,
So that I have to put it into words?
Did I not tell you that the veilèd lady
Into whose house I went revealed her face—
When you remained outside? Did I not tell you
How I conversed with her, that she is both
Intelligent and lovely? whose reserves
Of beauty do not need to give exemption
For lack of understanding? Did I not tell you
That Pedro had informed me she was rich
And comes of noble birth?
Luis: Yes.
Hipólito: How can you then
Be doubtful of my movements? Am I not bound
To linger in her street—say, rather, enter
The shining sphere of that most perfect sun
Whose rays wreak sweet destruction—the feather
Consumes in flames, and the wax melts, so that
I share the fate of Icarus.
Luis: Don't you believe

Don Pedro's warning that your suit is vain
Because of her perfect virtue?
Hipólito: That's one more reason
Why she is worthy of love. The hopelessness
Of my pursuit encourages me more,
And makes me more determined.
Luis: But is it right?
And suitable?
Hipólito: Is it not right and proper?
The lady's rich and handsome, noble, virtuous,
And well-reputed, so within the month
I can be married to her.

                                                [*Exeunt*]

Scene 2: A street in which are situated the houses of Pedro and Ana

[*Enter Inés, wearing her cloak*]

Inés: My mistress wrote the letter quickly, and even more quickly I've followed the gentlemen. So far I've dodged them and reached the street where the lady lives—and that's her house. They're stopping over there. I don't want them to see me at their backs, lest they realize I've followed them, so let the lady's house serve once more as a sanctuary for my misdeeds.   [*She enters Doña Ana's doorway*]

[*Don Hipólito and Don Luis enter the street*]

Hipólito: This is the fortunate street! But who could doubt
That Flora lived on Garden Street? Here is
The balcony where Dawn may well appear
At any hour, appareled in sunflowers,
And garlanded with jessamine and lilies,
For surely it is here, behind her portals,
Where Dayspring rises.
Inés: [*Emerging from the doorway*] [*Aside*]   Since any suspicion
that I've followed them is now allayed, I'll give him the letter as my mistress instructed. But I'll have to play the mute again.
Luis: A muffled woman has come out of her house.
Hipólito: And she is coming toward us.
Luis: She must be one
Of the silent ladies, for she's making signs.
Hipólito: No doubt these women only talk at home,
And give up talking when they leave their house.
[*To Inés*]   Is it me you want? Is it? Well, here I am.

What do you want? [*Inés gives him a letter*]   Wait for a moment,
woman.

[*Exit Inés*]

Luis: That sign means that you must not follow her.
Hipólito: She swiftly turned her back, to indicate
I should be silent and peruse the letter.
[*Reads*]   "A man's courtly manners were always the truest guarantee of his nobility; and yours give me assurance that you are
entirely trustworthy. Therefore I need to see you, in order to
entrust you with a secret. Procure a sedan chair and bring it as soon
as possible to St. Sebastian Street. Then find a house where I can
talk to you. God be with you!—   "THE SILENT LADY."[15]

What do you make of that? Now try to make me
Believe Don Pedro and give up my suit!
Luis: You are engaged upon a notable exploit!
Hipólito: I told you that I had a way with women.
Luis: What are you going to do?
Hipólito: Just what she asks.
So let us share the tasks between us both,
For that's what a friend is for. So, Luis, go
As if your very life depended on it,
For the sedan chair—for we didn't know
That we would need it—and await as asked
In Saint Sebastian Street, and tell her when she comes
That I confided in you, to avoid
Confiding in a servant. In this way
We'll make a virtue of necessity,
So that it's like a compliment to her;
And I will wait for you at my house.
Luis: But what
If Doña Clara should call there by chance?
Hipólito: You're right to raise that point. If she found out
About my plans, there'd be the devil to pay.
What shall we do?
Luis: Well, since Don Pedro's house
Is very near, the best thing we can do
Is take her there.
Hipólito: You're right. So, at all costs,
Get the sedan chair, while I negotiate
About the house.
Luis: Look! Two more women are emerging
From Doña Ana's house.
Hipólito: You see, they take it
Quite seriously. Let us not spoil our chances,

But go before they see us, lest they should be
Reluctant to go to the place that was arranged.
Luis: I'll see about the chair.

[*Enter Ana, Lucía, and Pernía*]

[*Exeunt separately*]

Lucia: What is your purpose, madam, to leave the house
In this disguise?
Ana: Love drives me to it. I'll enter
Don Pedro's house, for I'm resolved to find
Whether Don Juan is hiding there.
Lucia: Where are you going?
Here is the house.
Ana: How can you be so foolish?
We'll go the long way round to avert suspicion,
In case a neighbor saw me leave the house.
He must not see me going to Don Pedro's.
[*Aside*] O Juan! O Love! What troubles you have cost me!

[*Exeunt*]

Scene 3: A room of Don Pedro's house.

[*Enter Juan and Pedro*]

Pedro: What a state you're in!
Juan: How should I not be so,
Since I'm near death from jealousy, Don Pedro,
At the wrongs I suffer, while my hands are tied,
My grievances unspoken?
Pedro: I have examined
What caused your jealousy, and brought you proof
That it is groundless. Why do you still complain?
Juan: Because for me there can be no release
From my suspicions.
Pedro: Well, I can assure you
That simply for your sake, and with due caution,
Standing as proxy for your jealousy,
I made discreet inquiries of the servants
Of Doña Ana, to find if she went out
This morning to the Park; and they all say
She did go out, but only in her coach
To attend mass, at eleven o'clock, and no one
Has told a different tale.
Juan: Then what has made
Hipólito tell lies.

Pedro: Confine yourself
          To getting at the truth, and do not try
          So foolishly to find out why he lies—
          Enough that he is lying.
Juan: Do you want to see
          How sensitive I am in my distress?
          For though I still believe the worst has happened,
          I have been calmed by what you've told me now,
          So that although I did not want to see
          Doña Ana before, I do now want
          To meet at sunset and converse with her;
          To tell her, since she's brought me to death's door,
          The cause of death, and all my grievances.
Pedro: Now you are set on meeting her, I'll tell you
          There has occurred to me a means to effect it.
          Write her a letter—my servant will deliver it—
          I'll tell you later. There is someone knocking.

          [*Enter Arceo*]

Arceo: Don Hipólito is coming, sir.
Pedro: You know the danger if he finds you here.
          I'll go to speak with him.
Juan: No, don't do that.
          I must hear what he says.
Pedro: Do you not trust me?
Juan: Of course I do. It is my love distrusts.
Pedro: I am so sure of Doña Ana's honor,
          I think he has returned now, to retract
          What he has said; and so there's little risk
          For you to overhear him. But withdraw,
          And do not show yourself.
Juan: Pity me, heavens!
          May one who listens now to jealousy,
          Listen as well to joy! [*Juan hides behind the door of his room*]

          [*Enter Don Hipólito*]

Hipólito: As always, Pedro, in fortune or misfortune,
          I come to seek you out; and since I trust you,
          And you're my friend, assist me. Doña Ana—
Pedro: [*Aside*] What a muddle! [*Aloud*] Say no more. You need
              not
          Inform me she is resolutely opposed—
          And rightly so—to your untimely suit.
          I well believe it.
Hipólito: You do not comprehend

My happiness and pleasure, for I've come
To tell you just the opposite.
Pedro: [*Aside*]   Good Lord! What's this?
Juan: [*Behind the arras*] I'll wait for him to finish.
Pedro: [*Aside*]   What shall I do?
I fear that this will lead to violence.
Hipólito: Doña Ana in fact—
Juan: [*Aside*]   My misery
Is without bounds.
Pedro: One moment. [*He locks the door behind*
which Juan is concealed]
Hipólito: Why lock the door?
Pedro: I do not like to leave that door unlocked
When I am going out. [*Aside*] This settles one
Of two immediate problems: jealousy
And danger. With God's help I should prevent
The danger, but the jealousy remains.
Hipólito: Doña Ana asks me in this letter
To find a place where I can talk with her;
And since my happiness is at the flood
I come to ask you, let me use your house
For meeting with her. She will come disguised.
I've need of Arceo to come with me
Since I should have a present ready for her
When she arrives. I know you will agree
To aid this lucky chance. So God be with you.
With such great happiness within my grasp,
If I'm not mad with joy, I must be mad.
Pedro: Stay a moment.
Hipólito: My desires allow
No lingering, and you should not expect it.
I will take Arceo with me.
                          [*Exeunt Hipólito and Arceo*]
Pedro: What can I do? My help is pledged to both.
One friend has asked to use my house; the other
Is hidden there already; and both of them
Have put their trust in me. I open the door
With sad reluctance, and beset with doubts
Of what is best to do. [*He unlocks the door*]
Seeing you threatened, Juan, by two disasters
From different quarters—O horrible dilemma!—
Your happiness destroyed, I tried to avert
One of the two disasters. Lest you came out
Through jealous rage, and risked your life—

Juan: All this
Was needless. After I had heard him speak,
Even suppose the door had been unlocked,
I would not have come out. After the shock
Of disillusionment, it was apparent
That I must bide my time. It would be folly
Unparalleled to fight him when his words
Have nearly struck me dead.
Pedro: I'm in a dilemma.
I do not know how I can carry out
Conflicting duties. In a single day—
Merciful Heavens!—Hipólito entrusts
His happiness to me, and by this token
The anguish of your heart. I put myself
Into your hands now. Where does my duty lie?
For heaven's sake, advise me.
Juan: I do not know
What I would do, if I myself were faced
With such a quandary. But I know well
What *I* must do: respect your house's honor,
Although my soul's afire with jealousy.
But once outside your house, I will dispatch him.
For in love's rivalries a rigid code
Of honor rules; and it demands redress.
Although it is the woman who offends,
It is the man who dies.
Pedro: You must not leave.
Juan: It is in vain to argue. I'm resolved.
Pedro: You are in mortal danger.
Juan: If I stayed
Would not the danger be as great for me?
Do you really want me on this very day
To look my own misfortunes in the eyes?
Very well; so be it. I'll remain
And be a witness of my agony.
Let Doña Ana come, I say—in love
With another man—I was about to say
Much more than this, but I will say no more.
Pedro: That does not seem right, either.
Juan: Well, my friend,
If you would have me neither go nor stay—
I'm desperate and half out of my mind!—
What would you have me do?
Pedro: I do not know.

Juan: Neither do I.
Pedro: I only wish to say
  That though I seem to expect the worst misfortunes
  I have such confidence in the lady's honor
  That I consider Don Hipólito
  Must either be deranged, or else some error
  Is causing him to think his love's requited.
Juan: Where do you get such groundless confidence?
Pedro: From the simple fact that Doña Ana is
  A woman of noble birth.
Juan: You are a fool
  To think along those lines; for you yourself
  Began by calling her a woman. Indeed,
  She is a noblewoman only second,
  A woman first and foremost. Look now, look,
  There can be no deceit. Here come two women.
Pedro: I'm in despair. We've thought of desperate measures;
  We've talked a great deal, but resolved on nothing,
  And now the crucial moment is at hand.
  I don't know what to do—but hide yourself.
Juan: I have no reason to conceal myself.
Pedro: You don't want them to see you?
Juan: Can there be
  Misfortunes greater than the ones I've suffered?
Pedro: Do this for me, until we ascertain
  The truth of the matter. After that, we both
  May die defending your offended honor.
Juan: Well, I consent, as token of my friendship;
  But on condition—alas!—that I remove
  The key from the door, and that it stays unlocked.

                                                      [*Exit*]

      [*Enter Ana, Lucía, and Pernía*]

Lucía: Listen, Pernía, stay at the door.
Ana: Don Pedro Girón, you will be astonished
  To see a woman thus invade your house.
  You are gallant, and also are discreet,
  And you appreciate as well as any
  How love extreme inexorably leads
  To more extremities. And since I must
  Confide in someone, there is no one better,
  Don Pedro, than yourself, who are so noble,
  So prudent, and so courteous.   [*She unveils*]
Pedro: [*Aside*]   No hope remains,
  Dear God! It's Doña Ana, as I feared.

Juan: [*Aside, half-opening the door*]   And I'm expected to keep
   silent!
Yet, since it must be so, burn, burn my heart
To ashes, since there's nothing I can do
To succor you.
Ana: Now I've revealed myself,
Don Pedro, hear the story of my sorrows,
Accompanied by tears and sighs. You know
I'm here; learn now—with shame I tell it—
The reason why I come to meet a man,
For I know for certain I can find him here.

[*Enter Juan*]

Juan: Enough, Don Pedro—to put me on the rack
Of jealousy, and yet expect my silence,
That is a harsh addition to my pain.
So I confess, if that is what you seek,
That I am guilty of the crime of love!
Ana: Don Juan! My lord! My source of happiness!
Juan: Doña Ana,
My source of misery, and cause of death.
Ana: O take me to your arms!
Juan: Hold! Do not use
Your arms to stretch me further on the rack,
For I already have confessed the truth.
Pedro: [*Aside*]   Great heavens! I do not know what I should do;
But so that nobody can leave or enter,
I'll bar the door.
Juan: Don't bar the door, Don Pedro,
For I intend to leave.
Ana: You must not go.
Yes, bar the door. Is this the thanks I get?
Such cruelty for the favor I have done you
In coming to see you?
Juan: To see whom?
Ana: Why, you!
I knew that you were here.
Juan: Bravo! You've found
A fine excuse! Ungrateful, cruel woman!
How quickly women learn the art of lying!
Ana: Don Juan, if you are angry with me still
For grievances of old, and if you shun me
Because you think that you were then betrayed,
I can convince you that it was not so.
The man you killed—

Juan: It was not him I spoke of.
See, see where your deceits are leading you!
I make complaint about one treacherous act,
And you begin to excuse a different one;
And since your treacheries are so numerous
That it is hard to tell one from another,
Do not attempt to put on a defense
Of any one of them, for I had rather
Continue being aggrieved about them all.
When all is said and done, a man who's left
With a total sense of outrage is far better
Than if he's given only vain excuses.

Ana: I do not understand you. If the cause
Of your complaint is not what I imagine,
Then tell me what it is. What new occasion
For grievance have I given you? But, sir,
I myself cannot have given you any;
So what have my unlucky stars decreed
To give you more distress? Stay, sir, and tell me
What it all means.

Juan: It signifies betrayal—
Your betrayal of me. But I do not
Regret your treacheries because through them
I've come to lose you. What I do regret
Is—I must say it—that another man
Should in a single day get the reward
I never managed to achieve in years.
And yet from this I take some consolation:
Since he has won the guerdon of your favor,
He is not truly capable of love.

Ana: It seems, Don Juan, that my evil fortune
Has furnished you with further evidence
Against me, which is quite beyond my knowledge
Or comprehension. How then can I convince you
By answering the charge? By heaven above,
I swear that people have been lying to you.

Juan: Not so. It is the truth.

Ana: Who told you so?

Juan: The lover you have come to meet.

Ana: It's you,
Don Juan, I have come to meet.

Juan: Of course,
Of course!

Ana: Because I knew that you were here.

Juan: Who could have told you that? Tell me from whom.
Ana: This maid of mine.
Juan: If only you had found
    A witness other than your maidservant;
    For all you maids and mistresses conspire
    To tell lies when it suits you.
Ana: I speak the truth.
Juan: Who could believe it?
Ana: One who loved me well.
Juan: By such a reckoning I must love you ill.
Ana: Then let me die, unhappy that I am!
Juan: And let me die, too, of my misery!
Arceo: [*Offstage*]   Open the door.
Pedro: This is still worse, O heavens!
    What shall I do, for Don Hipólito's here?
Juan: Ungrateful woman, do you still pretend
    That I've been lied to? Here comes the gallant
    You want to see.
Ana: I'm glad that he has come,
    Because he cannot be, as you suppose,
    The man I came to meet. So open up,
    Don Pedro, let him in; and let Don Juan
    Find for himself that whosoever held
    So low opinion of my lofty virtue
    Was telling lies.
Juan: May God assist me now
    To find out whether I must live or die.
    I'll overhear your conversation now,
    Since hiding is become my way of life.
        [*Don Juan hides and Don Pedro unlocks the door*]

    [*Enter Arceo with a salver of sweetmeats*]

Arceo: Why were you so slow in opening up? When someone knocks
    with his feet, it's a sure sign he's carrying something. Bless my
    soul, that Portuguese's sweet-shop has been stripped bare![16]   [*To
    Ana*]   My lady, Don Hipólito is coming. But can I believe my
    eyes? Doña Lucía here in my house?
Lucía: For once it seems a duenna's gossiping will lead to men being
    killed.

    [*Enter Don Hipólito*]

Hipólito: [*Aside*]   I wonder if Don Luis has arrived
    With the sedan chair. Yes, I spy the lady.
    Ah, Love! 'Tis as I planned.   [*Aloud*]   Welcome, my lady,

To this humble place, which by your presence is
A canopy of May and of the sun,
A sphere in which spring's green hues are displayed,
And the dawn's rosy tints.

Ana: [*Aside*]   O heavens! what is happening? Is not this
The husband of the woman who begged asylum
In my house this morning?

Juan: [*Aside, holding the door ajar*]   Was there ever such
A cruel occurrence?

Pedro: [*Aside*]   Everything's gone awry. I don't know how
To put it right.

Hipólito: Don Pedro, do not keep
This lady in distress. Do you not see
She can't speak openly while you are here?

Pedro: Then, since I'm in the way, I will depart.
[*Aside*]   But I intend to keep an eye on things.

Ana: Don Pedro, do not go. You must remain
To judge what happens!   [*To Hipólito*]   I have hardly seen you.
And it's gone hardly with me ever since.[17]
Since I have suffered much on your account.
Say, do you know me?

Hipólito: Yes, and no; for now
I know you, and yet know you not. I know you,
Because I'm well informed of who you are,
And yet I do not recognize you, madam,
Seeing you talk so strangely to me now.
'Twas in the Park I first conversed with you;
Then in your house; then I received a letter
Requesting me to come and talk with you;
And since I had you brought here, you have come.
Why is it, then, that you are so surprised
To see me, when you came to meet me here?

Juan: [*Aside*]   How should they think that I can see and hear
All this and not appear? By heaven above,
It is an outrage on the name of love!

Ana: To meet you, sir? Be careful what you say.
You'd best not sting me to refute your lies,
For you alone will suffer. In all my life
I never went to the Park, nor saw you there,
Nor spoke with you. You came into my house:
If you are wise, you will not ask me why.
Though I could tell you, you are meant to be
The last to know the truth. Suffice it then
To say you are deluded. Leave me, sir.
Perhaps your wife is cause of this confusion.

Hipólito: My wife! I understand now your annoyance.
I was wrong to bring you here. Though you are welcome
To keep up your pretense of ignorance,
I will not be encumbered with a wife,
For that's a shock I won't recover from.
Pedro: [*Aside*]   She cannot even manage to invent
A plausible lie.
Juan: [*Aside*]   Nor am I managing
To keep my temper. But if I emerge
I'll break the law of friendship and destroy
Her reputation. I shall be undone
To no good purpose. For Pedro and his servant
Will get involved, and there will be a row,
The outcome doubtful. Yet I cannot bear it.
Could any man alive stand idly by
And listen to another paying court
To her he loves? Yet there might be a way
Whereby myself alone would be undone
If—but the deed will be more eloquent
Than any words. I know now how to do it.

                                                                    [*Exit*]

Ana: In God's name, leave me, sir; and so that you
May better realize it's you I shun,
And just how far a woman like myself
Will dare to go, I now proclaim aloud
It is the man who's hidden in that room
Who is my lord and love; and it is he
Whom I had come to meet; and it is he
I deeply love. For I have never written
To you, sir, in my life; nor ever met you,
Nor ever really talked with you; and so
By this action I shall both allay
The danger he is in, and show he's wrong
To think I scorn him.
                   [*Exit to the room where Juan is, followed by Lucía*]
Hipólito: She has locked the door.
Was there ever such a cunning woman?
From the first moment I set eyes on her
I guessed she was a schemer.
Pedro: [*Aside*]   She's made a wise decision: in this way
She can prevent Don Juan from emerging,
Which I have been afraid of for some time.
Hipólito: I am perturbed and know not what to say.

   [*Enter Don Luis*]

Luis: I'm sure that my arrival is most welcome,
  Hipólito; the lady is outside
  In the sedan chair.
Hipólito: What lady?
Luis: Why, the one
  You are expecting.
Hipólito: What do you say?
Luis: She entered
  The sedan chair in St. Sebastian Street
  And she is here outside.
Hipólito: You are mistaken.
  The lady that I came to see was here
  When I arrived.
Luis: But how can this be so?
  The lady whom we met in the Park, the one
  We followed and conversed with, at this moment
  Has just arrived with me.
Hipólito: How can that be,
  Since I've just seen and talked with her unveiled,
  And she's just gone into the neighboring room?
Luis: I've nothing more to say, except she's coming.
Hipólito: Dear God, I am ill-starred.

  [*Enter Clara and Inés, veiled*]

Luis: Now tell me whether she's the one or not.
Hipólito: Either she is, or there are two of them.
Pedro: Do you see, Hipólito, do you see now
  The lady who came here today, did not
  Come to meet you.
Hipólito: You'll drive me mad.   [*To Clara*]   Veiled lady
  In duplicate, in case I'm so unlucky
  As to lose the original, I am supplied
  With two of you. Did you not talk with me
  In the Park today? Was it not you I followed?
  Did I not see you in your house?
      [*Dona Clara makes signs to indicate an affirmative answer
      to all three questions*]
  Once more I'm utterly perplexed.
Clara: [*Unveiling*]   My gallant sir,
  Now I'm unveiled I'll speak to you in words.
  I'm the dumb lady, who behind her veil
  Explained herself in dumb-show. I believed
  It was small matter for congratulation
  That one mere male should lord it over us,
  And so I sought an opportunity

To snatch some laurels from him. I chose to triumph
By my disguising. You imagined—vain
And foolish as you are—that in a trice
You had transfixed the hearts of all the beauties
Parading in the Park. Not so, Sir Flirt.[18]
Now learn your lesson; recognize the fact
That your behavior gives a bad impression
Of love which you profess. This healthy lesson
Leaves Phyllis now avenged for Fabio's scorn.[19]
And were it true I was in love with you
And came to seek you out of jealousy,
The pleasure I received from my revenge
Would be enough to root out any love
That I had left for you. I am avenged
So long as you're aware my jealousy
Was of myself, and no one else. For nothing,
And no one, surely, could inspire a woman
Such as I am with jealousy, unless it freed her
From love as well.
Sir, take away this lavish show of sweets
From Portugal, which now have proved so bitter.
The wedding's postponed forever and a day.
But don't forget to thank this devil's pander
For all the trouble he has taken for you.
He did quite admirably what you required.
There he was, exactly to the minute,
Ready and waiting with the chair. He played
His role superbly, always emphasizing
The need to be discreet and circumspect.
He's a fine friend of a false-hearted lover.
And so farewell. Let no one follow me;
For if I don my veil, go down the street,
And turn the corner, if I choose to start
Another piece of trickery, I can make you
Believe I'm quite another lady—even
Take refuge in some lady's drawing-room,
Some lady of discretion, as I did
This morning, when I forced you to believe
That someone else was I, by making use
Of a small white hat, and nothing else besides.

                                        [*Exit Clara*]

Hipólito: Listen a moment! Hear me out!
Luis: In all my life I've never met a man
      Who has such winning manners with the ladies!
Hipólito: Is this a time for joking, when I feel

As though I were dying. Stay a moment, Inés.
Inés: It would be useless, for we're very angry.

                                        [Exit Inés]

Hipólito: I don't know what to do in such a fix.
But yes, I do know; for I must rely
On my persuasive eloquence to disarm
The annoyance of one woman; and then later
Resume my courtship of the other woman.

                         [Exeunt Hipólito and Luis]

Pedro: Thank God that this at last has put an end
To the jealous wrangle between Doña Ana
And Juan, for they must have heard it all;
And it has put an end to my love, too,
For Clara came to meet Hipólito,
So that, without even trying, I have had
My jealous fears confirmed.
Arceo: And if, indeed, the lady and gallant
Have learned the truth, the play is at an end.
Pedro: *[Going to the room where Juan had been hidden]*
Don Juan, have you heard the truth at last?

    [Enter Ana and Lucía]

Ana: I'm not so fortunate as that.
Pedro: How so?
Ana: When first I entered I was just in time
To see a man, both bold and resolute,
Leap from the window to the roof below.
Arceo: So, after all, the play's not over yet.[20]
Pedro: What a strange and terrible reaction
That springs from love and jealousy! *[Aside]*   He's gone
To intercept them. I must follow after
To avert a fatal ending to their meeting.

                                            [Exit]

Ana: My fortune now is even more malign!
For when I come in search of your sweet words,
Don Juan, all I find are bitter blows
From my hard fate. For when you are beset
With false suspicions, you await them boldly;
And when true explanations seek you out
You turn your back and flee. Who is this woman,
For pity's sake, who came into my house
Only this morning? And who is this man
Who firmly swears that I came here to meet him?
Oh! If the springtime is the cause of this—

All these deceptions and displays of anger—
I wish there were no more flower-scented mornings
Of April and May.

                                                    [*Exeunt*]

ACT III

Scene 1: A room in Doña Ana's house. The room is in darkness

[*Enter Don Juan*]

Juan: Nothing goes well with me. Could even a rock
Withstand such multitudinous buffetings?
I came into the street—leaving the room
Where I was witness to my own misfortunes;
Impossible to endure them, but equally
Impossible to avenge myself—to await
In jealous desperation that gallant
Who crowned himself with such abundant blessings.
I leapt through the skylight, so that people there
Should not deny my jealousy its revenge.
I thought that by descending from the roof
I'd reach the gateway without difficulty,
But leaping to a patio beneath,
I lost my way, and I have ended up
In someone else's house. A door is opening—
People are coming in, and by their lights
I can perhaps discover where I am.
Good heavens! What a thing to happen! This
Is Doña Ana's house! That my tossed bark
Should seek a refuge in the very gulf
Where it was wrecked before! Yes, it is she.
Heavens! What shall I do? It is not right
That she should find me here, and should suppose
That, coward-like, I've come here to bewail
My jealousy, while not avenging it.
Was ever man so utterly bewildered?
What shall I do? For it befits me not
To go, nor yet to stay.   [*He hides*]

[*Enter Doña Ana and Doña Lucía, the latter with a light*]

Ana: Take off my cloak.
Thanks, fickle Fortune, that you've granted me,

Unhappy that I am, a single instant,
Just one, in which to weep, a little space
In which to wail my woes. Now I'm alone,
My tears and my complaints be storms and oceans
Between the earth and air!

Lucía: Madam, if you proceed
To such extremities, though justified,
Then Death will triumph over love. Your sorrows
Can find some consolation; for, indeed,
There is no grief that cannot be consoled.
And if Don Juan leaped out of the window
To pay the dues of friendship to Don Pedro,
Don Pedro, Arceo, and Pernía now
Have left in his pursuit, lest the two rivals
Should kill each other.

Ana: Even if my fears
Should be assuaged, 'tis only for a while.
How can they ever cease? Or how can I
Erase the memory of his jealous wrath
For which I gave no cause?

Juan: [*Aside, behind the arras*]   I can't interpret
A word of what they're saying.
I only fear that they'll make plain to me
The extent of my misfortunes and my griefs,
Confirming my suspicions. How could I then
Suffer in silence?

Lucía: Go and lie down, I pray you,
And take some rest.

Ana: There is no rest for me.
Besides, I must await Don Pedro here;
I asked him to inform me what has happened
About Don Juan: they all went after him.
There is a knocking now. Open the door.

[*Enter Pedro, Arceo, and Pernía*]

Ana: Don Pedro, what's been happening?
Pedro: All's been vain
And useless.

Ana: How is that?
Pedro: We haven't found
Don Juan, and that's very strange indeed.
To reach the gateway, leaving by that window,
Which overlooks the patio, there's a door
Through which he had to pass, but it was locked.

So it has proved impossible to find him;
Yet if he is not still inside my house,
He could not have got out into the street.
Arceo: To tell the truth, my lady, we've not looked in the right places. If
you want to find a jealous man, you must needs look for his
drowned body at the bottom of a well, or hanging in an attic.
Pernía: I've already told you to mind your Ps and Qs. Shut your mouth
when I'm about.[21]
Arceo: And I've already said my piece to you, you weird old wiseacre,
about treating a lackey as a bull, and drawing your cutlass to play
the matador with him.[22] That's all I have to say.
Lucía: My hand will be a broadsword to separate you two ruffians.
Pedro: In short, it's proved impossible to find him.
Ana: Don't be dismayed. My sorrows are the cause,
And well do they proclaim that they are mine.
For they know well to arrange appearances
To prove my guilt, and give my love offense.
But may the Lord forsake me and destroy me
If ever in my life before today
I saw that man, who followed from the Park
A woman to this house—and it was me
He found. But what's the use of saying this—
Great heaven—when Don Juan cannot hear me.
My pleas are wasted on the empty air.
Pedro: God be with you. In case he should come back
To seek me at my house, I shall return there.
What do you command?
Ana: It is not right
I should command you—but entreat you, yes,
To come back here tomorrow and recount
What has occurred.
Pedro: God be with you, madam.
Ana: And with you.

                                                    [*Exit Pedro*]
                    Lucía, lock the doors,
Then come to undress me. For I shall rise
Early tomorrow, since I have to go
To the Park, on business. I wish the feather bed
That now awaits me might become instead
A marble tomb for this my living corpse.[23]
                                                    [*Exit*]
Juan: [*Aside*] To the Park in the morning? Alas! that what has served
To undeceive me should not prove enough;
That, though my griefs recede, the danger presses.

Arceo: You're the cause of all these muddles and quarrels, Doña Lucía, for it was you who told your mistress that Don Juan was staying with us.

Lucía: The man who told me that is most to blame, for in telling me what's going on, he knew perfectly well that to tell me to keep a secret is the same as telling me to tell everyone.

Arceo: You're such a model duenna that from now on, you could serve as a mold for making more of them.

Lucía: You shameless flunky!

Arceo: You duenna!

Lucía: Madman!

Arceo: Duenna!

Lucía: Scoundrel!

Arceo: Duenna!

Lucía: Buffoon!

Arceo: Duenna!

Lucía: Villain!

Arceo: Duenna!

Lucía: Rascal!

Arceo: Duenna! Duenna! And don't try to go one better than me in insults, because you'll never manage it.

Lucía: Why not? You're a—

Arceo: Go on, say it.

Lucía: A poetaster!

Arceo: Hold on, hold on! Did you say poetaster? Goodbye, duenna. Now we're quits.[24]

Lucía: Are you off then?

Arceo: Well, what do you want?

Lucía: Wait here while my mistress finishes her preparations for bed. Then I'll come back to have a chat with you.

Arceo: I'll wait here.

> *[Exit Lucía, with the light]*

> O mothers! You who have borne sons
> To be nocturnal lovers of old women,
> Behold in me exemplum of misfortunes
> For which they have been born. For I await
> A fearful apparition, perturbed and scared
> In solitude that's peopled by my sighs.[25]

> *[Enter Don Juan, from the room where he was]*

Juan: Now is the time, O doubts, to give me counsel
> Whether what's happening is truth or falsehood.
> What matters most is that I've kept my presence
> Hidden from Doña Ana. She does not know

That I was listening; and by the sighs
Which issued from her heart, and which her lips
Falteringly pronounced, she's given me
Some evidence that she laments my fate,
And that she sympathizes with my griefs.
These servants cannot be deceived, nor be
Deceiving me; and since it was Arceo
Who told Lucía that I was concealed
In Pedro's house, and she told Doña Ana,
That's proof enough that she went seeking me.
But if that's so (as such signs seem to prove)
Why, alas, did Don Hipólito
Declare she went in search of him; and who
Can this other woman be? and, finally,
Why now does Doña Ana wish to go
To the Park tomorrow, so that I am kept ⌐
In a state of anxiety? By heaven, I swear
I'll find the reason for it. While I'm here,
I cannot both keep hidden and keep silent;
And if I am discovered, it will be
Impossible to solve the mystery
Of why she's going to the Park. And so
It's vital that I leave. Arceo here
Is waiting for Lucía. Before she comes—
Since she has not yet locked the door—I'll try
To slip into the street; then follow Doña Ana
Wherever she may go. If I am caught,
Or killed, nothing, I say, is more important
Than that I find the truth.

Arceo: I hear a step. Welcome, Lucía. Give me a kiss.   [*He kisses Don Juan*]   But you've acquired a beard. Who is it?

Juan: Be quiet. It's no one.

Arceo: What do you mean, no one? I'm so polite I'd rather believe that there are many of you, good sirs. Help! Help!

Juan: I swear I'll kill you if you don't keep quiet.

Ana: [*Within*]   What noise is that?

[*Enter Lucía, who collides with Don Juan in the dark*]

Lucía: [*Whispering to Juan*]   You're an odd fellow! Are you so scared that you had to cry out? Be off with you, lest they find you here. Come, follow me.

Juan: [*Whispering to Lucía*]   Let's go.
[*Aside*]   I must keep silent till I know the truth,
For that's a lover's proper attitude.

[*Exeunt Lucía and Juan, who bumps into Arceo on the way out*]

Arceo: Another devil here! All these mysterious exits and entrances remind one of *The Phanton Lady.*²⁶

[*Enter Doña Ana, half-undressed, with a light*]

Ana: Who's there? Does no one answer? But—Good heavens!

Arceo: [*Aside*]   I'll hide my face, so as not to be recognized.

[*Enter Doña Lucía*]

Lucía: [*Aside*]   The danger's past, for Arceo is now outside in the street. But isn't this he? If he's here, who was the man I put out in the street?

Arceo: [*Aside*]   Now I'm for it!

Ana: You, sir, who hide your face, and violate
This noble sanctuary, if desperate need
Has driven you to these extremities,
I'll willingly hand over all the keys
To jewels and wardrobe; slake your monstrous thirst
With diamonds and silks. But if you covet
My honor more than wealth, then I entreat you
Not to disdain (Ah, woe is me!) the honor
(I'm terrified) of an unhappy woman,
Victim of great misfortunes. If you've come here
To offend my honor, then by all that's holy,
Before you speak a single word to me,
Before you can insult the man I love,
With my bare hands, I'll kill you. If tears alone
Will not suffice to melt your diamond heart,
I'll rend my breast and use my blood instead
To work it to my will.

Arceo: You need not work it,
Since I can work it for you. It wouldn't do
For a lady to play the pelican, or an angel
To play a working woman.²⁷ Matters of import
Have brought me to your house. I did not come
To steal your jewels, nor to outrage your honor.
And therefore that you may be quite assured
Of my discreet intentions and be safe,
Farewell! God keep you, lady!²⁸

                                                      [*Exit*]

Lucía: What's this?

Ana: Has he gone?

Lucía: Yes.

Ana: Turn the key in the lock; and since bright dawn
Comes forth to vanquish darkness, I do not wish

To go to bed. Don Juan, had you seen that—
Who ever could have managed to convince you
That I am not to blame?

[Exeunt]

Scene 2: The Park

[Enter Doña Clara and Inés, dressed as in Act I]

Inés: So you're returning to the Park?
Clara: Yes, Inés,
Though there's no rule, nor rhyme, nor reason for it,
I'm going back to where I lost my life
To find my life again.
Inés: What you have suffered
Is reason enough; and if I'm not mistaken,
You're piqued because your splendid plan miscarried,
Through yesterday's strange occurrence.
Clara: It would be useless
To hide with words the pain my tears confess.
I sent for Don Hipólito, presuming
To make a mock of him. He brazened it out
And made a mockery of my stratagem,
Although it's true he offered me excuses
Which I made shift to credit at the time,
Only to save my face; for he admitted
That he had come because another woman
Had summoned him. And therefore my enjoyment
Was turned to anguish. I myself, alas,
Kindled the fire in which I am tormented,
Prepared the poison which I drank myself,
Yes, roused the monster that has torn me up,
Nursed at my bosom the serpent which has stung me.
Well may she burn, moan, suffer, and so die,
Who lit, concocted, nourished, and aroused
Poison, fire, serpent, and wild beast.²⁹
Inés: From this
Might all who see you now assert we women
Only love well when we are treated badly.
But why have we come here, despite your anguish?
Clara: To see if Don Hipólito comes today.
Inés: A splendid object!
Clara: If I can obtain
Today some respite from my doubts, I'll deck
Mornings of April and May with thankful flowers.   *[Exeunt]*

[Enter Don Hipólito and Don Luis]

Hipólito: I followed Doña Clara to her house,
Even as you saw, and made excuses to her
For the deception I was victim of,
And asked her what offense there was in going
To see a woman who had summoned me,
To find out what she wanted. Then by acting
The part of passionate lover—at which I'm expert,
For there is nobody these days, Don Luis,
Who is not practiced in that role—I left her
Appeased, amenable to my explanation.
And so, resulting from her stratagem
To do me down, she was herself deceived,
For she believed my show of passionate love;
Whereas I must confess that Doña Ana
Has robbed me of my soul, my life, my will.
For as at first I thought that it was she
Who bade me come, to find her there indeed
Made me resolve to cling to the belief
That she had summoned me.
Luis: You're a cool fellow!
Hipólito: Would it have been more sensible to admit
That I had been defeated?
Luis: No—but if
I had experienced about these women
What you have done, I would have been upset
And so ashamed that I would never wish
To see them again.
Hipólito: That would have been absurd.
You have such foolish scruples, you are like
An absolute provincial gentleman.[30]
We'll see if you'll conform to modern modes:
To spend your wealth, and love a host of women,
All for your pleasure, none to your regret.

*[Enter Doña Ana (dressed the same as Clara) with Doña Lucía.
They talk together aside]*

Lucía: Now that we're in the Park, you can inform me
Why you have come here to this lovely spot.
Ana: Since you will soon discover it, why do you want me
To tell you now? It is superfluous
To say things twice, especially when the things
Are just about to happen, for the man
I'm looking for is here.

Lucía: That is the man,
My lady, involved in yesterday's deceits,
Unless my eyes deceive me.
Ana: It's he I mean.
For I've come out to see and talk with him,
So that his duty as a gentleman
May make him give me back my reputation;
For gentlemen who are most courteous
Are those who shield the honor of a lady.
Lucía: Did you leave your house and come to the Park for this,
When, if you're seen here, you'll incur fresh blame?
Ana: Wherever Don Juan should chance to be,
He'll be in hiding, and not venture here
Where there are crowds of people; so it's here
That I can talk with Don Hipólito
In greatest safety.
Lucía: I hope in heaven's name
That you are right.
Ana: Put on your veil and call him.
Say that a lady wants to speak with him
Alone, without his friend.
Lucía: [*To Hipólito*]   Sir, a veiled lady
Wishes to talk with you alone. She's here.
Follow us then.
Hipólito: [*Aside*]   It's Doña Clara, sure;
The dress is hers. So she has tried again
Yesterday's trickery, but she won't succeed
This time.   [*He comes forward and addresses Doña Ana*]
Good Lord, you are a most peculiar creature
Since you won't trust a man who much esteems you,
And gives you no offense. But if you seek
More satisfaction than I've given already,
You need not follow me, for you are ever
Here in my heart.
Ana: You have mistaken me
For another woman, as your speeches prove.
I'll undeceive you promptly.   [*Unveils*] Do you know me?
Hipólito: You asked me that same question once before
When it was more embarrassing. I replied
Both yes and no. And now it seems to me
That I am still in doubt, and the reply
Must always be the same. Yes, I know you
Since I am seeing you. Yet I do not know you,
Because good fortune often turns to bad,
And now the opposite is taking place.

Ana: Follow me to the Flower Garden: it is best
That I should talk with you alone; so tell
Your friend to stay behind.

[*Exeunt the two women*]

Hipólito: Don Luis, you may now congratulate me
On a new love affair. That veilèd lady
Is Doña Ana. I can't be self-deceived,
For I have seen her plainly with my eyes.
Do you not see it is the self-same woman
As yesterday? That she has come to meet me?
Wait here; and now dispute if you are able,
That I've a way with women.

[*Enter Doña Clara and Inés, their faces veiled*]

Inés: [*To Clara*]   Don Hipólito is here.
Clara: Well, go no further.

[*Hipólito, misled by their dress, believes the women are Ana
and Lucía, waiting for him to follow them. He comes up and
addresses them*]

Hipólito: I'm following, Doña Ana. Lead the way.
For since I go with you, O lovely goddess
Of these green meadows, any place will be
The Flower Garden; for the green and purple hues
Are dim beside the sparkle of your eyes,
And fountain's pearl and crystal far surpassed
By your foot's snowy whiteness.
Clara: [*Aside*]   Oh dear, oh dear!
He said "Doña Ana." What new trick is this?
Why wonder when one can discover it?
The Flower Garden is the place to meet,
And I should take him there.   [*Aloud*]   Come, let's go.
Hipólito: [*Aside*]   Fortune, my love is much indebted to you,
Since while I'm safe from Clara's jealousy
You offer me a rendezvous with Ana!
A glorious triumph for your deity!

[*Exeunt all, except Don Luis*]

[*Enter Don Juan*]

Juan: Doña Ana came down to this place.
Though I lost sight of her amidst the crowd,
She cannot hide from me. I've spoken truly
For even though appearances might lie,
My luckless fate would yet reveal the truth.
She talks with Don Hipólito. No hope

Is left me. Torn with love and jealousy,
Let me now die of rage!

Luis: [*Aside*]   Heaven preserve me!
What do I see? Is not that man Don Juan?
[*Aloud*]   Don Juan de Guzmán! Sir!

Juan: Who calls?
[*Aside*]   What a horrible dilemma! That
Is Don Luis.

Luis: Wheresoever I find
A man who stains my honor and my name,
I greet him with the sword, and not with words;
Dispensing with courtesies, because the sword
Is Honor's clearest voice. Unsheathe your own—
So that I may more honorably obtain
My vengeance.

Juan: I have never in my life
Refused to answer with my sword the man
Who greeted me with his. If you've a mind
To kill me, then make haste. If you delay,
Another wound may take away your chance.
For no man can die twice.

Luis: I do not answer you;
My sword must speak.

Juan: [*Aside*]   Don Hipólito
Went with Doña Ana to the garden.
Invidious torture! Who could have believed
That I would be affronted over there,
While here a man is trying to take revenge
On me.
          [*They fight*]

Luis: My sword is broken.

Juan: I could kill you.
But so that you may realize how a man
Of knightly valor acts—and how I acted
When I dispatched your cousin (for a man
Who acted basely once, would do it twice:
Cowardice is not a temporary failing)
Go find another sword. I will stay here.

Luis: [*Aside*]   How awkward! Since the man who gave offense
Makes me beholden to him; the injurer
Does me a favor. I know what I must do.
[*Aloud*]   Wait here. I'll soon return.

Juan: You know the risk
If I'm found here, and therefore to avoid it,
I'll wait in the Flower Garden.

Luis: I'll meet you there,
      In a mere moment
                                                    [*Exit*]
Juan: What shall I do?
      In this atrocious situation, where
      One problem's dogged by another. When I try
      To solve one, then I forthwith find another,
      And know not what to do about them all.
      Whatever I do will be the worse for me.
      If I go after Don Hipólito,
      Then, like a fool, I break faith with Don Luis;
      And if I wait for *him*, I break my faith
      With my own jealousy. But why indeed
      Should courage falter? Since, in either case,
      The end is death. Kill me first who can,
      Whether it's Don Hipólito or Don Luis,
      For since the man I injured seeks me out,
      It's right that I should seek my injurer.
                                                    [*Exit*]

Scene 3: The Flower Garden

[*Enter Doña Clara and Don Hipólito*]

Hipólito: Here on the margin of this flowery arbor
      Which spring embellishes with so much art,
      You may inform me now, what is the cause
      Of your request, for you are well aware
    . That I am at your service, Doña Ana,
      And do not let that veil, that tactless cloud,
      Affront your beauteous rays. Let the sun rise
      Since day has dawned.
Clara: I'll do what you command.
      Not to obey such elegant conceits
      Such gallant compliments would be unseemly.   [*She unveils*]
Hipólito: Good Lord! It's Doña Clara!
Clara: Why are you so abashed? Why this surprise?
      It's I. Go on. Your little speech is splendid.
Hipólito: I'm not abashed, and I am not surprised—
      Save only that you should suppose that I
      Had failed to recognize you all the time.
      I wanted to avenge myself on you
      For coming out like this, so I addressed you
      By a wrong name.
Clara: Indeed! A likely tale!

Hipólito: By heaven I swear that when I asked Don Luis
 To stay behind, I told him who you were.
 Let him appear and if he won't confirm
 What I have said, then punish with your scorn
 The faults I have committed. I'll go for him,
 And he will say—
Clara: Whatever you want him to.
 Don't call him.
Hipólito: Why not?
Clara: Because he is like
 The proverbial Muñoz, "who's a bigger liar
 Than you yourself."[31]
Hipólito: No, no, it would be best
 For him to come and let you know the truth.
 [*Aside*] That's not the reason, but I need a break
 For my relief; experience to the full
 My shocked astonishment that in a trice
 Women can change identity like that.

             [*Exit*]

 [*Enter Don Juan. On seeing him, Doña Clara veils herself*]

Juan: [*Aside*] I've searched each nook and cranny of the garden,
 Embellished with its variegated hues
 And I have not been able to confront
 The object of my jealousy. Oh heavens!
 When jealousy has been importunate
 Why does it hide now when I seek it out?
 It flees, perhaps, because it's been revealed.
 But is not that Doña Ana? My wrath is futile,
 Futile my vengeance, too, since I have found her
 Alone. It's unbelievable that I
 Should be so foolish as to grieve to see her
 Unaccompanied by Hipólito.
 I will withdraw. But heavens! I cannot do it.
 Jealousy hinders me. [*Aloud*] My cruel foe,
 False siren, harpy, lying sphinx, you serpent
 That lurks within your beauty's snow and roses,
 Where is that constant lover who adores you,
 So that I may revenge myself on you
 By using my sword on him, rather than taking
 Vengeance on him by striking you with words.
Clara: You're deceived, sir, in your anguish and presumption,
 Since I have never given you cause to dare
 To speak so foolishly, and with such scorn
 [*Unveils*] —Because you do not know me.

Juan: You are right. I have been impudent and foolish.
I took you for another. A cloud can veil
Either the moon or sun. I found the moon
Wearing the sun's disguise. Forgive me, madam,
My words were not for you.

[*Enter Doña Ana and Doña Lucía*]

Ana: I can vouch for that:
His words were meant for me.

Clara: Well, if his words
Were meant for you, let him address you now,
And there's an end of my displeasure, sir.

                                                                           [*Exit*]

Ana: I'm overjoyed, Don Juan, that you've come
Just at the time your own eyes have deceived you
And undeceived you. Since you've made this error
You must perforce believe that it can happen.
For you to think another man could not
Believe what you've believed, would mean you thought
That he was more intelligent than you.
And you more foolish, and there can be none
With such a poor opinion of his brains.

Juan: How foolish, Doña Ana, to attempt
To undeceive me so. For though it's true
My eyes deceived me, I equally perceive
Your explanation is itself an insult,
Since you have brought it here in person now.
So your deceiving and your undeceiving
Are equally deception: you can't excuse
The insult to my jealousy, for now
I am as much annoyed by your attempt
To undeceive me, as I was at first
By your deceit. Although that was an insult,
This vain attempt of yours to undeceive me
Is downright contumely.

Ana: My coming here
Was neither to deceive you, nor offend you.
I came on your account.

Juan: How could you know
I would be here?

Ana: I couldn't have known; but yet
I might have guessed that you'd turn up to find me
If I came here to make Hipólito
To seek you out.

Juan: To what end?

Ana: That he himself
Might explain matters to your satisfaction.
Juan: A foolish stratagem! A second lover
Who tries to assuage the jealousy of a first
Makes him more jealous still.
Ana: Do not compile
A roll of lovers. I am not a woman
To have a second one.
Juan: Enough of that!
For I recall one night—I'll say no more,
For silence is more eloquent than words.
Ana: I would to God my truthful explanation
About that night would be convincing to you.
But if it cannot, there's a surer way:
Reminding you that I am who I am.
Juan: If only that sufficed.
Ana: It would be so
If you loved me truly.
Juan: It is because I love you
I can't believe you.
Ana: Well, let us suppose
A man was hidden in my house last night,
Who entered it because—
Juan: Because of what? Tell me.
Ana: Because he fled from officers of justice.
Moved by my tears, or of his own accord,
He went away; and had you seen him leave,
It's certain I'd have paid the penalty,
Though I was innocent of the offense.
Juan: No, you would not, if he had been a man
Like Arceo, and it was he who lay
Hidden by Doña Lucía in your house.
Lucía: [*Aside*] Heavens! They've found me out,
Ana: What's that you say?
Juan: The truth, that's all.
Ana: What impudent behavior!
Juan: But yet the man I killed that other time
Was nobly born; and entered with a key.
I would not mention this, and like a serpent,
Poison the air I breathe. Farewell. May heaven
Spare you, Ana, for some other lover.
You offer far too many explanations
For one man to take in, and he must flee.
[*Aside*] I'm only going, so that I can wait
For Don Luis nearby.   [*Exit*]

Ana: Pray stay, Don Juan.
Listen. My sorrows are beyond belief. [*She veils herself*]

[*Enter Don Hipólito, and Doña Clara behind*]

Hipólito: [*To Ana*] I could not find Don Luis anywhere
Within the Park—
Clara: [*Aside*] I'll follow Don Hipólito to see
Whither his tricks are leading.
Lucía: [*Aside*]   Who could imagine
That such a wicked scandal-monger was abroad?
Hipólito: [*To Ana*] But yet, by heaven, Clara, it is true
I recognized you from the very first.
Ana: No, you did not; for if you really had
I think my honor, Don Hipólito
Would not have been in jeopardy. Behold!
It's me you've been addressing. [*She unveils*]
Hipólito: [*Aside*]   What trick is this?
Clara: His words were meant for me, and not for you.
And what you said to me, I can repeat
To you; because I also have a man
Who addresses me. [*She unveils*]
Hipólito: Good Lord!
The two of them have got me on the hook!
Ana: Although you imitate the words I spoke,
I shall not follow you in everything,
And leave at once. I shall not leave you both
Until I find out what is going on.
Lucía: [*Aside*] Who would believe there were such tittle-tattlers?
Hipólito: Who are you waiting for?
Ana: Someone as witness;
One who must hear and see this for himself—
And here he comes. I owe to heaven at last
This single act of mercy.

[*Enter Don Pedro, Arceo, and Don Juan*]

Pedro: You must not slip away now I have found you,
After I've searched for you the whole night through.
Juan: I have some urgent business, and my honor
Depends upon it.
Pedro: Hear Doña Ana first.
Arceo: [*Aside*] What's happened, Lucía?
Lucía: Tittle-tattle, Arceo.
They've found out everything.
Ana: Thank God, Don Juan, that for once you've come
In time to recognize that I am truthful.

Doña Clara, tell him. Is it not true
That yesterday you came into my house,
Fleeing from Don Hipólito? and he thought
I was the veilèd woman he pursued?
Clara: Yes; and since I wished to play a trick on him,
I therefore wrote a letter in your name
And went to see him in Don Pedro's house;
And what took place there, he himself can tell you.
Ana: Don Juan, this means that I have given you
All the explanations I can give;
And for the rest, it's up to heaven, since
They're known to heaven alone.

[*Enter Don Luis*]

Luis: Don Juan de Guzmán!
Pedro: [*Aside*]   This makes matters worse.
Arceo: [*Aside*]   O Lord! Don Luis has recognized him now!
Hipólito: [*To Luis*]   Is this man Don Juan de Guzmán?
I'm sorry that I did not recognize him,
Or, in your absence, I would—
Luis: Stop! One moment.
Nobility is victor in this quarrel,
And not the sword.
Juan: You might have waited for me
Until I was alone.
Luis: We should have witnesses
Of what I purpose. You gave me the chance
To fetch another sword when in the duel
My sword was broken. If I'm late, I have
A good excuse—to write this document
Of my withdrawal from the legal action
In which I sued you. You were in my debt
For a life you took; but you have given me,
With prudence and nobility, one back.
So that I have no longer any claim
Against your life. And if I did not say so
At once, it was because, being weaponless,
I would not have you think that it was fear
Which made me pardon you. And so, Don Juan,
I hand you now this paper, when my sword
Is at my side.
Juan: You give me back my life,
And honor, too. And now you see the lady
Who was the cause of all these happenings.
And if my gratitude seems less than heartfelt,

She may express it for me by the warmth
Of her embrace.[32]

Ana: So with your friendship sealed,
We all shall seal it, too.

Clara: No, we do not.
Since there's no longer one who makes me jealous,
I do not have a man whom I could love.

Hipólito: What more is there for me to say, except
I do not love you either

Ana: Arceo and Lucía
Must marry right away.

Arceo: But when women called Lucía join with men called Arceo,
won't their offspring be Lucifer?[33]

Juan: This is the end of MORNINGS OF APRIL AND MAY.
Pray you forgive its shortcomings.

[*Exeunt*]

THE END

No hay
burlas con
el amor

No Trifling with Love

DRAMATIS PERSONAE

Don Alonso de Luna   Moscatel, valet
Don Juan de Mendoza   Don Pedro's daughters:
Don Luis Osorio   Doña Beatriz
Don Diego   Doña Leonor
Don Pedro Enríquez   Inés, maid

The scene is set in Madrid

ACT I

Scene 1: A Room in the house of Don Alonso

[*Enter Alonso and Moscatel (looking very depressed)*]

Alonso: The devil take you! Why do you go about
Forever in the grip of foolish fancies?
You're never here on time, nor give straight answers
To what I ask; and what is doubly wrong—
If I don't call you, you turn up; and if
I do, you hide. What is this all about?
Explain yourself.

Moscatel: Alas! It's all about these sighs
Due from the soul.

Alonso: What! Does a rogue now dare
To sigh like that?

Moscatel: Don't rogues possess souls, too?

Alonso: Oh yes, for feeling, and for crude expression
Of acute suffering; but not for sighing;
For sighing only suits a noble passion.

Moscatel: And have I not the right to noble passion?

Alonso: What a mad idea!

Moscatel: But is there any passion
   Nobler than love?
Alonso: I might say yes; but yet
   To avoid an argument I will say no.
Moscatel: No? Well then, if I aspire to love, my passion
   Must needs be noble.
Alonso: You're in love?
Moscatel: In love.
Alonso: If that's the reason for your madness, I
   Could laugh more at your melancholy now
   Than I laughed yesterday at all your jests.
Moscatel: Since you have never known what 'tis to love,
   And always set such store upon your freedom,
   You've taken pleasure in pretending love,
   And mocked at men who mean what they profess.
   So, since I truly love, you mock me now.
Alonso: I do not want a lovesick servant. You
   Will leave my house today.
Moscatel: Take heed.
Alonso: There's no more to be said.
Moscatel: Look here—
Alonso: What do you want to say?
Moscatel: That fate has changed
   The usual plot; for always on the stage
   It is the master who's the one in love,
   The servant fancy-free. I'm not to blame
   For such an alteration. So let the public
   Behold a novelty today. I'll act
   The lover, you'll be fancy-free.[1]
Alonso: You'll not remain here
   A single day.
Moscatel: So quickly sacked! Will you not give me time
   To find another master?
Alonso: No more words!
   You shall be gone this instant!

   [*Enter Don Juan*]

Juan: What's the matter?
Alonso: It's this rogue here, who has committed
   The worst of rogueries, the basest deed,
   The blackest perfidy that was ever found
   In the heart of man, the greatest treachery
   That could be imagined.
Juan: What was it?
Alonso: He's fallen in love.

Am I not right to abuse him in this way?
For a man commits no greater roguery,
Baseness, and treachery than to fall in love.
Juan: Yet, it is love that makes a man courageous,
Generous, prudent, gallant.
Alonso: The devil take it!
You have composed for me a piece entitled
"Love's Wonders,"[2] but it's based upon a lie,
For nothing ever made a man so wretched,
So miserly, so cowardly as love.
Juan: What are you saying?
Alonso: Just listen, and you'll see
Which of our views is sounder. A man in love
Wants all he gets for the lady he adores,
Not thinking of a friend's or servant's needs,
But of his selfish pleasure. And so it follows
Love makes a miser of him, for true virtue
Is not unfairly generous, and there is
No greater skinflint than the man who's generous
For his own pleasure only.
Juan: I do not want,
Alonso, to refute your sophistries,
Lest I insult my own distress, which springs
From love; and if I told you all about it
I fear I would be worsted. I do not wish
To cause another's triumph over me.
I came here to consult you on a problem;
But since, alas, it's one that's born of love,
I will not speak of it; because a man
Who gives a servant such a punishment
Will not be sympathetic to a friend
In the same case.
Alonso: He certainly will listen
With sympathy. For you to be in love,
Juan, is not the same as for this knave;
For you are noble, gallant, rich, and prudent;
Your sort of love consists of tenderness
As well as passion. Wherefore should base churls
Warble love's praises? To make you realize
I can be serious on serious matters,
As well as laugh when laughter suits the bill,
I'm wholly at your service. [*To Moscatel*] You, get out!
Juan: No, let him stay. I've come to see you both.
Alonso: Well then, proceed.
Juan: Listen. You know, Alonso,

How I, submissive to the yoke of love,
Drew Venus' chariot—so easily
She gained the victory, that I do not know
Which happened first: the will to conquer me,
Or the victory—they seemed to coincide.
You know the reason for my noble yielding:
The sovereign loveliness of Leonor,
The daughter of Don Pedro Enríquez,
Of whom my father was the intimate friend.
This wondrous beauty, lovely paragon,
Is the good fortune that I wish to gain,
The glory I desire. I do not say
That I am fortunate and deserve her favors.
It would be impudent discourtesy
To say I merit them, though I enjoy them.
Enjoyment and desert are not the same,
And though I say I have them, I cannot boast
That I deserve them. Fortune, and not merit,
Enabled me to achieve the impossible.
Lapped in this state of sweet illusion, soaring
Upon the wings of my desire, caressed
And guarded by the night, welcomed by shadows,
Applauded by silence, I go to visit her
To whom I owe more favors than to the sun,
The light, the day itself. The consciousness
That I am dying of love keeps me alive,
Till I can openly declare myself
And ask her noble father for her hand.
I do not doubt that he will give consent,
Since love already had made up the match,
And there's equality in wealth and birth.
There is no reason for delay. And yet
The reason I have not asked for her hand
Nor married her—and here's the obstacle
To my content, the modicum of wrong
In my good fortune, and the single snag—
Is this: that Leonor has an elder sister,
And since a man can hardly be expected
To marry off his second daughter first,
I haven't yet approached him. For if I asked him
For one of his two daughters (for, of course,
I must not say which of them I adore)
He's bound to give me Beatriz, the elder;
And if I say she's not the one I want,
But Leonor, my suit will be suspect;

And his suspicions, slumbering peacefully,
Will be aroused. So I may lose the freedom
Of entry to his house I now possess.
If, indeed, it's not already lost
Because of the unfortunate event
Which happened last night—and that's why I came
To see you. Listen closely. Beatriz,
Leonor's sister, is the oddest creature
Madrid has ever seen. Though she is lovely
And very intelligent, both beauty and brains
Are being spoiled by the extravagance
Of her strange disposition. Beatriz
Is so conceited that I don't suppose
She ever looked a man in the face; because
She is convinced that the mere sight of her
Would be enough to kill him on the spot.
And she is so enamored of her wit
That to pay court to it, she studied Latin,
And composed verses in Castilian.
As for her dressing, she is so affected,
She tries all fashions, but discards not any.
She curls her hair at least three times a day,
And she is never satisfied with it.
The Affectations of Belisa (which
Lope has dramatized so brilliantly)
Are very trivial compared to hers.[3]
And though she's irritating in these ways,
That's not the worst of it. It's the way she comments
Affectedly, like poets she's been reading;
Long-winded as she is, she adds so many
Qualifying glosses that one needs
An explanation of her explanations.[4]
The flattery and applause of fools have made her
So proud and arrogant that she disdains
The goddess of love, proclaiming independence
From her dominion. This obsession of hers,
This irritating manner makes her so hateful
At every hour, that never were two people
So contrary, opposed, and so at odds
As these two sisters, that their drawing-room
Is all the time a setting for a duel;
I don't know whether it's from foolish envy
Or from mistrust, that she has started now
To accompany Leonor, so every moment
She's in pursuit and asking what she's doing.

So much so, that she seems to be the shadow
To the bright sunshine of her sister's eyes.
And so last night, I went into her street,
Secretly, in disguise, and near the balcony
Where I was wont to speak with Leonor,
I gave the signal. Leonor forthwith
Opened the casement, and I was alert
To seize the opportunity. I drew near
To talk with her. But hardly had my voice
Begun to utter all the sentiments
(Prepared, but not well mastered, which my heart
Could not contain), when Beatriz in pursuit
Clamored for Leonor to leave the window,
Making innumerable silly comments,
Which, if I understood her curious style,
Meant that she'd tell her father of this outrage.
I don't know whether I was recognized,
And so in my anxiety I'm afraid
Of knowing, and not knowing, of the outcome
Of this affair. I've not been to the house,
Afraid of her anger; but I'm not resolved
To stay away, for if she's been informed
Of my intentions, Leonor's very life
Would be in jeopardy. And therefore, since
There's danger in both going and not going,
I've chosen another way—to send this letter
Secretly, and cunningly (it's not
In my own hand). So I want Moscatel,
With all the cleverness at his command,
To carry it to Inés, Leonor's servant.
And since he won't be recognized as mine,
There's nought to fear. So what I ask of you,
Alonso, is to give him leave to go,
And that you wait with me outside the house;
For if I find that Leonor's in danger,
I am resolved to take her from the house,
In spite of all the world. I've chosen you,
Since you are brave, to aid me in this deed.
You are my friend, and I am well aware
That though you take a fashionable delight
In frivolous pleasure, you're quite serious
When it comes to swordsmanship.

Alonso: Moscatel,
Take that letter; gain access to the house
Of Don Pedro Enríquez, by any means

You can devise, and give it to the girl
   Don Juan mentioned.
Juan: Arranged so quickly?
Alonso: If it must be done, is it not best
   To do it immediately? [*To Moscatel*] Take the letter,
   And come with us.
Moscatel: [*Aside*]   Although I'm not afraid,
   Since it is Inés whom I go to find,
   The mistress of my heart, may Love inspire me
   With boldness.
Alonso: Lead the way.
Juan: What a true friend!
Alonso: [*Aside*]   How tedious are these stupid love affairs!
   What if they heard me? No, they didn't. I
   Am fortunate indeed, for I have never
   Made love where there's a risk. I've only wooed
   A girl or woman for the "right true end,"
   And no holds barred. I loudly knock for entrance
   On my first visit, and speak loudly too;
   And whether I'm instilled by the affair
   With fear or boldness, rests upon one thing:
   Whether the lady has—or has not—money.

                                             [*Exeunt*]

Scene 2: A street

[*Enter Alonso, Juan, and Moscatel*]

Juan: This is the street. We will conceal ourselves
   Behind this doorway, lest we should be seen.
Alonso: You're right.

[*Enter Don Luis and Don Diego, who raise their hats as they pass*]

Who are these men who stare at Leonor's house?
Juan: That is Don Luis de Osorio
   Whom I have often seen here recently—
   To my extreme annoyance.
Alonso: Well, should we not
   Annoy him too?
Juan: No, this is not the time
   For things like that. Let us walk slowly past,
   And give no cause for comment.
Alonso: Pass it is.[5]
   Although I think we could have come out trumps.

Juan: [*To Moscatel*]   Turn now; go back at once and give the letter
    To Inés.
Moscatel: I'm afraid.
Juan: You have no cause.
    There is the place. Deliver the letter quickly.
                              [*Exeunt Alonso, Juan, and Moscatel*]
Luis: This is the perfect sphere, the heaven in little,
    Where dwells the deity, the loveliest planet
    The sun has e'er beheld, since it was born
    Flaming upon the deep, until its death
    Ablaze on icy waves and white with age.
    Yet, though her beauty is incomparable,
    It is of no importance. She might be ugly:
    Such is her intellect, it would not matter.
Diego: But do you serve this intellectual lady
    With thought of marriage?
Luis: I pay court to her,
    Not only for love, but from expediency.
    As for the outcome, my relations are
    Negotiating now.
Diego: I am not sure
    You're doing the right thing.
Luis: Why ever not?
    Seeing I find in her nobility,
    Virtue, great beauty, and great intellect.
Diego: Because her intellect is in excess.
    I wouldn't wish my wife to have more knowledge
    Than I myself. I'd rather she knew less.
Luis: But when has learning ever been a fault?
Diego: When it was inappropriate. For a woman
    Should know the way to spin, to sew, to darn,
    But doesn't need to know about stylistics,
    Nor how to write in verse.
Luis: But yet to practice
    Such intellectual activities
    Is not a fault; for when excess of wit
    Takes such a noble form, there's no objection.
Diego: I'm not convinced her intellect's like that.
    I know the contrary from the cruel disdain
    With which she treats you.
Luis: I adore her scorn.
    Let us walk down the street again. No, wait
    Until these gentlemen have passed. I view them
    With some concern.
Diego: Let's go then.

Luis: Lovely focus
Of all my thoughts, which shelters the indifference
I so adore, I shall return betimes
To seek your threshold.

                                                                    [*Exeunt*]

Scene 3: A room in Don Pedro's house

[*Enter Doña Leonor and Inés*]

Leonor: Is my sister dressed yet?

Inés: She was still dressing her hair a moment ago; and as she, out of vanity, consulted her mirror again and again, I left her, so as not to die of boredom.

Leonor: If she is often foolish, so is her mirror.

Inés: How do you mean?

Leonor: If one is consulted in a difficulty and doesn't freely give advice to anyone who asks for it, isn't that foolish, Inés? Every day I have asked advice of Beatriz, but she never once replied to my persistent requests. So she is very much a fool.

Inés: I've just thought of a reason for it.

Leonor: What can it be?

Inés: It's simply a case of mutual misunderstanding. She talks learnedly and you talk plainly; so the two of you are at cross-purposes all the day long.

Leonor: How happy I would be if that were my only cause for concern! Oh, my dear Inés, I'm dreadfully afraid that that affected creature, that exasperating critic, will tell my father what she heard me saying on the balcony last night.

Inés: The fact that my master left the house so early prevented that from happening, for there was no opportunity for him to find out. So let us devise some scheme to discredit her tale in advance.

Leonor: I have been trying, but without thinking of anything practicable. How can I, when it was she herself who caught sight of Don Juan?

Inés: It is just what she saw that must be emphatically denied—so as to undo its effect. What hasn't actually been witnessed, my lady, need never be denied.

Leonor: The best means, alas, that occurs to me, Inés, is simply to make her the confidante of my love, my conduct, and my hopes; for to confide a secret is surely to create an iron door to lock it in. Oh dear! What am I to do, Inés, if this is the only resource left to me?

Beatriz: [*Within*]   Hullo, there! Is there a retainer about?

[*She enters, carrying a mirror, looking at herself in it*]

Inés: What is it you want?

Beatriz: That from my dexter hand
You take this magic glass and bring my *gants*.

Inés: Pray, what are "gants"?

Beatriz: Why, they are gloves. Oh, that I should be forced
To use such common parlance.

Inés: I'll know it another time. Here they are.

Beatriz: O, how I have to war with ignorance!
I say, Inés.

Inés: My lady?

Beatriz: Bring Ovid from my library.
Not the *Metamorphoses*, nor yet
The *Ars Amandi. Remedio Amoris*,[6]
Yes, that one, that's the work I'm studying.

Inés: How can I recognize a book—if that
Is what you ask—who cannot even read
A playbill?

Beatriz: You unenlightened, idiotic,
Uninformed creature, has cohabitation
With me effected no improvement yet?

Leonor: [*Aside*] This is my cue. [*Aloud*] Sister.

Beatriz: Who speaks to me?

Leonor: One, sister, who obedient to your will
Throws herself at your feet.

Beatriz: Stop! Draw not nigh; for you will surely tarnish
The gleaming whiteness of my chaste *persona*,
Profane the rites my honor's altar claims.
A woman trusting in the shadows' chaos,
Dishonoring day by her nocturnal deeds,
May not attract the attention of my gaze
With voice profane, for she will be a serpent
In human form, who poisons with her breath.[7]

Leonor: Prudent and beauteous Beatriz, you are my sister.

Beatriz: That I am not—because I cannot have
A libidinous sister.

Leonor: What is libidinous, sister dear?

Beatriz: A sister with a flickering lamp, a solar viceroy,
Who dares to ope a window, and whispering through it
With sensuous lips gives the bright planet Venus
Something to talk about, and the chaste stars
Something for reticence. I shall diminish
The scandal by imparting to our sire.

Leonor: And did you recognize him?

Beatriz: No, and how could I? For I'm unacquainted
With any of the masculine gender.
Leonor: Well,
I wish to tell you who he was, and why
He talked with me.
Beatriz: What impudence! Must I
Endure this insult?
Leonor: Though you may not want to,
You'll hear it nonetheless. It is not fair
To my good name that foolish fantasies
Should make you think my honorable conduct
Was scandalous behavior.
Beatriz: Honorable?
Leonor: Listen—
Beatriz: I refuse to lend an ear
Directly to your voice.
Leonor: Directly or indirectly.
You're going to hear it all.
Beatriz: If I were forced
To hear your secret, I would have to keep it
Clandestine, and it is not in my nature
To commit a sin so grave.
Leonor: I'm speaking to you.
Beatriz: I'm like a snake that does not heed the charmer.
I am not listening, I am not listening.

                                                    [*Exit*]

Leonor: Listen—But who is that who has come in?
Inés: No doubt he seeks my master.
Leonor: See who it is,
While in my sadness and anxiety
I pursue that horrid creature.

                                                    [*Exit*]

        [*Enter Moscatel*]

Moscatel: [*Aside*]   O love within, how cowardly you are!
Not even the safeguards every envoy has
Can check your fear.[8]
Inés: How dare you, Moscatel,
Enter this chamber!
Moscatel: Since you do not know
What has impelled me to this step, your harshness
Is somewhat premature.
Inés: Is it not enough
That you have entered?
Moscatel: Yes and no.

Inés: Well!
What do you mean by no and yes?
Moscatel: No, because
You don't know why I've come. Yes, because
You are annoyed with me. No, because
You'll soon know why. And yes, because I'm slow
In telling you. Although I might have come
Drawn by your beauty, brought here by my love,
Distraught by thought of you, I come in fact
To bring this note, indited by Don Juan
To Leonor, entrusted to my care
Because I am not known to be his servant—
Unless it was because he recognized
The nature of my malady—lovesickness—
For one who does not know what 'tis to love
Makes a poor go-between.
Inés: Well, tell him then
You've given me the letter, and that I'll hand it
To Leonor. And now be gone at once,
For I'm afraid, unlucky as I am,
That Beatriz—
Moscatel: I'm going. Though I adore
Your presence, I am so obedient
That I'll give up your cruelty as price
Of your dismissive scorn, and so perhaps
Your scorn can then be bartered as a step
To gain your favor.[9]
Inés: Though I might reply
That I have not been so ungrateful to you
As I perhaps have seemed, I'm so afraid
At finding you here, and I'm in such a state,
I'll save up my reply; it's time that—
But, alas, my master's coming up the stairs.
He must not find me here, nor see you here
Talking with me.

                                             [*Exit quickly*]

Moscatel: Wait, hear me, listen, tarry—

[*Enter Don Pedro, an old man*]

Pedro: Who has to wait and hear, listen and tarry?
Moscatel: Someone who should have spoken. As it is
I am the one who may be forced to speak.
Pedro: What are you doing here?
Moscatel: [*Aside*]   What do you think?
Can you not see for yourself?

Pedro: Why don't you answer?
Moscatel: I was thinking up an answer.
Pedro: What are you seeking?
Moscatel: [*Aside*] Why should this have to happen?— [*Aloud*] I
     was looking
For my assassin.
Pedro: Why do that?
Moscatel: Because
     I've never in my life found anything
     That I was looking for.
Pedro: Who are you?
Moscatel: That
     Is the first suitable question you have asked.
     I'm a gentleman's man, sir, and honorable;
     If nowadays there can be such a thing
     As an honorable man.[10]
Pedro: Whom do you serve?
Moscatel: I don't serve anyone,
     Although I call myself a servant.
Pedro: How so?
Moscatel: Because it is my master serves my turn.
Pedro: To talk to me in such a fashion is
     Flagrant impertinence. My righteous anger
     Can brook no more.
Moscatel: [*Aside*] Oh heavens! This is a nasty business!
     What if he takes a swipe at me here and now?
     I'm sure he will, and those two in the street
     Are powerless to help me.
Pedro: Either you tell me now without delay
     Both who you are, and what you want, and why
     You've come into my house, or in this house
     At my hands you will die.
Moscatel: Since in your rage
     You've signed my death-warrant, and you intend
     Its immediate execution, I'm Moscatel,
     A servant to a certain gentleman,
     Called Don Alonso de Luna.

     [*Enter Don Juan and Don Alonso*]

Juan: [*Aside to Alonso, at door*] Since Moscatel is here and we have
          seen
     Don Pedro enter too, I had to seize
     The opportunity.
Alonso: I am prepared
     For anything. I'll go and hold the door.   [*Exit*]

Pedro: Well, proceed.

Juan: [*Coming forward*] What is the matter, sir?

Moscatel: [*Aside*] That's a relief

Pedro: [*Aside*] I must restrain myself. [*Aloud*] I found this man
here.
I don't know what he's after.

Juan: Do you not?
He will soon tell us what it is, or die
Upon my sword. [*Aside to Moscatel*] Now you must lie a little:
It's most important for me.

Moscatel: [*Aside*]   What a way
To come to my rescue! [*Aloud*] I'm looking for a man.
No one was here to answer me, and so
I went in, came upstairs, and there was still
No one to ask. But here I met a girl—
[*Aside*] A modicum of truth will serve me here—
[*Aloud*] She thought I was a thief and fled from me.
It was to her I called out "listen, wait,
One moment—"

Juan: This could be what has happened.

Pedro: [*Aside*] Though I'm not satisfied that he has told me
The truth, it would be mad to let Don Juan
Discover from my sword and from my face
That I have entertained suspicious thoughts,
And so I must pretend that I've believed
His explanation. Then later I'll pursue him
Less circumspectly, find out who he is,
And banish my anxiety. [*Aloud*] Well, sirrah,
Why, if you came here looking for some man,
Were you so much abashed at seeing me?

Moscatel: Because you set on me, and I'm a man
Who's easily abashed.

Juan: Go on your way.

Moscatel: God be with you, sirs.

Juan: [*Aside to Moscatel*]   Tell Don Alonso
To get away from here.

                                              [*Exit Moscatel*]

Pedro: I will return,
But now I'm in a hurry.

Juan: Where are you going?

Pedro: To search for a lost letter.

Juan: You shall not leave
Without my company.

Pedro: [*Aside*]   He has perceived
That I am angry, so I needs must try

To banish his suspicions. [*Aloud*] Come with me, then.
Juan: [*Aside*] So far so good. He doesn't suspect me. I
Can stay with him no matter what.

[*Exeunt*]

[*Enter Inés, and later Leonor*]

Inés: I am confused by what's been going on.
A rigorous inquisition first, and then
To become quiet! To talk with Moscatel
So threateningly, and then pursue him gently.
What sudden changes! What will happen next?
Leonor: [*To Beatriz offstage*] God help you for an interfering fool!
Inés: My lady, what has happened to enrage you?
Leonor: Beatriz refused to listen to me.
She's rude to me, and proud, and quite as tiresome
As usual. She says she'll tell my father
About the whole affair.
Inés: When troubles come,
They never come alone, but intertwined.
The first is eve to one upon the morrow.
The man you left here, so that I could find out
Who he was, had come in quest of you,
To give this letter to you—
Don Juan would not take the risk of sending
A servant of his own—A moment after
He'd handed me the letter, your father came,
Encountering the fellow. Then Don Juan
Came to the rescue and persuaded him
To give all kinds of silly explanations;
But though my master wanted to appear
Convinced, he was not so; and he has gone
To follow him.
Leonor: How true what people say
About misfortunes. One alone's enough;
For, like the phoenix, where one dies, the tomb
Becomes the cradle where another's born.
Give me the letter, since I want to answer
At once, to tell Don Juan of my danger.
Inés: Make haste and read it. It may tell you something
To help you with your problem.
Leonor: You are right.
I'll open it. There's nothing to be lost
In doing so. [*Reads*] "How badly, my beauteous beloved, can
I express or communicate to you. . . ."
Inés: Your sister's coming.

Leonor: Unlucky that I am!

[*Enter Beatriz*]

Beatriz: What is this missive which you crumple up
And hide from me?
Leonor: What? I?
Beatriz: Yes, sister, you.
Leonor: I don't know what you mean.
Beatriz: Obstinate creature,
You've twice recalcitried with base excuse.
That sullied sheet on which a goose's quill
Has traced a few brief lines in Ethiop liquid
From vessel of chalcedony, that paper
I must behold![11]
Leonor: You'll try in vain to see it.
In any case it would be doubly foolish.
You take offense at anything I say,
Refuse to listen when I want to tell you.
While treacherously desiring to discover
What I am trying now to keep from you.
Beatriz: By my sororal privilege and duty
I take no notice of your speech, but only
Of your behavior; for the first may lie,
The other must perforce reveal the truth;
And therefore on this critical occasion
I'm not disposed to listen to your words,
But rather to reveal what you'd conceal.
Leonor: How will you do it, since I will not let you?
Beatriz: Like this.   [*She grabs the letter and the two women struggle
for it*]   Give me the epistle.
Inés: It's not the Epistle but the Gospel to her![12]
Leonor: Although, you beast, you're using force to see it,
You shan't, if I can help it.
Beatriz: Give me the letter.

[*Enter Don Pedro, just as the letter tears, each woman
holding half*]

Pedro: What letter's that? Why are you quarreling,
You wicked girls?
Inés: [*Aside*]   The building has collapsed,
As the losing gambler says.
Pedro: Give me that piece,
And you, the other one.
Leonor: [*Aside*]   O love, assist me
To get out of this fix!

Beatriz: The fragment, sir,
Which from my fragile hand you thus abstract
Will soon inform you of the great disgrace
Your honor suffers.
Leonor: I am ignorant
Of the letter's contents; and since she is not,
Can there be any doubt that it is hers?
And she was reading it when I came in—
Beatriz: What! I?
Pedro: Be silent.
Leonor: And on seeing me,
She hid it with so much embarrassment,
She made me want to see it. I tried to take it;
She tried to stop me. You must not think that this
Was overbold of me. For since I learned
That Beatriz has a man who writes to her
And talks with her beneath this balcony
At night, my outraged virtue has allowed me
To treat her in this way, though I'm the younger.
Inés: [*Aside*]   Leonor has won this trick hands down,
Although the cards were even.
Pedro: Beatriz!
Beatriz: I am amazed and know not what to say.
Her words construct a simulàcrum of me,
Made up of fire and ice, for all the sin
She heaps on me is her own phantasy.
Leonor: Well, was not Inés here? She knows the truth.
Beatriz: Inés was here. Can she not tell the truth?
Inés: [*Aside*]   Yes, I was present in this present matter.
Pedro: [*Aside*]   How unfortunate I am!—confronted
By two opposing evils, both bad for me,
Both armed against me. For if I discover
Which of the girls is guilty, I shall not thus
Be saved from my distress, for in this fix
They've so beleaguered me,
Besieged and harried me in my misfortune
That, since my death is unavoidable,
Knowing the perpetrator is not enough
To avert it. [*Aloud*]   Beatriz, now get you gone.
And you, too, Leonor, be off with you.
Beatriz: Sir, I—
Pedro: No words!
Leonor: [*Aside*]
I pray the letter won't confess the truth
Which I have been denying.   [*Exit*]

Beatriz: Mendacious sister,
You are to blame for everything.

                                             [*Exit*]

Pedro: Inés!
Inés: [*Aside*] Now it's my turn.
Pedro: Wait.
Inés: [*Aside*] I'm not the sort to leave one in the lurch.[13]
Pedro: Since you're the only witness to this scene,
Which of them read the letter?
Inés: [*Aside*] I'm not a girl to make or break the rules,
But I'll do what I ought.
Pedro: Why do you hesitate?
What are you frightened of?
Inés: [*Aside*]   It's a maid's duty
To aid the one who lies.[14] [*Aloud*]   Sir, I arrived
Just before you, and I could not determine
From word or gesture whose the letter was.
That's a true statement, made as under oath
By any servant called upon as witness
In a court case.
Pedro: [*Aside*]   I cannot even get
A modicum of ease for my distress,
Which knowledge might have brought. [*Aloud*]   Inés, begone.
Inés: [*Aside*] Long live the winner.

                                             [*Exit*]

Pedro: But yet the letter will inform me now
What you and they refuse to tell. I'll join
The pieces of this snake which stores its poison
In separate halves.   [*Reads*]

"How badly, my beauteous beloved, can I express or communicate
to you my worry, since your sister overheard us last night. Let me
know at once if she informs your father, so that I can bring you to a
place of safety."

The letter could apply to either of them,
Which but augments my grief; for if I knew
Which of them was behaving wantonly
I then at least could recognize the virtue
Of the other girl. In this way my distress
Would be reduced. But heaven was willed that I
Should believe neither, but suspect them both,
So that my suffering should not be less.
To find a servant here, and to perceive
His scare at sight of me; to let him go

When Don Juan arrives, to follow him
Only to lose him and to come home then
Prey to confusion and uncertainty—
All this demands a wise investigation.
And therefore since I know the fellow is
Don Alonso's servant—always assuming
He wasn't lying out of fear—I must
Inquire about this nobleman, keep watch
On his behavior. Till I am possessed
Of what the truth is, or else take revenge,
May Heaven aid me!   [*Exit*]

ACT II

Scene 1: A street

[*Enter Don Alonso, Don Juan, and Moscatel*]

Alonso: We've had a lucky escape.
Moscatel: I am the one
Who had the lucky escape; but first I had
The wretched luck to get in such a fix
And stare death in the face.
Juan: But fortunate,
Seeing you were in jeopardy, that I
Decided to enter after Don Pedro.
Moscatel: Fortunate
For you, too, sir; for if you hadn't entered
I would have blurted out the sorry truth.
Alonso: Would you indeed?
Moscatel: Indeed I would have done,
And more besides.
Alonso: Observe, Don Juan, now
Whether a lover can be cowardly.
Juan: Is it possible for a man in love
To be a coward?
Moscatel: Quite easily so.
He risks a life that is no more his own,
But pledged to his sweetheart. If a lover's life
Is pledged to her to lose it in her service,
It is a fraudulent act to mortgage it
To settle any other debt.

[*Enter Inés, veiled*]

Inés: Don Juan, sir.
Juan: Who calls me?
Inés: It is I. [*She unveils*]
Juan: Welcome, Inés.
Inés: I've scoured Madrid to find you.
Juan: What has happened
To make you seek me?
Moscatel: [*Aside*]   That is little Inés.
I only hope my master doesn't catch
A glimpse of her.
Inés: I've come to bring this letter.
Good bye.
Juan: Wait till I've read it.
[*Juan reads, while Moscatel stations himself between
Alonso and Inés*]
Alonso: By Jove!
That's a pretty little wench.
Moscatel: [*Aside*]   He's seen her now.
I wouldn't bet a farthing on my honor.
Alonso: [*Aside*]   Listen, Moscatel.
Moscatel: Sir.
Alonso: If this girl were yours,
I would forgive you—were there ever love
Deserved forgiveness.
Moscatel: [*Aside*]   Steady, jealousy!
Slow down, and do not slay me with such rage.—
[*Aloud*] You fancy her?
Alonso: Is she not very handsome
For a servant girl?
Moscatel: No, she is not at all
But very ugly. If you could see my girl,
I'll bet an arm that you would then declare
It was a sin, of the most unnatural sort,[15]
To think she could compete.
Alonso: What lies you tell!
Juan: I've finished reading it.
Alonso: And what is in it?
Juan: Lots of complaints from Leonor; but yet
She tells me I can go and visit her,
Since by some trick—she does not tell me what—
I'm not suspected. I'll come back afterward
And tell you all about it. [*To Inés*] Let us go.
                                        [*Exit*]
Alonso: [*To Moscatel*] Don't let her go. Stop her.
Moscatel: [*Aside*]   Worse than ever, jealousy!

Alonso: Hi! beautiful!
Inés: What do you want?
Alonso: I wish
      To see that pretty face of yours.
Moscatel: [*Aside*]   O heavens!
Inés: My face requires a lot of scrutiny,
      And I am in a hurry.
Alonso: I know the way
      To take a quick look.
Moscatel: [*Aside*]   And then to follow it up.

      [*Enter Don Luis and Don Diego*]

Diego: [*To Luis*]   That girl's her servant.
Luis: I have seen her leave
      The house and followed her, to try to give her
      A note for Beatriz.
Inés: [*Aside*]   I wonder what Moscatel is trying to tell me
      By making signs.
Diego: She's talking to Don Alonso.
Luis: As I suspected. For Beatriz's servant
      To come like this in search of him; for him
      To haunt her street, be always at her window
      Together with his friend; and then to see
      When he departs, the others stay to talk—
      Can only signify a love affair.
Diego: What do you mean to do?
Luis: I do not want
      To be seen; for after all I have received
      No favors from her. I am not committed.
      And for a lover who has met with scorn
      To fight a duel would be absurd bravado.
Diego: You're right, and maybe the base jealousy
      Besieging you is lying.
Luis: Jealousy
      Is never base.
Diego: That is a novel viewpoint.
Luis: Is anything more noble than to speak
      The truth? Well, only jealousy's endowed
      With such nobility, since it cannot lie.
                         [*Exeunt Don Luis and Don Diego*]
Inés: All right. Good-bye, for it is very late.
Alonso: Allow this servant to accompany you;
      Don't go alone.
Inés: Well, let him come with me.
Moscatel: [*Aside*]   That I should have to listen, and see this!

Alonso: Moscatel.
Moscatel: Sir.
Alonso: Listen to me.
  Inés has given permission for you to escort her
  On my behalf, to her house. Go with her, then,
  And tell her on the way that if she happened
  To call at my house there would doubtless be
  A present for her.
Moscatel: Do you mean it?
Alonso: Yes.
  For since I must accompany Don Juan
  In his pursuit, it suits me for the while
  To have a girl to give me some amusement.
Moscatel: I'll tell her.
Alonso: I will wait for you to hear
  How you get on.

                                                [*Exit*]

Moscatel: [*Aside*] We're in a cleft stick, honor!
Inés: Come on. What are you waiting for?
Moscatel: Let's go.

                                                [*Exeunt*]

Scene 2: Another street

[*Enter Moscatel and Inés*]

Inés: You've been so downcast that you've scarcely raised
  Your eyes to look at me. What is the matter?
Moscatel: Ah, lovely Inés, enchantress of my soul!
  What agony you cost me!
Inés: What is wrong?
Moscatel: Both love and honor; for I love and serve,
  And now today I have to choose between
  My lady and my master. I must cease
  To serve, or cease to love.
Inés: I cannot follow
  This gibberish you speak.
Moscatel: I will make you do so.
  My master saw you, Inés, and I wish
  He had been stricken blind—though this would make me
  A blind man's boy.[16] He saw you, and of course
  He fell in love with you:
  Not for your infinite beauty, but because
  Of his too finite love—your face is new.

He sent me with you—here I am tongue-tied—
To—say to you, that if you go to see him
You will receive—alas—if in the morning
Your lunch, and if it's in the afternoon,
Your tea.

Inés: You boorish madman, stop such talk.
What have you seen in me that you should dare
To speak so loosely to a girl like me.
Inform your master I am who I am,
And that there's nothing he has would induce me
To go to his house.[17] I'm not one of those light wenches
Who can be bought with lunches or with teas.
I am a girl of independent mind,
And that's my answer to him.

Moscatel: You say that?
Inés: I say that. Now get away from here.
They must not see you—we are near the house.
Moscatel: You're leaving me in anger?
Inés: Don't follow me;
Don't look at me.
Moscatel: Well, I must needs obey you.
Since Inés leaves me in dejection now,
Eyes, weep your fill, and with no sense of shame.

                                                    [*Exit*]

Inés: Here is my house; and at the door I'll doff
My cloak—and for that reason I suppose
Beneath our skirts we favor farthingales.[18]
Now even though my mistress—the foolish one—
Has missed me for a while, she will not guess
That I have been abroad.   [*To the audience*]   And none of you,
I charge you on your consciences, must tell her.[19]

                                                    [*Exit*]

Scene 3: A room in Don Pedro's house

[*Enter Don Juan, Doña Leonor, and Inés*]

Leonor: This lie has cut our problem down to size.
Juan: Thanks to your wit! It was a clever ruse.
Leonor: My life was lost, but by this stratagem
I've managed to revive it. For what was proof
I turned into uncertainty. It's quite a feat
Of eloquence to turn a certainty
Into its opposite.

Juan: And so your father
Was left in fact suspicious of you both.
Leonor: So much so, that he wanders in and out
Worried and listening to each in turn;
But yet he has not ascertained so far
The writer of the letter and for whom
It was intended. Inés, the only one
Who knew that I was guilty, did not tell him,
And left him in the dark.
Inés: I did not say
The letter was addressed to Beatriz
Because it might have given me the lie.
I merely stuck to your account.
Juan: How fortunate
The letter had been couched in such a way
It could have fitted either. For I remember
I did not mention you by name, nor write it
In my own hand. But tell me, Leonor,
How Beatriz has taken this?
Leonor: I think
That so subjected to appearances
She'll lose her reason, if she's any left;
For with her crazy and affected ways,
She's vain about her beauty and her wit,
And now she's made the object of suspicion
She will dissolve in tears. I am so pleased
To see her thus, that I'd give anything
If this imaginary love affair,
For which I've had her blamed, could be a real one.
Inés: Can you suggest, sir, what we now can do
To drive her further to a state of frenzy?
Leonor: It would be advantageous to our love
If she were kept confused and in disgrace;
For by this means she'd cease to persecute me
And hold her tongue.
Juan: I wish to play a part
In furthering your revenge; and to that end
I'll bring a friend to keep her occupied,
And I—but here she comes. I'll tell you later.
Now mum's the word.
Leonor: Go then, don't let her see you;
For though you aren't suspected, I am sure
We should be on the alert to hide our love.
Juan: Goodbye then, lovely Leonor.
                                        [*Exit*]

Inés: Santiago!
    Charge! Let's get at her. [20]

                              [*Exeunt Juan and Inés*]

    [*Enter Doña Beatriz*]

Beatriz: [*To herself*]   Since like the phoenix
    I am alone—because imagination
    Is not a real companion—I will today
    Soliloquize on my unhappiness
    And on my natal horoscope. My honor
    Was like a sun illumining the day,
    So, when it was eclipsed, I was the one
    Who suffered then. My brilliant, flaming planet
    Is now obscured, its epicycle shaken
    By Leonor's lie.
Leonor: What do you want of me?
Beatriz: Although, in talking to myself, I named you,
    I did not call you; although name and call
    Are normally synonymous, today
    I deviate from the normal sense of call
    And, with my worries, mean the opposite.
Leonor: Why do you use such cruel words of me?
Beatriz: Since you presume, mendacious one, to ask me,
    Then take the consequences. Were you not
    The one to whom the letter was addressed:—
    As love's your witness, speak.
Leonor: Yes.
Beatriz: Did you not
    In answer to the paternal fiat, say
    The letter was for me?
Leonor: Yes.
Beatriz: Did you not
    So validate a lie as to dilute
    The purity of truth?
Leonor: Yes, Beatriz.
Beatriz: Why are you then surprised that I deplore
    Your fraudulent conduct.
Leonor: Listen. It was your temper
    Brought this about. I would not have attempted it
    If you had helped me to deceive our father
    About my love. But once the harm was done
    I had to save myself. I don't deny,
    Beatriz, between ourselves, that I was guilty;
    But I will not admit it to another.
    I love, and I adore—I die of love.

[*Don Pedro appears on one side behind Beatriz;*
Leonor sees him and he retreats]

Leonor: [*Aside*]   Oh dear! my father.
Pedro: [*Aside*]   I heard Leonor say
    "I die of love"
Leonor: [*Aside*]   I'll try and put things right.—
    "I die of love": you tell me to my face
    "I am in love."
Pedro: [*Aside*]   That I should see this thing!
Leonor: "I desire him!"
Pedro: [*Aside*]   That I should hear it too!
Leonor: To think a lady of your birth should say
    "I die of love." My father must be told;
    For though you've said you'll not confess to him
    What you have told me, he shall know it now.
Beatriz: What do you say?
Leonor: Stand back and draw not nigh me.
Beatriz: It's *difficile* for me to comprehend
    Your strange behavior, Leonor.
Leonor: Do not tarnish
    The gleaming whiteness of my chaste *persona*.[21]
Beatriz: What is this metamorphosis?
Leonor: How dare you
    Give vent to such profanity.
Pedro: [*Aside*]   Leonor
    Is the virtuous one.
Beatriz: Sister, listen to me.
Leonor: Do not address me so; I cannot have
    A libidinous sister.

                                  [*Exit*]

Beatriz: Who has ever seen
    Such hysterical behavior? Who has seen
    Such an emotional outburst? Such pretenses?
    And all in quick succession?
Pedro: Yes, Beatriz,
    I saw these things, and so my careful watch
    Has not been fruitless.
Beatriz: Sir, were you here?
Pedro: I was indeed.
Beatriz: And did you overhear
    What Leonor was saying?
Pedro: I did indeed.
Beatriz: Then you will know the truth about me.
Pedro: Yes,

For I have found today your younger sister
Has cause to scold you.

Beatriz: That such a thing should happen!
I'm fate-oppressed and ill-starred.

Pedro: What do you mean?

Beatriz: Sir.

Pedro: Beatriz, enough! Enough of affectation,
Enough of irritating pedantry,
Enough's enough! For that is what has been
Your own worst foe, that causes the defeat
Of your good name. It is apparent now
That one who does not talk like other people
Will not behave like them. I know your problem
And all about the letter you received
From that affected foolish nobleman—
Too free with you, and not the least bit pleasant.
I overheard when Leonor scolded you
That you're in love with him. The blame is yours,
And also partly mine. But I will soon
Set things to rights. So here's an end to study!
Poetry's finished. All Latin books are banished.
I'll see to it. It's enough for any woman
To have her *Hours* in the vernacular.
Sewing, needlework, embroidery,
Are all a woman needs to know.[22] Leave study
To men. It's no good looking so amazed,
For I will kill you if I hear you call
Something other than its normal name.

Beatriz: Subordinated by profound respect,
A sunflower turned toward your face, I swear
Never to phrasefy. Notwithstanding,
Allow me to disperse appearances
Created by deception, and which malice
Has made to seem like truth, unjustly acting
To captivate your dear benevolence.

Pedro: Beatriz!

Beatriz: Incline your ear to my entreaty.

Pedro: I see you're much reformed!

Beatriz: I do assure you
By your maternal ancestry—

Pedro: I do believe
You'll drive me mad today.

                                        [*Exeunt*]

Scene 4: A room in Don Alonso's house

[*Enter Don Alonso and Moscatel*]

Alonso: The rogue said that?
Moscatel: Inés was as insulted
By your advances, as if she were the daughter
Of Prester John himself.[23] "Inform your master,"
Said she, "that he will not prevail upon me
For I am far too grand to be his mistress,
Too low to be his wife."[24]
Alonso: There's not a duchess
Of Amalfi, Mantua, or Milan
Who does not make a similar response
To kings in plays, but not a roguish maid
From Picardy![25] The devil take you, minx!
Why not regard it as a stroke of luck
That one with a clean shirt should thus approach you?
Moscatel: But, sir, a person's underwear desires
It's like.
Alonso: And how did you get on with Celia?
Moscatel: She was at her window, and she must have been
A trifle tipsy, for she asked why you
Had failed to visit her—a sign that she
Was hardly sober. Why go and see her now
When you did so only three days since?
Alonso: My constancy is ever my undoing!
All of these women think because I take
A gallant leave that I'll be their gallant
For life.—What happened to me was better still.
Doña Clara, passing in her coach,
Called out to me, so I approached to hear her.
She bade me—what a silly thing to do!—
To send her twenty lengths of lamé cloth,
Because she wanted to run up a gown
In honor of me. Half-jesting, I inquired
"Of what color?" She replied, "You choose."
And so I improvised this apt quatrain:
       Though I would gladly give (as you propose)
       A gown whose color I unprompted chose,
       Alas! My fright has left my cheeks so pale,
       That my non-color hardly would avail.
So I escaped from buying her the cloth.
Moscatel: A fine way that to vent one's feelings, sir!
Alonso: How so?
Moscatel: By paying debts with mockery.

Alonso: Do you know what stuns me and amazes me?
    That while men customarily refuse to give,
    Women as customarily make requests.
Moscatel: By custom they're devout in their petitions.
    [*Aside*]   How quickly he's forgetting Inés. Farewell jealousy!
Alonso: Moscatel.
Moscatel: Sir.
Alonso: Do you want the truth from me?
Moscatel: If you can manage that, then tell it, sir.
Alonso: Little Inés has pricked me.[26]
Moscatel: Is she so sharp?
Alonso: And I shall conquer just to laugh at her.
    Go back to her.
Moscatel: What! I?
Alonso: Yes.
Moscatel: [*Aside*]   Not farewell
    Jealousy—not yet.
Alonso: You'll say to her—

    [*Enter Don Juan*]

Juan: Thanks be to Heaven that I can for once
    Bring happy tidings; for love cannot always
    Consist of woes; and now its grievances,
    Its sorrows and reproaches all are ended,
    Because, since Love's a child, the blubbered face
    Of yesterday is full of smiles today.
    Yesterday I asked your valor's aid
    When honor was at stake. Now things are better,
    I must employ you in a happier role,
    Using your courtly manners, taste, and wit,
    So that you may experience equally
    The two extremes of my distress and joy.
Alonso: What's happened to you?
Juan: Clever Leonor
    Has cunningly transferred her guiltiness
    To Beatriz; their father's left uncertain
    To whom the guilt belongs. What was clear-cut
    Has ended up confused—one daughter's word
    Against the other's. To help along this plot
    With regard to Beatriz, and keep her busy
    (For sister's quarrels always are the worst)
    She's asked me to produce another man
    To pretend love for *her*; it's vital for us
    For her to be blamed still, or, failing that,
    That someone should distract her. So, Alonso,

You must be the lover. Leonor
Will help you to gain access to the house.
So from today you must walk up and down,
And stand in adoration at her window,
Badger her maids, follow her goings-out,
Write to her—
Alonso: Stop! I'll never in my life
Talk to her, court her, follow in her footsteps,
Stare at her. What! to gaze like an idiot
All day at her window, playing the fond lover,
Till a pitcher of cold water cools my ardor?[27]
I to bribe a maid to tell her lady
Of how I suffer? I to proffer friendship
To some long-bearded steward? Pursue a woman
To find where she hears Mass, or does not do so?
(I've never bothered, Juan, to discover
Of any of my ladies if they've been
Properly christened; and they are delighted,
Because they do not wish to speak about
Their place of baptism).[28] Am I the sort
To write a letter that is meant sincerely,
Not full of inanities, but one in which
Love and happiness are discussed with reason?
Talk at a window one cold night for hours
To beg to hold a hand, and the reply
Will be, inevitably, "It's pledged to another."
And then, in spite of my insistent pleas,
Casts in my face her tardy maidenhood.
Better to die than follow such a one,
Importune, loiter, gaze, or talk, or write!
I wouldn't give two figs for any love
Unless I have free access, take a chair
On my first visit, on the second a stool,
And on the third a settle, to recline
Upon the cushions, the lady's lap for pillow,[29]
One who will scratch my head if it should itch.—
Apart from this, just think how well-informed
And how amusing is the specimen
You're offering me! Who talks outlandishly,
So that a man who has to listen to her
Requires a Latin dictionary.[30] So find
Some duel perhaps for me to be of service;
I'd rather fight with ten plain men at once
Than to come up against a learned female;

For any woman I would choose to know
Must have a guarantee that she's direct,
Plain-spoken, and without a trace of learning.
Juan: Does it not often happen in the city
That a man helps along his friend's affair
By flirting with the lady's bosom friend?
Alonso: It also often happens in this city
That one may lose his fortune in assisting
A friend in such a lottery of love.
Juan: I'm not suggesting you should get involved
In a genuine affair—but just pretend.
Alonso: The idea is attractive—to make a mock
Of a silly woman, so vain and so conceited.
Moscatel: [*Aside*] How quickly he has found it right to accept
This opportunity! What a crazy time
Now lies in store for us!
Alonso: All right—so long
As it is all pretense. But if you think
I'm going to woo in earnest, and put up
With her responses, you're imagining
What is impossible.
Juan: No one is forcing you
To do that.
Alonso: I'll begin to talk to her,
Starting today.
Juan: Let's go to her house now,
And on the way I'll tell you all the things
That you should know; and I'll arrange for you
To enter, and talk with her.
Alonso: Let's go at once;
For at the thought of how she will respond
Sincerely to my insincerities,
I'm dying of laughter.
Moscatel: Let us hope that love
Does not end up in tears.
Alonso: What do you mean
By tears, you fool, since all is make-believe?
I merely wish to aid Don Juan's love,
Avenge the lovely Leonor, and deceive
The beauteous Beatriz, while having fun
With little Inés.
Moscatel: [*Aside*]   That can only be
By robbing me of all my happiness.

Scene 5: Beatriz's room, with a cupboard

[*Enter Beatriz and Inés*]

Inés: Your melancholy, my lady, is very great.
Beatriz: How could mine be otherwise than great?
Have I not ample cause? Because of Leonor,
My own paternal parent casts upon me
The aspersion of love. That anyone should think
(Although it is my pride to be Disdain)
I would have hearkened to a lover's vows,
That I received a billet-doux, bestowed
Favors upon a man, opened a casement
To let him enter, and permitted him
To touch my cloud-encompassed dexter hand.
These are such things on which I dare not have
Even a private flicker of a thought.
So this retreat, in which I scarcely see
The light of day, will be a lugubrious sphere,
Ambivalent hermitage, in which, though living,
Perhaps I die, unostentatious dwelling
Wherein by feigning that I am not dying,
I might still live. The sun—Narcissus, clad
In jessamine and scarlet—from its first
Morning refulgence to its final paroxysm
In the cold night, where its reflection waits,
Must not behold my visage, unless perchance
Its covetous light should penetrate this chamber
Where my profanèd honor is kept hidden.
Here let my eyes beweep ambiguous signs,
By which I mean the fierce vexation caused
By another's misbehavior, blamed on me.
Inés, I ask you, have I not complained
In a plain style, an ordinary way?
And had my father heard me, ah, how much
He had perceived improvement in my speech.
Inés: How much indeed! But a few words remain
Which ought to be avoided.
Beatriz: Which are they?
Inés: I noticed paroxysm, lugubrious,
Ambivalent, casement—and others I don't recall.[31]
Beatriz: There is enough stupidity about
To drive me mad! Are not these words so basic
That every common doorman knows them? Yet,

I vow, despite of Saturn, from now on
To doff my buskin and to don a clog.[32]
Inés: [*Aside*]   Little by little, her style is on the mend.
Beatriz: And should you hear me use a phrase forbidden
To common women, and you see more coming,
Tug at my sleeve.
Inés: I will. And I promise you
I'll be your censor.

[*Enter Leonor, Alonso, and Moscatel*]

Leonor: [*Aside*]   That is Beatriz;
And since you've come to keep her occupied
By wooing her in sport, you will be able
To talk here safely. I'll be over there,
Conversing with Don Juan, and on the alert
For any difficulty that may crop up.
I'll guard your rear.
                                                    [*Exit*]
Alonso: [*Aside*]   Who would have believed
That love, though merely feigned, could strike me dumb?
Inés: [*Aside to Moscatel*]   What does this mean?
Moscatel: [*Aside to Inés*]   To administer the
      drug
Which has been prescribed.
Inés: Why have you come?
Moscatel: Because
I love you: keep out of my master's line of fire
Unless I'm sentinel.
Beatriz: [*Seeing Alonso*]   What does this mean?
Inés: A daring man has entered.
Beatriz: In my domain!
What are you doing?
Inés: Tugging at your sleeve.
Beatriz: That's silly. Stop it. I simply meant my room.
Alonso: Lovely Beatriz, do not lift your voice
And send your plaints, released from lips' red jail,
Unto the heavens. Lend a compassionate ear
To my distress; and be not angry with me.
Cruelty has not always been the heritage
Of loveliness.
Beatriz: You seem to be obsessed
With rhetorical substitutes and synonyms.
Inés: Two tugs for that.
Beatriz: All right.   [*To Alonso*]   Impertinent,

Who dared to violate the sanctuary
Wherein the sun, the phoenix and the pyre,
If it should enter, would retire in fear,
And had it not the excuse of bringing daylight,
Would never enter, even in particles,
What audacity, or what bravado,
Directs your treacherous foot?

Inés: [*Aside*]   This is where
He starts deceiving.

Moscatel: [*Aside*]   I hope he makes a bolt.

Alonso: Most brilliant Beatriz, sweet enigma,
Who renders words superfluous, compliments
Supererogatory. I'm the man who's been
For two long years a human sunflower
In your beauty's sunshine—fragrant when I see you,
Wilting when you are absent; for the distance
'Twixt death and birth is not more than between
Seeing you, and not seeing you.

Inés: [*To the audience*]   Ladies, take heed.
How can you tell if one is lying or loving,
If this is falsehood?

Alonso: I have come today
Unceremoniously, because your father
Met with my servant, bringing you a letter.
Mindful of my honor, and of the danger
In which you stood, I seized a chance that offered,
And dared to enter.

Beatriz: Stop, for I must know
(Although I take the risk of breaking Honor's
Inviolable law)—what letter was it?
And what servant?

Alonso: This was the servant here.
The letter was the one that Leonor
Opened, though it was yours, since Inés
Gave it to her.

Inés: I did not give it to her.
She took it from me.

Beatriz: It was your servant?

Alonso: Yes.

Beatriz: The letter was from you?

Alonso: Yes.

Beatriz: Meant for me?

Alonso: Why do you doubt it?

Beatriz: I do not doubt it, sir.
I know too well that you have been my death,

The murderer of my peace, you cruel man,
Tyrant, who caused my good name to be doubted.
If you are kind and courteous, then depart,
For if my sister finds that you are here,
You'll be the death of me, for she'll make truth
From lies of yesterday.
Inés: [*Aside*]   How easily
Has she believed the story he has told,
Which I confirmed!
Moscatel: [*Aside*]   There's nothing easier
Than to deceive a woman.
Beatriz: Do not expect
A greater triumph o'er my vanity
Than that of seeing that on your account
I shed these tears—indeed a man can cost
A woman tears without her being in love.
Tears are no proof of love. Go.
Alonso: [*Aside*]   I desire
More fervently than she to do just that.
I'm quite distracted, as I do not know
How to reply to her.
Beatriz: Don't bring more scandal
Upon my house; for this concupiscence
Which I have heard about is quite enough.
      [*Inés tugs at her sleeve*]
Stop it. Leave me alone, for heaven's sake.
You seem determined to pull off my arm!
Alonso: By leaving you in courteous obedience,
I act as planet to myself opposed,
In token of humility in love—
So long as you know my love.
Beatriz: Well then, goodbye;
I know it already.
Alonso: [*To Moscatel*] Not a bad beginning.
Moscatel: [*To Alonso*]   But not a happy ending. There
are people coming.
Inés: Oh, my lady! Do not let him go.
Beatriz: Why not?
Inés: Leonor, Don Juan, and your father
Are talking together, and coming to this room.
Moscatel: [*Aside*]
Of these three enemies, it is the father
Who is the devil.
Beatriz: O heavens! This will be
A fatal day if they should see you here.

The heavens have brought such evidence against me,
Accusing me of guilt I never dreamed of.
This room's adjacent to my father's chamber;
You cannot leave this way, nor go the other.
And so, before they come here, you must hide.
Alonso: Is this a comedy by Calderón
In which there has to be a hidden lover
Or a veiled lady?³³
Beatriz: My honor is at stake.
Alonso: Must I hide?
Moscatel: [*Aside to Inés*] This trick was a bad idea.
Inés: [*Aside to Moscatel*]   Yes, very bad.
Beatriz: I would be much indebted.
Alonso: [*Aside*] Heavens above! Consider: this is not fair
To give me real distress for unreal pleasure.
Beatriz: Why do you tarry?
Alonso: You ask me why? To find
The place where I must hide.
Inés: The place for you
Is the china cupboard.
Beatriz: A good idea!
Alonso: So I'm to be a ducal dish, or else
A piece of Mayan pottery.³⁴ I'm to go
Into the china cupboard? Heavens!
Beatriz: It's essential.
Inés: Get in.
Alonso: It is impossible without a shoe-horn.
Inés: You get in too.
Moscatel: Is this a cupboard
Which will seat two, like a hired mule?³⁵
          [*They get into the cupboard, and some of the dishes break*]
Inés: Be careful:
You're breaking dishes.

          [*Enter Pedro, Leonor, and Juan*]

Pedro: Ho! Bring some lights here.
Juan: [*Aside*] Heavens! I do not know what I can do
If Pedro finds Alonso here. I know
This room has not another door; and since
I've got him in this fix, and he's my friend,
I don't know where the remedy will lie
If he's still here.
Leonor: [*Aside*]   Oh, had I never thought
Of getting even! It started as a jest,
But now it's very serious.

Pedro: When do you retire
At this time of the year?
Juan: Early. [*Aside*]   That's a hint
For me to go away. I must comply.
I leave Alonso in the greatest danger
Through being my friend. But yet I cannot stay.
What I shall do is keep on the alert
To see what happens.   [*Aloud*]   I will say good night.
Pedro: Good night. Light the way for Don Juan, Inés.
Juan: There is no need for you to come.
Pedro: I know
What I should do.

> [*Inés goes out, lighting the way;*
> *Pedro follows, accompanying Juan*]

Leonor: [*Aside*]   Where has Beatriz hidden Don Alonso?
I cannot see him.
Beatriz: [*Aside*]   That a stranger to me
Should cause me such alarms!

[*Don Pedro returns, with Inés, bearing the light*]

Pedro: Bring that light
Into my room, Inés.
Leonor: [*Aside*]   Now, without a doubt
He will discover Don Alonso in his room.
Pedro: Come, both of you: I have to talk with you.
> [*There is the sound of breaking china coming from inside the*
> *cupboard. Inés, hearing it, lets her lamp fall*]
But what is that?
Inés: I've dropped the lamp.
Pedro: You never pay attention
To what you're doing.
Inés: But I do, sir.[36]
> [*Exeunt Don Pedro and Doña Leonor*]
Beatriz: Listen, Inés.
Since my father is retiring early,
See that these men get out of here at once,
Without my sister finding out.
Inés: She won't find out.
But how can this be done? Because my master
Did not accompany Don Juan down
Just for politeness, but to lock the doors,
Beatriz: But nonetheless arrange for them to leave
By hook or crook.

> [*Exit*]

Inés: I know how they can go.

[*She opens the cupboard*]

My sore-pressed sirs, you can unfold yourselves.

Alonso: By God, you rogue, for two pins I'd have killed you.

Moscatel: I couldn't help it if I broke the china:
    It was only crockery.

Inés: Come with me.

Alonso: Oh, Inés, if the fright which I have had
    Had been for you, it would have been well worth it.

Moscatel: No, it would not; it would have been ill worth it.
    How can you trifle at a time like this?

Alonso: I cannot help myself. Let's go.
    But lest the opportunity be lost,
    Take this kiss.

Moscatel: [*Aside*] A man has often seen her
    With mutton in her arms, but not till now
    Has a sheep's-head like me, seen her with her arms
    About a man.[37]

Inés: Let's get you out of here.

Alonso: A good idea!

Inés: Although my master locked the doors, you two
    Can still get out. Jump from this balcony
    Without being heard. Quick!

Alonso: Must we do that now?
    Shut in a cupboard, then from this balcony
    To leap into the street?

Inés: It must be so.

Moscatel: And could the person tell us, is it high?

Inés: You're only on the first floor here. Be quick!

Alonso: But what if I should break a leg? [*To the audience*] You
        men,
    Who fall in love, if such predicaments
    Are hateful to a lover, what must they be
    To one who's not in love. Curse all true lovers!

                                    [*Exeunt*]

ACT III

Scene 1: A room in Don Pedro's house

[*Enter Beatriz and Inés*]

Beatriz: What are you saying?

Inés: I'm saying that after—

Beatriz: Good heavens, Inés! What has happened?

Inés: —after those two had fallen like Lucifer, some men burst on the scene and challenged them. And then—so expert both master and man at swordsmanship—they defended themselves, one by the use of his head, the other by his heels.

Beatriz: Who told you this?

Inés: This epic tale of the gallant with the broken foot, metrical or otherwise, was recited to me by his servant;[38] for since the leap from the balcony left him lame, I went to see him at his house.

Beatriz: Tell me who vulnerated—wounded—him?

Inés: That isn't known.

Beatriz: And so he lies debilitated?

Inés: Yes. Leg and head were both damaged—but he is now much better.

Beatriz: Will he be disjunctive for life?

Inés: How should I know the meaning of "disjunctive"? Are you never going to be shot of such a bad habit?

Beatriz: How idiotic! Was there ever so illiterate a woman? A man who is disjunctive does not have feet that move alternately one after the other, but rather perambulates in a halting fashion.

Inés: I don't care what the word means, or what it doesn't mean. All I know, to my dismay, is that he's wounded.

Beatriz: Alas! I suffer with him. He came into my chamber,
Bold and resolute, having discovered
My hidden anxieties. This was a deed
Which both offended me and put me under
An obligation to him. For when love,
When thinking to offend, defends as well,
A sense of obligation is set up
Which comes to counterbalance the offense.
My father entered, and there might have been
A tragic outcome if the gentleman
Had not obeyed the rules that I imposed,
Hid for my sake, and jumped on my account,
Fell for my sake, and for my sake was wounded.
My sense of grievance, therefore, is quite equaled
By sense of gratitude. Which should be given
The preference?

Inés: What is the trouble now?
What ails you that you're melancholy?

Beatriz: How else
Should I behave?

Inés: My lady, do not squander
Dawn's dewdrops now. They may be needed later.

Beatriz: Oh dear, Inés, oh dear goodness, Inés!
        If only you could keep my secret close
        I'd tell you of my torment.
Inés: Tell me, then—
        For though the place I come from does not treat
        Secrets as sacrosanct—as holidays—
        But gives them a hard day's work for loosened tongue,
        Yet I will canonize Saint Secret now
        And keep his feast day.[39]
Beatriz: Well, if that is so,
        I will confide in you. I would reward
        That gallant gentleman for what he's suffered
        On my behalf, but would not have him know
        I'm sorry for him. For to feel compassion now
        Does not imply that one is not still cruel.
        I'm faithful to my debt and to my honor
        Which now permits me to inquire about him,
        Not for his sake, but mine.
Inés: Of course.   [*To audience*]   Ah, sirs,
        At last she's melted.
Beatriz: I'd like you now, dear Inés,
        To go and see him, as of your own accord,
        And find out how he is.
Inés: What else?
Beatriz: I'd like you
        To take a ribbon, and tell him that you stole it.
Inés: I'll play my part as well as if yourself
        Were doing it. Give me the ribbon, then,
        And you will see how fast my tiny shoes
        Will carry me.
Beatriz: I'll go to fetch the ribbon,
        But never breathe a word to Leonor.
Inés: I will say nothing to her.

                                              [*Exit Beatriz*]

        [*Enter Leonor*]

                               Hurrah! For Love has triumphed.
Leonor: Why so pleased?
Inés: I'll tell you later—no,
        It's best to tell you now. God knows, I'm bursting
        With trying to hold it in. Our stratagem
        Has had a great effect on Beatriz.
Leonor: What effect?
Inés: She has entrusted me
        With a deadly secret; and the very fact

She told it me in confidence is enough
To make me want to tell it on the spot—
Quite naturally, for though I might not tell it
Just for the sake of doing so, I would for sure
Because she's charged me to the contrary.
Don Alonso has already triumphed
Over her pride. His rhetoric was such.
That in her own despite she's sending him
A ribbon by me. When all is said and done,
A woman is a woman. And though I'm telling you,
You must know nothing of it.

Leonor: Mum's the word.

                                                                    [*Exit Inés*]

[*Enter Don Juan*]

Juan: I overheard that, so I realize
How vain it was to look for loyalty.
I see now there is but a set amount
Of love to share; and so, to keep it happy,
When there's decrease of it in Leonor,
In Beatriz it increases.

Leonor: Why do you say
My love's decreased?

Juan: It has indeed decreased;
For though till now I've borne my ills in silence,
It was because I hoped to ascertain
The truth from you without revealing them.
But since inevitably I must endure them
Without avenging them, let me not die
Without confessing them. Alonso came—
At your request—to talk with Beatriz.
I do not argue, nor seek to demonstrate
Whether this stratagem was right or wrong.
To avoid offending her, and to the detriment
Of his own good name, he leapt from a balcony.
To find out how this contretemps would end
I waited in the street, and as he fell,
Two men turned into it. I moved away,
Lest they should be disturbed at sight of me.
So, standing some way off, I heard the clash
Of weapons, and ran up to aid my friend.
But yet, despite my haste, when I arrived,
I found the strangers were no longer there,
Alonso wounded. Judge, therefore, Leonor,
If my suspicions could have greater cause.

Through his pretense of love, I had discovered
My own true jealousy. I call the heavens
To witness to the anguish I endured.
A man who leaves this house to be attacked
By other men can only mean one thing,
And that to my dishonor. I desired
To keep it dark for your sake, and for mine,
Till I could ascertain (as I have said)
The name of the gallant. Since I have failed,
And since I know it's useless to endeavor
To keep my jealousy from letting slip
Some hints of my dishonor, I want my tongue
To speak, since hands have failed to act. Farewell,
Ungrateful woman, for now that I have spoken,
I will not stay to listen to excuses.

Leonor: But have not I a sister, who might be
The reason—

Juan: No, for if there *were* a sister
Who had a lover, you would never try
To make her suspect, for it would not do,
Either in fun or earnest to accuse her;
And as, indeed, you wanted to pretend
She had a lover, I assume from that,
That you would not have introduced a bogus lover
If she had had a real one.

Leonor: Would to God—

Juan: I do not ask you for excuses, Leonor.

Leonor: Nor will I give you any. That would be wrong,
Since I have never injured you at all.

Juan: You are the cause—so leave my love to die.

                                    [*Exeunt*]

Scene 2: A room in Don Alonso's house

[*Enter Alonso and Moscatel*]

Moscatel: What ails you, sir? What are you thinking of?
Or what imagining? Tell me, sir.
You, of all people, to be melancholy!
You abstracted! What a transformation!
Has one sword-cut proved so efficacious?
A wound achieved so much? A balcony
Had such an effect? that these have put a stop
To your gay jesting?

Alonso: Oh, dearest heaven! I simply do not know

What it is I feel. Although it's good,
It yet seems bad. It gives me pleasure, but
Seems to bring anguish.
Moscatel: Did you not say to me
The lady was not nearly so affected
As Don Juan pretended.
Alonso: That is true.
Moscatel: And have you not extolled her beauty?
Alonso: Yes.
Moscatel: And are you not aggrieved that there were men
In ambush in the street to set upon you?
Alonso: I don't deny it, but I have good cause.
Moscatel: Then it's a case of jealousy.
Alonso: No, it's not;
For I would not have minded in the least
About the men being there, if they'd delivered
The immaterial blows of jealousy,
Rather than blows of swords. And then besides,
At Don Juan's request, I went to make
A fool of her. It would not do at all,
If in the end I proved to be the fool.
Moscatel: Once upon a time, a would-be toreador entered the ring to
have a go, sponsored by a friend of his. He twirled his cape jauntily,
set his hat at a gallant angle, and boldly took up the lance some
twenty paces from the pen. A bull emerged and came face to face
with his horse, though it might as well have been rump to rump,
seeing that the effect of the thrust from the horn of the one, and the
blow from the body of the other was as if they had given each other
a purge, and both noisily emptied their bowels. Whereupon the
rider was thrown on the top of the bull, and his sponsor, meaning
to strike the bull, gave his protégé an excellent blow instead.
Whereupon the gentleman got up and cried out, "Does anybody
know who this noble sir is supposed to be sponsoring, me or the
bull?" Nobody had an answer. The moral is this. You went to
Beatriz's house, sponsored by Don Juan, but your skill proved
unequal to the occasion; and so nobody knows whether Don Juan
was your sponsor or Beatriz's. [40]
Alonso: Be quiet, I say. What a rotten moral you've given your tale.
Moscatel: Rotten or not, thank God you can no longer criticize my love,
for you have joined the same dance.
Alonso: If that is so, tell me, since another man is in love with this lady,
what's the good of my paying court to her? [41]
Moscatel: Oh no, sir, you can't get out of a tricky situation as quickly as
that.
                    [*Knocking within*]

Alonso: See who is knocking.
Moscatel: Who is there?

[*Enter Inés*]

Inés: Is your master at home?
Moscatel: [*Aside*] What's this I see? Inés! [*Aloud*] You faithless creature! [*The two walk together by the door*] Heavens above. You've come to see him.
Inés: What do you think I'd do? [*Aside*] I want to imply that it's true, for what I like best of all is to make him a tiny bit jealous. [*Aloud*] Yes, because it's important for my reputation that Don Alonso should realize that I know how to keep my word.
Moscatel: What an honorable sense of honor!
Inés: Out of the way!
Moscatel: You mustn't enter.
Inés: Stand aside.
Alonso: Who is talking to you?
Moscatel: Nobody.
Inés: You're lying, for I'm somebody.
Alonso: She is very much somebody. Inés, my dear, let me give you a thousand and one kisses.
Inés: I'll give you an equal number in return.
[*Moscatel pinches her*]
Ouch!
Alonso: What's the matter?
Inés: I caught against the handle of your dagger.
Alonso: I'm sure your visit will mean life and soul to me; for though you gave me an angry reply when Moscatel delivered my message, you know nevertheless that I love you, and you won't always be unresponsive.
Inés: I have never been so with you, for as soon as I got the message, I said I'd come to see you.
Alonso: You rogue! Have you been deceiving me?
Moscatel: What? me, sir?
Alonso: By heaven, I'll kick you into kingdom come.
Moscatel: Just as in the proverb—but no, I've not yet been told to start dancing.[42]
Inés: [*Aside*] As soon as he knows what I've come for, Moscatel will be undeceived. A pity his jealousy will be so short-lived!
Moscatel: In heaven's name, is the word of a trollop—?
Inés: You rogue, be more respectful. Don't forget I'm your superior. [*To Alonso*] I wish to talk to you alone.
Moscatel: [*Aside*] Alone!
Alonso: Go out and guard the door.
Moscatel: I'm to stay outside! God Almighty!

Alonso: What do you say?

Moscatel: That I'm a loyal fellow, and I refuse to allow such goings on, that you should go to the extremity of putting your life in danger for the sake of such a worthless woman.

Alonso: And since when have you been so concerned for my health? Go outside.

Moscatel: I'll not go even if you kill me, for your life's at stake.

Alonso: I've never seen you show such loyalty before.

Moscatel: I've been saving it up for an occasion such as this.

Alonso: That's enough. [*He grabs him and pushes him out*] Now we're alone, embrace me again, Inés.

Inés: Although you think I'm naughty in coming to see you, I don't come on your account, as I pretended, but to shield my mistress's good name.

Alonso: I don't know what you mean.

Inés: I'll explain in a few words. Beatriz found out that there was a fight outside her doors, and that you were wounded in it; so, moved to compassion by your wound, under an obligation to you, and anxious about your condition, she sent you this ribbon. It is a token from her, although she told me to ensure that you did not find out that it came from her. That said, good-bye.

Alonso: Listen, wait. Beatriz remembers me? Beatriz is grieved by my misfortune? Beatriz sends me tokens of her favor. That seems very strange.

Inés: Not to me; for once I knew that your love was feigned, I knew it would succeed; for as nothing ever turns out right, a man who pretends to love gets more return from us than one who loves indeed.

[*Enter Moscatel*]

Moscatel: [*Aside, behind the arras*] There's no rest for a jealous man, nor for an unhappy one. I'll see the naked truth for myself, for it's better to see it than to imagine it.

Alonso: Lovely Inés, since Beatriz today goes from one extreme to the other, let me do the same. For though I don't court her because I'm in love, I'll do it because I'm a nobleman, and *noblesse oblige*. Wait here while I write her a letter.   [*Exit*]

Moscatel: [*Aside*]   He's going into the other room. I'm relieved. [*Aloud*] Hircanian tiger of a kitchen wench, Egyptian crocodile, base serpent, Albanian lioness, how can my tongue find the arguments, my mouth find the words to complain about you?[43]

Inés: It can't.

Moscatel: Well, if words fail me, my hand can box your ears.

Inés: Your hand will do no such thing. But no more trickery! I was just getting my own back. I was only teasing.

Moscatel: Well, if you've been playing a game of bluff, let's reshuffle the cards for a change of luck. Kiss me.

Inés: With pleasure!   [*They kiss.*]

[*Enter Don Alonso*]

Alonso: What is this?

Inés: I'm doing my kissing on my own ground.

Moscatel: I was so delighted that that virago had been tamed—Pardon my curiosity, I listened to what you were saying—that I kissed Inés as a reward for bringing you the ribbon.

Alonso: Give this letter to your mistress, Inés, and take this diamond for yourself.

Inés: May you live even longer than the phoenix, the Arabian bird which reputedly is longer lived than any mother-in-law![44]

[*Exit*]

Moscatel: It's time we had a reckoning, sir, for I'll stay no longer in this house.

Alonso: Why ever not?

Moscatel: Because I don't want a lover for a master, one who neglects me in order to attend to his lady.

Alonso: What a way to repay me for having put up with all your idiocies!

Moscatel: It must be so.

[*Enter Don Juan*]

Juan: What must be so?

Alonso: He wants to leave my employment.

Juan: Why so, Moscatel?

Moscatel: Because he has committed the greatest infamy, the greatest crime, the greatest—

Juan: Stop! What has he done?

Moscatel: He has fallen in love. See how justified I am.

Alonso: He has got this mad idea into his head, through having seen how politely I have been wooing Beatriz for your sake.

Juan: Thanks to love that problem is now settled,
My anguish ended.

Alonso: How can you be free of it?

Juan: Because this very day my love was finished.

Alonso: But what of Leonor?

Juan: She is no longer
Throned in my heart. Since love is linked with fortune,
It suffers many metamorphoses.

Alonso: You must go with me to her house.

Juan: I won't.
I will not see or talk with her again,
As long as I live.

Alonso: On account of Beatriz,
I must return to see and talk with her,
Morning and afternoon. Though I'm the one
With a broken head, and your head is undamaged,
Will you not go with me?
Juan: No, I will not.
My jealousy's a wound more sharp and cruel
Which strikes my very soul.
Alonso: Let us exchange
Our wounds, for whether they are slight or mortal,
I'd much prefer to have a battered soul
Then have a battered pate. That's logical:
If a wrong treatment's given to a wound,
It kills you; whereas even a false cure
May yet revive a man who has been wounded
With jealousy.
Juan: Whatever the cause, Alonso,
Justified or not, I'll not again
Put you in such an awkward situation.
Alonso: You have no need to give up the affair
On my account. It doesn't bother me.
Juan: I'm giving it up for my sake, and for yours.
Your wound is cause enough.
Alonso: But thoroughbreds
Are not discouraged by a single wound.
Juan: I won't return to their street, or their house.
Alonso: I shall return, if not on your account,
Then to discover who was my assailant.
Juan: So far as your reputation is concerned,
We can pursue inquiries from outside.
Alonso: I'm even more concerned for my good name
In the ladies' eyes than with the gentlemen.
A lady as proud as Beatriz must not think
That I—
Juan: I'll find a way to disabuse her.
Alonso: Juan, Juan, let us be quite frank:
I am determined to see Beatriz.
Moscatel: [*Aside*] He'll talk thus wildly now, but come tomorrow
He'll say I made it up.
Juan: If it's so important to you,
What's stopping you? Good luck to you.
Alonso: How can I
If you and Leonor don't guard the rear?
Juan: I shan't go back to talk to her again.
Alonso: You must for my sake: for there's nothing odd

In talking with a lady for the purpose
Of helping a friend's courtship.

Juan: For your sake
I'll do a thing I never thought to do.
Well, for your sake I'll go. But yet take care
Of the cupboard.

Alonso: What does that matter?

Moscatel: And there's the jump
From the balcony, too.

Alonso: Very well.

Moscatel: And there's the sword-thrust.

Alonso: I hope not. But if Love has engineered
For a single lie so many things to happen,
Then, since the truth's involved, let sword and cupboard
Now do their worst.

                                        [*Exeunt*]

Scene 3: A street

[*Enter Don Luis and Don Diego*]

Diego: You know how willingly I've always served you.

Luis: Diego, I appreciate your friendship
And know it has been always exercised
With honesty and tact.

Diego: That being so,
You will not take amiss a mild reproof.

Luis: No, I shall not.

Diego: What happened that night, when—

Luis: Do you want to tell me it was madness? Yes,
I confess it. That's the best that can be said
In my excuse for having wounded one
Who did not act as though he were my rival.
This matter must perforce be remedied;
For anyone who lets his jealous fears
Burst out of all control on mere suspicion
Will not succeed in keeping them in check
On subsequent occasions.[45]

Diego: Tell me now
What are you going to do about the project
You broached before. 'Tis certain that Don Pedro
Knows what you had in mind.

Luis: What does that matter?
For if the holy sacrament of marriage
Can be annulled when it's been celebrated,

Why should I not annul my marriage plans
Before the event?[46]

[*Enter Don Pedro*]

Pedro: [*Aside*]   Obsessed with the icy feeling
Which burns me up, and with the burning passion
Which chills my heart, and with the wound to honor,
I'm late in coming out, with the intention
Of talking with Don Luis. Better to end
Suspicions at a stroke, than to await
Till a brash youth, the wonder of the district,
Comes up against me. Here he comes! How glad
I am to see him, noble and gallant.
Yes, he's the one.
Diego: Your father-in-law approaches.
Luis: Let us flee.
Pedro: Don Luis, I have been
Informed by your relations that you wish
To honor my house; and grateful, as is right,
I've come to seek you out, to demonstrate
How proud I am that I shoud merit—
Luis: Sir,
I'm one whose luck of yesterday becomes
Today's excuses. I confess that I
Aspired to greatness, and was fortunate
To be granted such an honor, but alas!
I've been unfortunate in my good fortune,
Since I'm involved in an affair of honor,
And this prevents me now from entering
The state of matrimony.
Pedro: An affair of honor
Makes you withdraw? [*Aside*]   Alas!
Luis: Yes, that is so.
Pedro: How can that be? What can you have against
My daughter Beatriz? [*Aside*]   I'm dying.
Luis: You must not take it
In that way, sir. For in your anger, you
Misunderstood my meaning, when I spoke
Of honor.
Pedro: In what way?
Luis: Because, sir, I
Have been informed His Majesty (whom Heaven
Protect as this sphere's sun, this kingdom's planet)
Intends this spring to wage a holy war,
And knowing that a noble lord (to whom

I am related) is now mustering troops,
I begged him for a company to lead.
He's given it me. This is the undertaking
Which makes it impossible for me to marry.
A man who is a soldier and a husband
Is either a poor soldier or poor husband.
If I should come back safely, I shall be
More worthy for you then to make me happy.
To marry Beatriz now conflicts with honor.

[Exeunt Don Diego and Don Luis]

Pedro: "To marry Beatriz now conflicts with honor."
Heavens! What is this that I have seen and heard?
Alas! there's little I can feel that—But it's wrong
So to torment myself; for if his honor
Is now involved for the reason that he gave,
My fears deceive me; and, when all is said,
Are the worst thoughts that pass through a sad mind
Inevitably true?

[Exit]

Scene 4. A room in Don Pedro's house

[*Enter Beatriz and Inés*]

Beatriz: But why did you accept the letter?
Inés: Because, my lady, I always accept everything I'm given.
Beatriz: Doubtless you told him you were sent by me!
Inés: Your suspicions are groundless. I kept silent
About the ribbon being from you, and also
About your sending me, out of respect
For you; as I'm accustomed to keep silent
Concerning any secret.
Beatriz: If that is so,
How is it, Inés, that you brought this letter?
Inés: [*Aside*] Heavens! she has me there. But yet I know
How to get out of it. [*Aloud*] He asked me to bring it
And, if the opportunity arose,
To give it you, my lady; and I took it
To make sure that I was on his side.
And since I brought a ribbon he supposed
I'd stolen from you, well might he believe
That I would undertake the easier task
Of bringing you a letter.
Beatriz: I'm quite pleased
With your explanation.

Inés: [*Aside*]   That is what is called
  An honorable get-out! [*Aloud*]   Leonor
  Is coming, madam.
Beatriz: It would not be fitting
  For her to see me with this letter—

  [*Enter Leonor*]

Leonor: Well might I say now, but with greater reason,
  "What is this missive which you crumple up
  And hide from me?"
Beatriz: And I might well retort:
  "You'll try in vain to see it." For anyone
  Who does not wish to know what I would say
  Should not expect to learn what I would hide.
            [*She retires and hides behind the door*]
Leonor: What is all this, Inés?
Inés: I've been dying
  To talk to you.
Leonor: Quick! What was that letter?
Inés: Thank you for nothing! Can't you wait for me
  To tell you without being asked to do so?
  I suffer pricks of conscience, unless I tell
  Before I'm asked a secret.
Beatriz: [*At the door*]   It's not safe,
  But I must listen to their conversation.
Inés: I went to see him; and I first informed him
  That Beatriz had sent me.
Leonor: You did well.
Beatriz: [*Aside*]   But I did not do well, in trusting one
  Who pours my secrets out to Leonor.
Inés: Then secondly I gave the ribbon to him,
  And said it was from her.
Beatriz: [*Aside*]   Unhappy creature!
  What have I heard?
Leonor: There is a noise next door.
Inés: It is Don Juan. He has just come in.
Leonor: How can that be? He left here in a rage
  And said that he would never see me more.
Inés: Are you so green still that you do not know
  That when a lover furiously proclaims
  "I'll never see you more, ungrateful beauty!"
  He's dying then to see her.
Beatriz: [*Aside*]   Now I've begun
  To hear my sorrows, let me hear them through
  To the bitter end.

[Enter Don Juan, Don Alonso, and Moscatel]

Juan: Doubtless, Leonor, you will suppose
My jealousy has brought me here to see you
And talk with you, because, to put it coarsely,
Jealousy is love's carrier, who carts off
And brings back, too. But no, I have not come
To listen to excuses: it's unpleasant
In things of love to voice one's grievances.
I've crossed your threshold for another reason
(For griefs will never lack some kind of reason
To advertise themselves). My friend, Alonso,
Who, for your purposes, feigned himself a lover
Of Beatriz, and whose first visit here
Went badly for him, is concerned indeed
Lest Beatriz in her vanity should think
He's too discouraged and, indeed, afraid
To come back to this house; so he has asked me
To accompany him to see her. How could I
Refuse to do for him, what he had not
Refused to do for me?

Leonor: You're much indebted to him,
And should repay him.

Juan: He's coming, Leonor,
To carry out his purpose; and lest my griefs
Should ever suspect, my sorrows ever imagine,
Or my misfortunes ever think I came
Out of a wish to find you, I'll remain
During his talk with Beatriz in the street.
So he may clear his name of this suspicion
And show his honor in its proper light.
Come in, Alonso. Now that the dying sun
Has passed with agony into the shades
And lies a cold corpse in the arms of night,
Converse with Beatriz, but yet take care
Don Pedro does not find you here.

Leonor: Stay, Don Juan,
Wait.

Juan: What do you want? Why should I wait?

Leonor: For my excuses.

Juan: They will be in vain.

Leonor: For explanations.

Juan: They will be no use.

                                                    [Exit]

Leonor: Don Alonso, I'll go after him

And then return. Forgive me. He is jealous
And I must undeceive him.

[*Exit*]

Alonso: Must I go then
Without a word with Beatriz?
Moscatel: You have said it,
Not soon enough for me. But do not tell me
We're going to end up as we did last time
In a shocking mess.
Alonso: Inés, tell me where Beatriz is
That I may talk with her.

[*Enter Beatriz*]

Beatriz: Here is Beatriz,
Who has just overheard the outrages
Done to her by a base sister, a false friend,
An infamous lackey, a treacherous maidservant,
And a scheming lover. How horrible it is
That among Leonor, Juan, Inés, and Moscatel,
There was not one who would bring consolation
For all my griefs, or help me find excuses
For my behavior! Here and only here
Shall I attempt to voice my sense of outrage
About the worst of insults offered me,
My worst misfortune. Are my qualities
Of birth and fortune of such little merit,
And am I worth so little—I must say this—
That any man should dare to look on me
And court me with a vain pretense of love,
To make a mock of love—to trifle with me.
Alonso: Beautiful Beatriz, you are so attractive
In your annoyance, and do me such favor
That it will be easy now to prove you wrong,
And so repay you.
Beatriz: How can it be easy
To prove me wrong, when you have courted me
Merely to mock me.
Alonso: If you will hear me out,
It will be done. perhaps a man may dare
To enter the sea, that looks a garden of foam,
A forest of snow, without imagining
That there is danger in it; then to his horror,
And suddenly, that garden and that forest
Cause him to drown. And love is like that too—.
It follows then, in pleasure and in pain,

If one should never trifle with the sea,
So equally there is NO TRIFLING WITH LOVE.
Or take a man who manufactures fireworks
For fun, or for experiment: he makes
A bolt by which he dies in agony
From its fierce fire. Love's like a blazing bolt
Annihilating its artificer.
Then just as there's no trifling with the fire,
So there's NO TRIFLING WITH LOVE. Or take a man
Who draws his sword for fencing with a friend,
Who wounds him inadvertently, as though
He were an enemy. His swordmanship
Proves his undoing, and it was a blunder
To use it so. For love is like a sword:
If there's no trifling with an unsheathed sword,
There's NO TRIFLING WITH LOVE. Of if a man
Plays with a wild beast when he thinks it tame,
The more he pets it, the more it will revert
To its previous fierceness. Love's like a wild beast,
And since one cannot trifle with a beast
When it seems friendly, there's NO TRIFLING WITH LOVE.
And so in jest I went into the sea,
Kindled a firework, fenced with a naked sword,
And played with a wild beast; and I therefore drowned
In the sea, suffered the bolt's blazing heat,
The violence of the sword and of the beast.
So if wild beast, cold steel, fiery bolt, and sea
Can kill a man, there's NO TRIFLING WITH LOVE.[47]

Beatriz: In reply to that argument—

[*Enter Leonor, in a panic*]

Leonor: O heavens! Don Juan
Hurried into the street, and while I called
I saw my father coming in. It's necessary
To hide.
Beatriz: No, Leonor, it's too late now.
Leonor: Don Alonso—
Beatriz: My father will discover
What has been going on, and he'll be told
About your tricks.
Leonor: If you should try to tell him,
I'll know the way to put the blame on you,
And come off blameless. Since the risks are even,
Let us join now to find a remedy.

Beatriz: I'll do it, just to set a good example.
  I'm forced to side with you.
Moscatel: I beg for sanctuary,
  In the cupboard, since there's no church handy.
Alonso: I will do no such thing. I'd rather—
Inés: He's coming.
  This room will keep you hidden—
Moscatel: And me, too.
Alonso: [*Aside*] How boring are such amorous complications
  To a young bachelor.
Moscatel: Once we are hidden,
  Go, Inés, and find out if anyone
  Is lurking in the street to break our pates.[48]
      [*The two men go into hiding*]

  [*Enter Don Pedro*]

Pedro: So late and no lights lit! Go Inés,
  And see they bring some light.
Inés: I have already.
Pedro: [*Aside*] Insult me to my face! Affront me so!
  Merciful heavens, give me patience now
  Or give me death.
Beatriz: What ails you, Sir?
Leonor: What weighs upon you?
Pedro: Honor ails me, insults weigh me down.
  But that's not accurate. I'm not the one
  Who comes weighed down by insults. They have come
  Into my very house and wait for me.
Leonor: [*Aside*] Oh dear! He must know everything.
Beatriz: Will you not tell me, sir, what is the cause
  Of such an outburst?
Pedro: Your mad conduct, Beatriz,
  Is the sole cause, for now I must speak out,
  Because on your account an arrogant youth
  Has today dared to impeach this house's honor.
Leonor: [*Aside*] There's nothing now that he has not found out.
Beatriz: I, sir?
Moscatel: [*Behind the arras*] Things are going badly.
Pedro: Yes, for because of you, Don Luis scorns
  Both it and me.
Beatriz: [*Aside*]   The situation now
  Is starting to improve.
Leonor: Oh! that is better:
  I can breathe again.

[*Enter Don Juan*]

Juan: [*Aside*]   Any affair can go wrong once. But no one,
   When there are but two possibilities,
   Can make the same mistake a second time.
   I shall not wait this time until the doors
   Are closed, and Don Alonso has to jump
   From off the balcony. I'll put matters right
   Before it comes to that.   [*Aloud*]
   Don Pedro, if the obligation now
   Your friendship with my parents once imposed
   My house and blood inherit—
Leonor: [*Aside*]   What is he doing?
Beatriz: [*Aside*]   I'm dying to discover.
Juan: —then it's your duty
   To succor and protect me. I've been insulted
   By some men at your doors, and it's important
   I should not go alone to seek them out.
   I know I can confide in you, because
   I know you burn like Etna, though outside
   You're capped with snow.
Pedro: There's no need to say more.
   For I am well aware that in our time
   I am constrained by the laws of blood and honor
   Not to desert a man who looks for help.
   Let's go.
Juan: You are, as I supposed you were.
   [*Aside to Leonor*]   When I have got your father in the street,
   Get rid of Don Alonso.
Alonso: [*Aside, appearing at door of adjacent room*]   These must be
   The men who tried to kill me. It's not fitting
   For me to stay behind, nor go with them.
Pedro: Night has fallen. Wait here while I fetch
   A buckler from that room, a special treasure
   Left over from my youth.
Juan: Pray fetch it quickly.

[*Don Pedro enters the room where Don Alonso is hiding*]

Beatriz: He's in a worse predicament, through the means
   By which he tried to escape it.
Pedro: Who is there?
Alonso: [*Within*]   A man.

[*Don Pedro, Don Alonso, and Moscatel emerge*]

Moscatel: What he says is true, for the person with him
  Is nobody, no sort of man at all.
Pedro: Don Juan, since I was prepared to help you
  Against your enemy, you have now the duty
  To come to my assistance, above all
  Because the affair is much more serious.
  This man has harmed my honor, and it's vital
  That I should kill him.
Alonso: Faced with this dilemma,
  You know, Don Juan, where your duty lies.
  I must protect my life, defend these ladies.
Leonor: Dear goodness!
Beatriz: How unfortunate I am!
Juan: [*Aside*]   Whoever found himself in such a plight?
Pedro: [*To Juan*]   Do you hesitate?
Alonso: [*To Juan*]   Do you waver at this time?
Pedro: But I am quite sufficient to take vengeance
  Without your help.

  [*They fight. Don Juan interposes*]

Juan: Hold, Don Alonso; hold, sir!
Pedro: What! Do you stop the fight!
Alonso: What! Do you act so basely against my interests?
Luis: [*Offstage*]   There is a clash of swords within the house.
Diego: [*Offstage*]   Don't delay; let us go in, Don Luis.
Luis: [*Offstage*]   Hold there!
Pedro: People are coming.
Alonso: What a crisis!

  [*Enter Don Luis and Don Diego*]

Luis: What does this mean?
Pedro: It means, Don Luis, that I
  Am taking satisfaction for the affront
  I heard about from you; for if your honor
  Forbids you to wed Beatriz, it befits
  My honor that I take revenge and satisfaction.
Luis: Now you must realize I had some cause
  To make excuses; and this had to do,
  Perhaps, with an encounter in the street.
Alonso: Then it was you who wounded me.
Luis: It was.
Alonso: I'll be revenged.
Juan: Well, since it is God's will
  My jealousy should prove to be unfounded,

Let Leonor live again within my heart—
And so I must defend her from your anger.

Pedro: Don Juan, Don Juan, no one in this house
Defends my daughters, unless it is the men
Who mean to wed them.[49]

Alonso: I'll take you at your word.

Juan: The remedy is simple. I pledge myself
To Leonor.

Alonso: And I to Beatriz.

Pedro: [*Aside*] I must keep silent; once the damage is done
There is no other remedy.

Moscatel: So the most carefree man
Emerges from his trifling wounded, lame,
And, worst of all misfortunes, bound in wedlock.

Inés: And so the silliest, vainest, and most arrogant
Of women emerges willy-nilly from the trifling,
A woman in love and, worst of all, subjected.

Moscatel: Inés, give me your hand. If this must be,
Let us not think, but act. Have done with trifling,
For love is actually a serious matter.

Alonso: Let no one trifle with love. Be warned by me,
For everyone should shield himself from love.
Forgive the poet, prostrate at your feet.

THE END

Notes to the Plays

A House with Two Doors Is Difficult to Guard
(Casa con dos puertas mala es de guardar)

1. Lisardo's opening speech is typically Calderonian in that he accumulates a series of comparisons, then finishes with a recapitulation of their key elements: sun, polar star, magnet, etc. For other examples of this stylistic technique see Clara's speech, Act III scene 2, of *Mornings of April and May*, and Alonso's monologue near the end of *No Trifling with Love*.

2. Silvia's word-play is more forceful in the original, strengthened by the fact that in Spanish the verb *perseguir* can mean both "to pursue" and "to persecute."

3. Calabazas puns in his turn by using the word *encarecido*, whose stem is meant to recall *caras*, the horribly ugly faces just mentioned. Hence our translation of *encarecido* as "barefaced exaggeration."

4. In Spanish *cu-* is a shortened form of *culo* ("backside"). Calderón may have had in mind the popular saying "que le pague el culo del fraile" ("take it out of the friar's backside," or "you're not getting anything more out of me." Silvia clearly realizes that she will not receive much material reward from Calabazas in return for her favors, and she is, as she says, a demanding girl (*-pido* means "I ask for" in Spanish). Doubtless Silvia is also implying that Calabazas, despite his manliness, would have difficulty in satisfying her sexual demands. Northup (*Three Plays by Calderón*, ed. George T. Northup [Boston: D.C. Heath, 1926]) found the wordplay here so obscene that he omitted three lines from the text.

5. Evidently a reference to Calderón's own play *La dama duende* (*The Phantom Lady*), written in the same year as *Casa con dos puertas* (1629). Yet critics disagree as to which of these two comedies was written first (see our Introduction, pp. xiii-xiv).

6. Philip IV was noted for his fondness for lavish spectacles and tourneys. Doubtless many such were staged for his entertainment while he was in residence at Aranjuez (see note 12, below). In the original, Calabazas uses the verb *mantener* in two senses: "to defray the costs of" and "to defend oneself in the lists." Several critics, including Northup (*Three Plays* by *Calderón*, pp. xliii, 296), believe the comedy was performed at Aranjuez in 1629, presumably because of the allusions to Aranjuez which it contains and the fact that the play is set in Ocaña, only ten miles from Aranjuez. So far as we know, however, no documentary evidence exists of the first performance of *Casa con dos puertas*.

7. Here, as elsewhere in this play and in others, Calderón uses the *gracioso* to mock his favorite dramatic devices. On this particular occasion, he is mocking his own practice of including very long speeches in first acts to accomplish the dramatic exposition. This type of mockery served two purposes. First,

it jolted the audience into more thoughtful attention by reminding them of the difference between real life and the illusion of life represented on stage. Secondly, it was meant humorously to disarm those who might otherwise have grumbled about a lack of variety or novelty. Such mocking reference to the old tricks of his trade was so commonly used by Calderón that it became itself one of the conventions of his cloak-and-sword comedies. See our Introduction, pp. xvii-xx; *Mornings of April and May*, note 3; and *No Trifling with Love*, notes 1, 14, 19.

8. A Calderonian gallant frequently equates the arrival of his lady with the coming of dawn. See Introduction, pp. xxxii-xxxiii, and Robert ter Horst, *Calderón: The Secular Plays* (Lexington: Univ. Press of Kentucky, 1982), p. 17.

9. The comparisons and contrasts drawn between art and nature in this monologue are discussed by J.E. Varey in *"Casa con dos puertas*: Towards a Definition of Calderón's View of Comedy," *Modern Language Review* 67 (1972): 83 ff.; and by ter Horst in *Calderón*, pp. 23-24, who also offers a partial prose translation of the speech.

10. Similar imagery of storm, sea, and ship is used by Juan in the first monologue of *Mañanas de abril y mayo*. Some phrases are, in fact, identical ("viento en popa" and "tormenta de celos"), and strengthen our belief that *Mañanas de abril y mayo* was written only a few years after *Casa con dos puertas*. See Introduction, p. xiv; *A House with Two Doors*, Act I. sc. 2; and *Mornings of April and May*, Act I, sc. 1.

11. To be admitted into one of the great military orders was a high honor, much coveted by noblemen at this period. Calderón himself was made a knight of the Order of Santiago in 1637. Perhaps in 1629 he was already, like Lisardo, petitioning for such an honor.

12. The fleur-de-lis is Isabel de Borbón, the French queen of Philip IV; the other "bright and dazzling blooms" are the ladies of her court who accompanied her at Aranjuez. The king and queen went for regular visits to their palace at Aranjuez, where Philip IV could indulge his passion for hunting. See Félix's long speech describing the king's pursuit of falconry at Aranjuez (Appendix to *A House with Two Doors*).

13. Atlas, one of the Titans, supported the pillars separating Heaven and Earth. During his eleventh labor, Hercules stood in for Atlas for a time and held up the sky. Calderón likens Philip IV to Atlas in flattering recognition of the world wide Spanish Empire. The Herculean figure who lightens the king's burdensome responsibilities is the Conde-Duque de Olivares, Philip's First Minister and favorite until his fall from power in 1643. Calderón's excessive praise of Olivares here, together with his implausible declaration that petitioners for the royal favor always received "a fit reward," indicates that he may indeed have been petitioning for some honor for himself at the time of writing *Casa con dos puertas* (see note 11, above).

14. A reference to Cervantes' *Novelas ejemplares*, most of which are also *novelas de amor*. Calderón frequently alludes to Cervantes in his plays (compare note 43, below; and see ter Horst, *Calderón*, p. 71).

15. Doubtless Lisardo would have disapproved thoroughly of Hipólito in

Mañanas de abril y mayo, who boasts repeatedly of his success with women (see Introduction, p. xviii).

16. Many of Calderón's heroines show an acute awareness of themselves as characters performing in a play; several, including Marcela, even aspire to be dramatic collaborators in the work in which they figure. Marcela is sufficiently gifted as a play-maker to appreciate the value of dramatic suspense. She tells us that she has invented a remarkable piece of intrigue to entertain us, but refuses to reveal its nature in advance. It should be noted that Laura, too, makes her contribution to the script. The role played by her maid, Celia, in pretending to Félix that she brings him to meet her mistress in defiance of Laura's wishes, is created for her by Laura's dramatic inventiveness (see Act I, sc. 3).

17. For a description of the *estrado*, or drawing-room, where ladies sat, usually on cushions, to entertain their guests, see José Deleito y Piñuela, *La mujer, la casa y la moda* (Madrid: Espasa Calpe, 1946), pp. 34-36. Ladies of position usually had several *estrados*, and callers were received at one or another, depending on their status. Northup points out that in Calderón's time women were just beginning to use the chair (see *Three Plays by Calderón*, p. 303).

18. Philip IV is also associated with the fourth planet, Mars, in Félix's speech in Act III (see Appendix). For other planetary references to Philip, see *Mornings of April and May*, Act I, sc. 5, and note 14 to that play. Philip IV was known to his contemporaries as the Planet King (see R.A. Stradling, "The Planet King: Philip IV and the Survival of Spain," *History Today* 31 March [1981]: 16-23.

19. Laura means that she could only clear her own name by blaming Félix's sister, Marcela, and that would put Félix's honor at risk.

20. Here Calderón again uses Calabazas to make mock of *comedia* conventions and disturb the dramatic illusion. Calabazas is right, of course: in cloak-and-sword comedies the manservant traditionally accompanies his master when the latter goes to court his lady (compare note 7, above.).

21. Lisardo uses a technical term here, "hecha mi consulta baja," which indicates that the first or lower stage of the process governing his petition has been completed. The petition, however, must still be placed before the higher authorities for the *consulta alta* (see Northup, *Three Plays by Calderón*, p. 307).

22. Tailors had a reputation for dishonesty in the Golden Age, and were much satirized in literature (see, for example, Quevedo's *Los sueños*).

23. The phrase used by Calabazas ("aquí gloria y después gracia") is a deliberately comic inversion of the commonplace remark "aquí gracia y después gloria," meaning "so far so good." Calabazas' inversion signifies his absurdly blissful mood. He will never have it so good again. In bestowing upon him a ready-made suit his master has brought him heaven on earth.

24. In the original, Calabazas declares that they are going to Ireland, by which he simply means any outlandish place. Northup points out that the word *Irlanda* suits the a/a assonance of Calderón's ballad meter here (*Three Plays by Calderón*, p. 309). Another reason why *Irlanda* may have occurred to the playwright is that he has just been alluding, in Calabazas' anecdote about the

tailor, to the places famous for their linens, Anjou and Rouen; Ireland was another region with an outstanding reputation for linen. In Spanish the word for a particularly fine piece of linen is simply *irlanda*.

25. Marcela's apparently inexplicable knowledge of their movements sets Calabazas' superstitious hackles rising. One is reminded of the *gracioso* Cosme's reactions to the seemingly supernatural antics of Ángela, "la dama duende." Calabazas has already displayed a disposition to regard Marcela as the reembodiment of "The Phantom Lady" (compare note 5, above). Catalina de Acosta was a well known actress of the period who may well have played the part of Ángela on stage. She could also have played the role of Marcela in the first performance of *Casa con dos puertas*, hence perhaps the reference to her in the play. Why she should be looking for her statue, however, is more difficult to explain. Clearly some topical joke is involved, perhaps a reference to another role played by this actress, as heroine of some sacred piece in which a religious statue or image was lost, searched for, and recovered, doubtless with divine help. Religious dramas based on legends about wonder-working images were numerous at the period.

26. Marcela's life is in Lisardo's hands because if Félix finds out the truth about her behavior he will seek to kill his sister in the name of honor. In fact, he attempts to do so at the end of Act III when Laura reveals Marcela's secret (see also the Introduction, p. xxi).

27. This passionate exchange of protests, denials, and recriminations parallels a similar confrontation between the lovers in the previous act; but this time it is Félix who is offended, while Laura attempts an explanation (see the Introduction, pp. xxiii-xxiv). The reversal of roles brings about sufficient dramatic development for us to enjoy, without any sense of monotony, the full irony of the parallels.

28. Félix remembers Laura's similar response in an earlier scene (compare Act II, sc. 1 and note 19 above).

29. If Laura had in fact told Félix her story here, the denouement would have taken place at the end of the second act. But Marcela intervenes in the nick of time, and Laura's revelations are prevented. Calderón is a master at engineering the near-miss or near-disaster in order to create dramatic excitement and suspense. He pushes his plot to the verge of its dissolution, only to turn it back smartly to its safer middle reaches once again. He employs the same technique at the end of the second act of *Mañanas de abril y mayo*, where even the *gracioso* mistakenly believes for a moment that the end of the play is prematurely upon him (see *Mornings of April and May* and its note 20).

30. The declaration "I am who I am" is frequently made by gallants and ladies in Golden-Age plays. It expresses their sense of personal integrity and their commitment to the code of honor. Laura uses the phrase here to emphasize that she is incapable of the sort of behavior of which Félix accuses her. Compare Félix's use of the same phrase in Act III, sc. 5, when he acts to protect Laura (the woman he rescues is, in fact, Marcela), even though he firmly believes that Laura has been unfaithful to him. For a full account of the formula, see Leo Spitzer, "Soy quien soy," *Nueva Revista de Filología Hispánica* 1 (1947): 113-27.

31. The so-called Mar de Antígola was a smallish lake outside Aranjuez,

small enough for Richard Ford to describe it disparagingly as a pond (see Northup, *Three Plays by Calderón*, p. 313).

32. Celia amusingly adapts a well known *letrilla* by Góngora much glossed by Golden-Age playwrights, since it expressed a theme which deeply preoccupied the Baroque age: that of the fleeting nature of beauty, of happiness, and of life itself. There is a serious allusion to the same poem in *Mornings of April and May* (see Act I, sc. 4, and its note 13). Compare Celia's adaptation ("Aprended, damas, de aquí / lo que va desde hoy a ayer") with the first lines of Gongora's poem: "Aprended, flores, de mí / lo que va de ayer a hoy."

33. Clearly, Marcela is the more quick-witted, decisive, and enterprising of the two ladies, though, ironically, Laura imagines that she is deceiving her friend.

34. For our comments on the significance of these lines, see the Introduction, p. xiii.

35. Second-rate poet-playwrights (the normal word for a dramatist in Golden-Age Spain was *poeta*) were often satirized in *comedias*, as too were dandies and lovers. Like many *graciosos*, Calabazas is given a name which indicates his character (Calabazas means "simpleton" or "ignoramus"), and cannot resist making puns upon it. The reference to the type of lover who did his wooing at the palace probably had a topical significance which is now lost to us, though doubtless much illicit love-making did go on in Philip's palaces. The king himself was a notorious philanderer.

36. Similarly satirical remarks about duennas are to be found in *Mornings of April and May*, in which, indeed, a duenna, Lucía, is one of the characters (see notes 24 and 25 to that comedy).

37. Anti-Jewish remarks are commonplace in Golden-Age literature. In the original, the exact term used is "un judío de Orán." Orán was a Spanish possession from 1509 until the early eighteenth century.

38. Calabazas' inquisitiveness is stronger than his cowardice. Moreover, he is clearly determined to act his part as *gracioso*-lackey strictly in accordance with cloak-and-sword conventions (compare his complaints to Lisardo earlier in this scene; and see note 20, above).

39. Fabio's words are ironically rich in involuntary double meanings, as he imagines his daughter's distress at his return. The audience knows that Fabio's daughter is not, in fact, virtuously asleep at home, but hidden in the house of her lover, Félix (see the Introduction, pp. xxviii-xxix).

40. Card-playing terms are used with double meaning in the original. *Hombre* is the name of a card game in Spanish, in addition to meaning "man"; *espadas* means "spades" as well as "swords."

41. Calabazas refers mockingly to one of the rules of conduct in matters of honor. Northup explains the reference at length (*Three Plays by Calderón*, pp. 317-18). The point is that a man who insults another tempers the insult if he makes it with his sword already drawn, for he therefore concedes that the person whom he insults is of equal standing, and is capable of retaliation.

42. Lisardo, like Félix, mistakes the identity of the lady in question.

43. An allusion to Cervantes' exemplary novel, included in *Don Quixote*,

entitled *El curioso impertinente (The Curious Impertinent)*. Calabazas criticizes his own imprudent inquisitiveness in following the two gallants and therefore involving himself in danger. There may be an additional significance, since *curioso* can also imply "cleanly clad." Like many *graciosos* in Golden-Age plays, Calabazas appears to be insinuating that fear has caused him to wet his pants. Consequently, he is willing to surrender his trousers to Fabio, as well as the sword which the latter demands.

44. Light is coming metaphorically as well as literally, for the mysteries are about to be resolved. The actors of the period, of course, had to pretend to be in the dark, since plays were performed in broad daylight (compare the Introduction, p. xxxi).

45. The sound seems to come from Norway because it is made by a Norwegian bugle, an instrument much used at the time (see Northup, *Three Plays by Calderón*, p. 311).

46. This speech is extremely difficult to understand in places, owing to textual inaccuracies in the Osuna manuscript. We have found Northup's elucidations useful (*ibid.*, pp. 310-13); nevertheless, in certain passages the playwright's full meaning still escapes us.

Mornings of April and May
(Mañanas de abril y mayo)

1. Arceo's mysteriously muffled visitor reminds the lackey of the ghostly statue ("el convidado de piedra") which came from the afterworld to knock one night for hospitality at the door of Don Juan Tenorio's lodgings in Tirso's famous tragedy *El burlador de Sevilla [y convidado de piedra] (The Trickster of Seville)*. The intruder's stiffly courteous manner of address serves only to intensify Arceo's unease, for the similarly well-bred formality of Tirso's ghost proved to be ill-intentioned, terminating with a handshake of inexorable warmth which committed Don Juan to the fires of hell (see *El burlador de Sevilla*, 3. 946-70). This is not the only play by Tirso mentioned in *Mañanas de abril y mayo*. In Act II, Inés suggests to her mistress that she is acting the part of a woman jealous of herself, an allusion to the unlikely predicament of the titular heroine of Tirso's *La celosa de sí misma* (see Act II. sc. 1). According to Blanca de los Ríos, *La celosa de sí misma* is the forerunner of Calderón's cloak-and-sword plays, with their "damas duendes" and "casas con dos puertas" (see Tirso de Molina, *Obras completas*, ed. Blanca de los Ríos [Madrid, 1952], 2: 14). References are frequently made within Golden-Age plays to other dramas of the period, and such allusions may help to ascertain dates of composition (see, for example, our Introduction, p. xiv). Calderón was particularly fond of mentioning his own plays within his plays (see note 26, below, and *A House with Two Doors*, note 5).

2. True to type, the *gracioso* not only knows contemporary Spanish literature well but is also knowledgeable about ancient culture and legend. He alludes here to the Seven Sleepers of Ephesus. These were seven Christian soldiers reputed to have concealed themselves in a cave during the persecutions

of Decius (A.D. 250) and to have remained asleep there until the reign of the Christian Emperor Theodosius II (A.D. 408-450), when they awoke to bear miraculous witness to the Resurrection.

3. Like many Golden-Age *graciosos*, Arceo is intensely aware of himself as a traditionally comic type, performing before an audience conditioned to expect him to be a coward, an eavesdropper, a gossip, and so on. Calderón deliberately uses Arceo's self-consciousness about his dramatic role to spruce up worn jokes and threadbare comic situations. For another example of Arceo's entertaining self-awareness, see his conversation with the duenna, Lucía: Act I, sc. 4. "Ah well, no secret should be wholly kept, when you're a duenna, and I'm a lackey" ("¡Eh! No haya secreto entero, / que eres dueña y soy criado"). See also *A House with Two Doors*, notes 7 and 20. Arceo's inability to keep a secret contrasts comically with the meaning of his name: the Latin verb *arceo* means "I shut in" or "shut up."

4. A noteworthy characteristic of Calderón's dramatic technique is the inclusion of a lengthy monologue early in Act I, to provide the audience with background information necessary for understanding the plot. Such speeches are often addressed to a character who is already well aware of the story, and are, therefore, as in this case, punctuated with apologetic comments, such as "You know already . . . ," "As you already know . . ." or "I tell you now / what's known to you already" ("Ya sabéis . . .," "lo que vos sabéis os cuento"). At least on this occasion the speaker offers a soundly psychological justification for his repetitions, namely, that he derives some solace from the exercise of regularly expressing his anguish in words. Calderón makes mock of his own fondness for lengthy explanatory monologues in *A House with Two Doors;* see note 7 to that play.

5. The first of many references to real streets and places in Madrid. The Paseo de Prado was an elegant avenue, a favorite walking-place of the upper classes. Calle Mayor (Main Street), as its name implies, was the main shopping street and was much frequented by ladies of society. Topographical allusions are numerous in Golden-Age cloak-and-sword plays. Together with references to contemporary events, manners, attitudes, and fashions, they create a strangely realistic setting which dramatically enhances the sparkling improbabilities of the intricately worked plot (see our Introduction, pp. xvi-xvii).

6. The first of several repetitions of the play's title, intended to underline the mood and theme of the comedy. Titles are traditionally used in this way in Golden-Age dramas. See, e.g., *Casa con dos puertas*, Act I, sc. 3, Act III, sc. 4. For further comments on the title of *Mañanas de abril y mayo*, its origins, function, and meaning, see the Introduction, pp. xxxi-xxxiii.

7. The commonest punishment meted out to criminals in seventeenth-century Spain was that of forced labor on the king's galleys. Galley slaves are usually presented in a bad light in Golden-Age literature. One might recall Don Quijote's encounter with the galley slaves in Part I. He frees them from their chains, convinced that they have been wrongly punished, and is later robbed by them for his altruism.

8. For comments on the origin of this song, see our Introduction, p. xxxi.

9. Legal terminology is used in the original text here and obscures the sense. Calderón may be referring obliquely to some topical scandal.

10. At this period coaches were regularly used for illicit assignations by ladies of suspect virtue.

11. We are soon to discover that these amusing comments about Clara offer valid insight into her habits and personality. She likes to display herself, to observe, and to be observed in turn.

12. Another example of Calderón's mockery of the conventions of cloak-and-sword comedy (see *A House with Two Doors*, note 7). Clara's refusal here to behave like a lady in a comedy and her insistence that she is a participant in real life, besides being humorous, serve a more serious purpose, that of emphasizing her robustly individualistic personality.

13. Ana's words ("que aun sombra mía no soy") echo the refrain of a well known *letrilla* by Góngora, much glossed and quoted by Golden-Age dramatists. Calderón uses this same *letrilla* in *La cisma de Ingalaterra*.

14. Hipólito's references to Philip IV and Queen Isabel are so condensed that it has been necessary to expand them to make them understandable in English. Philip IV was often flatteringly associated with the fourth planet, Mars (compare *A House with Two Doors*, note 18).

15. There is an anonymous Golden-Age play entitled *The Silent Lady (La dama muda)*, evidently surviving only in an early eighteenth-century manuscript, which Calderón may have had in mind (compare note 1, above).

16. The reference is evidently to a high-class shop well known in Madrid at this period. The Portuguese were famed as traders in exotic spices, perfumes, and sweetmeats (see Clara's allusion later in this scene to "this lavish show of sweets / From Portugal" ("todo ese grande aparato / de dulces de Portugal").

17. Ana's comment depends on wordplay. In Spanish, *apenas* is an adverb meaning "scarcely, hardly," while the phrase *a penas* signifies "to or toward griefs, difficulties." An identical pun is used by Rosaura in the opening monologue of Calderón's *La vida es sueño* (1635), when she declares; "y a penas llega, cuando llega apenas" (Hardly does she come when she comes to grief/hardship").

18. The phrase used by Clara to describe Hipólito is "señor Para- todas," a description believed by E. Cotarelo y Mori to reflect the influence on Calderón of Pérez de Montalbán's book *Para todos (For Everybody)* (see *Ensayo sobre la vida y obras de D. Pedro Calderón de la Barca* [Madrid, 1924], p. 148). This collection of plays, poems, stories, and other forms, much read in its day, was first published in 1632. Calderón's linguistic ingenuity is such, however, that the phrase "señor Para-todas" (literally, "Sir For-every-lady") could well be a purely spontaneous creation. In the final act Hipólito reveals how appropriate is Clara's nickname when he advises his friend Luis to "love a host of women / All for your pleasure, none to your regret" ("querer por tu gusto a todas / por tu pesar a ninguna").

19. Phyllis (Filis) and Fabio are conventional names often given to ladies and lovers in Spanish pastoral literature to mask their true identities. In Lope's poetry, for example, Filis is regularly used as a pseudonym for Lope's mistress, Elena Osorio. A pastoral reference is appropriate here because Clara has just mentioned the beauties of the parks, that is, the beautiful women pursued there

by Hipólito. Parts of Clara's speech are difficult to understand, perhaps as a result of textual deficiencies.

20. Here, as elsewhere, Calderón teases his audience into believing for a moment that the play may end after only two acts, before revealing that this is not the case, that, after all, this comedy will conform to cloak-and-sword conventions. Accordingly, the tangled threads of confusions, deceits, and misunderstandings will not be straightened out until the last possible moment of the final act. Compare *A House with Two Doors*, note 29.

21. Pernía reacts angrily to Arceo's witty remarks about the behavior of jealous men. In love with Lucía, who favors Arceo, Pernía is a jealous man himself and believes that Arceo is making mock of him.

22. Arceo's retort mixes card-playing terms with bull-fighting terminology; in consequence, it defies precise translation.

23. Ana tends emotionally to overdramatize her situation, as her language here reveals. She speaks in a desperate manner reminiscent of that displayed by protagonists in Calderón's serious or tragic drama. The phrase "living corpse" (vivo cadáver") is used several times with reference to Segismundo in *La vida es sueño* (see also note 17 above).

24. The worst insult which Arceo can hurl at the duenna, Lucía, is to call her "duenna," a type much criticized and ridiculed in Golden-Age society. The *dueña* is frequently the butt of satire in literature of this period. Quevedo, for example, in his *Sueños* (*Visions*) satirizes duennas and consigns many of them to hell. In *Las zahurdas de Plutón* (*The Rubbish-Dumps of Pluto*) Quevedo deposits them in a huge lake of dirty water, and describes them as "ranas del infierno" (frogs of hell) becuase of their slimy appearance and the fact that they talk endlessly in a croaking monotone. Bad poets were also much satirized at the time. It is noteworthy that Arceo does not feel that Lucía has matched the insulting force of his cry of "duenna" until she calls him "poetaster." The phrase "mal poeta" also meant, of courst, "bad dramatist" in the Golden Age, since all Golden-Age drama was verse-drama (see Calabazas' comments in Act III, sc. 2, of *A House with Two Doors*; see also note 35 to that play).

25. Arceo continues to heap abuse upon duennas, while at the same time mocking lovelorn poetasters. In particular, he stuffs the end of his poem with clichés from contemporary love-poetry: "In solitude that's peopled by my sighs" ("aquí donde mis suspiros / pueblan estas soledades"). Specific parody of Juan's opening speech in Act III, in which he has expressed his perturbation, his fears, and his complaints, is doubtless also intended.

26. Another mention by Calderón of his famous comedy *La dama duende* (see our Introduction, pp. xiii-xiv, and *A House with Two Doors*, note 5). Arceo appears obsessed by fearful notions of supernatural beings. In Act I his mind has conjured up a ghostly statue (see note 1, above); in this act he has already imagined his mistress, Lucía, as a "fearful apparition" ("estantigua"); now he fancies that there is a "phantom lady" haunting the household.

27. Arceo plays on the different senses of the verb *labrar*, which means "to labor, to work on the land," but can also signify "to shape, form, rework" something, or "to influence" somebody. Arceo refers to the pelican because he remembers the legend about that bird. The pelican was reputed to rend its own

breast to provide nourishment for its young, a myth that developed because young pelicans pushed their beaks deep into the pouch of their parents while feeding on regurgitated fish. The pelican, in consequence, came to symbolize self-sacrifice and atonement. Celestina alludes to the self-sacrificing pelican during her first conversation with Melibea (see Fernando de Rojas, *La Celestina*, ed. Dorothy S. Severin [Madrid: Alianza Editorial, 1965], p. 95).

28. Arceo parodies the role of honorable gallant and speaks in suitably pompous fashion. For comments on this parody see our Introduction, pp. xvii-xviii.

29. Clara's speech is typically Calderonian in that a number of metaphors are accumulated, which are then reiterated in a more concentrated fashion to bring the speech to its conclusion. See *A House with Two Doors*, note 1. See also Kenneth Muir and Ann L. Mackenzie, *Four Comedies by Pedro Calderón de la Barca* (Lexington: Univ. Press of Kentucky, 1980), *The Advantages and Disadvantages of a Name*, note 1, p. 288.

30. The meaning of the Spanish phrase "caballero de ciudad" is difficult to convey exactly; the phrase might not simply suggest any provincial gentleman but one who has some official standing in his town, as a counselor, for example, or a magistrate.

31. Eleanor S. O'Kane lists a Spanish proverb: "Preguntaldo a Muñoz, que miente más que yo" (*Refranes y frases proverbiales españolas de la Edad Media* [Madrid: Real Academia Española, 1959], p. 168). There is evidently no accurate English equivalent. The sense is approximately: "That's the story, take it or leave it; it's the nearest you'll get to the truth." Clara believes, doubtless rightly, that Luis will loyally corroborate his friend's lies.

32. Juan's response here is ambiguous. It is not clear from his words whether he himself embraces Ana, or, on the contrary, rejects her and pushes her toward Luis. The difficulty of interpreting Juan's reply is aggravated by textual uncertainties. Some versions of the play offer: "ella os pague con los brazos / lo que con armas no puedo" ("Let her be the one to reward you with an embrace, since I cannot take arms against you"). However, the most reliable editions give these lines as follows: "ella os pague con los brazos / lo que con alma no puedo," and we have translated the lines accordingly. For our comments on the end of the play, see the Introduction, pp. xxxv-xxxvi.

33. The meaning of Arceo's final witty remark is somewhat obscure. It reads as follows in the original: "Mas ¿que nace el Anti-Cristo / de Lucías y de Arceos?." He may intend to satirize duennas again by suggesting that to marry a duenna is to run the risk of fathering Antichrist in person. Or he may be referring to the fact that he and Lucía have already had sexual relations outside marriage. According to some authorities the Antichrist will be born of fornication. Arceo may also be playing on the sense of his name and that of Lucía: *arceo* implies "to shut in, prohibit access to," while the duenna's name suggests *lux, lucis* ("light"). Thus, it could be argued that the effect of joining Arceo with Lucía is to shut away the light and let forth the evil darkness of Antichrist.

No Trifling with Love
(No hay burlas con el amor)

1. Comments from the *gracioso* designed to remind us that we are attending the performance of a play are commonplace in Calderonian comedy (see *A House with Two Doors*, note 7; *Mornings of April and May*, note 3). On this occasion Calderón breaks the dramatic illusion to promise us a play that will depart radically from cloak-and-sword tradition. He keeps his word. See our Introduction, pp. xxxvi-xl.

2. Another reference to play-making, this time by Alonso, to remind us that we are participating in dramatic make-believe. Ignacio Arellano, ed., *No hay burlas con el amor* (Pamplona: EUNSA, 1981), p. 193), suggests that Calderón may have had a particular play in mind when he referred to "Love's Wonders" ("Los milagros de amor"), possibly *Cuatro milagros de amor* of Antonio Mira de Amescua. Certainly Calderón often alludes to specific plays in his comedies (compare, for example, *Mornings of April and May*, note 1). But his intention here may simply have been to propose an alternative title for *No hay burlas con el amor*, which undoubtedly illustrates the wondrous transformations which love can accomplish in human behavior.

3. Lope's comedy *Los melindres de Belisa* was published in 1617. For comments on this play as a possible source of *No hay burlas con el amor*, see the Introduction, p. xl.

4. Calderón does not mention by name the poets whose style of writing has so adversely affected Beatriz's mode of speech, but it is obvious that he is referring to Góngora and his disciples. Their poetry was notorious for precisely those stylistic excesses mentioned by Juan in his complaints about Beatriz ("no habla palabra jamás / sin frases y sin rodeos"), namely, exaggerated circumlocutions and elaborations. Juan describes Beatriz in the original as a "crítico impertinente," a phrase which reminds us that the alternative title for *No hay burlas con el amor* is *La crítica del amor*. The word *crítico* meant rather more than "critic" in the seventeenth-century; it indicated a person who talked or wrote in an affected fashion (see our Introduction, pp. xv and xxxix-xl).

5. No exact rendering of Alonso's remark is possible in English, for he employs terms from card games to construct double meanings. Thus the phrase *poder ser hombre* is used in the sense of taking on all other players in a particular card game, besides meaning "to be capable of manly conduct," while the word *figuras* signifies "face cards" as well as human figures rather ridiculous in form (Alonso's view of the persons of Luis and Diego).

6. Ovid's works were much read in the Golden Age and greatly influenced poets such as Góngora. Ovid's *Metamorphoses* is the source of one of Góngora's best poems, *Fábula de Polifemo y Galatea* (*Polyphemus and Galatea*). It is easy to understand why Beatriz should reject the *Metamorphoses* and the *Ars Amatoria* in favor of the *Remedio Amoris*. Ovid's *Metamorphoses* poeticizes classical and mythological love-relationships (the love of Polyphemus for Galatea, the pursuit of Daphne by Apollo, and others), while his *Ars Amatoria* brilliantly illustrates methods of courtship and seduction for the benefit of the

rake-about-town. Beatriz claims to be opposed to love and love-making, and is therefore drawn to that work by Ovid which purports to offer correctivesa and antidotes to love. Obviously she does not appreciate the burlesque intention of the supposedly recantatory *Remedio Amoris*: but then, Beatriz has little sense of humor.

7. Not even Góngora was in the habit of indulging in such extreme hyperbaton as that employed by Beatriz here. She actually separates a possessive adjective from its noun by inserting a verb between them. The original lines read: "pues víbora será humana / que con su, inficione, aliento." We have not attempted to match Beatriz's degree of hyperbaton, for the result would have been incomprehensible in English: "for she a serpent will be human, who with her, poisons, breath" (see the Preface, p. x).

8. Then, as now, an envoy or ambassador was guaranteed safe conduct.

9. Moscatel uses the terminology of finance to describe the dealings with the woman he loves. There are other allusions to mortgages, interest, returns, and so forth, in this play (compare the *gracioso's* comment to Don Alonso at the beginning of Act II). Such references might seem to reflect the materialism which dominated and corrupted Spanish society at the period, the effect of New-World riches and attendant economic complications.

10. Moscatel's responses to Don Pedro are full of double meanings. Here he refers first to a "criado honrado" ("honorable manservant"), then to an "honrado criado," which can also mean "honorable manservant" but signifies besides a "well-bred man of honor" or a "born gentleman." The wordplay is difficult to convey exactly, but Moscatel appears too suggest that born gentlemen have become a rare species. This is not the only place in this comedy where Calderón casts a sharply critical glance at the society of his day.

11. Beatriz's tortuous allusion to Leonor's letter provides further evidence that Góngora has been a major influence upon her syntax and diction (see the Introduction, p. xl).

12. A play on words. The letter (or epistle, as Beatriz insists upon calling it) reminds Inés not so much of the Epistle at mass as of the Gospel, for any words written by Juan are likely to be received reverently as if they were, indeed, the Gospel according to Saint John (Juan).

13. Inés's words in Spanish are: "Honor, con quien vengo vengo," and these were doubtless intentionally chosen by Calderón to advertise his own comedy *Con quien vengo vengo*, composed about 1635, though admittedly the phrase was in popular use at the period, approximating in its meaning to our saying "A friend in need. . . ."

14. Inés's remark is another amusing reminder to the audience that they are witnessing merely a dramatic imitation of reality (compare note 1 above). It is, moreover, accurate. There are few maidservants in Golden-Age comedies who do not wholeheartedly assist their mistresses in their intrigues and deceptions.

15. The unnatural sin to which Moscatel alludes is that of sodomy ("pecado nefando"), punishable by death in the Golden Age.

16. Boys acting as guides to blind beggars were often badly treated by their masters; hence Moscatel's admitted reluctance to become a "mozo del

ciego." The most famous blind man's boy of Spanish literature is Lázaro, protagonist of *Lazarillo de Tormes,* Spain's first picaresque novel.

17. Inés hilariously parodies the outraged reaction traditionally shown by
the virtuous noblewoman in Golden-Age drama toward unwelcome sexual advances (compare Arceo's parody of the honorable nobleman in *Mornings of April
and May,* Act III. sc. 1). Besides the usual adjectives a lady would be likely to
employ in such a circumstance, such as "¡grosero, descortés, loco!" Inés does not
fail to include the set phrase "soy quien soy" (see *A House with Two Doors,* note
30).

18. Enormous farthingales were very much in fashion at the period. The
Spanish word *guardainfantes*—literally, "child-keepers"—derives from the fact
that pregnant women used these undergarments to conceal their condition.
Here Inés finds hers useful to conceal her cloak and thereby the fact that she has
been out of doors. The fashion in farthingales reached such extremes that laws
were introduced to ban them, but these proved unenforceable. *Guardainfantes*
were much satirized in poetry, prose, and drama.

19. It is not unusual in Golden-Age comedies for the *gracioso* or *graciosa*
to take the audience directly into his or her confidence in this fashion. Such
direct address emphasizes for us the distance between the dramatized world and
our world outside the play; yet, paradoxically enough, it serves at the same time
to draw us deeper inside the make-believe society inhabited by Inés and the
other characters.

20. Inés uses the traditional battle cry delivered by Spanish soldiers as
they moved in to engage the enemy: "¡Santiago, cierra España!" (literally: "St.
James, close in Spain"). St. James is the patron saint of Spain. The campaign
against Beatriz has begun.

21. Leonor deliberately parodies the display of virtuous outrage in which
Beatriz had engaged in the previous act, to the extent of reproducing her sister's
affected words and word order (see the Introduction, p. xix and Act I, sc. 3). Such
borrowed words as "libidinous" and *"persona"* are sufficiently bizarre and archaic
for the audience to enjoy their saucy repetition. Leonor similarly parodies her
sister's language in Act III, sc. 4.

22. Pedro lists the normal domestic occupations of a lady in seventeenth-
century Madrid. The *Hours (Horas)* to which he refers is the prayer book which
the lady would use at her devotions; it contained prayers mostly addressed to the
Virgin and meant to be recited at set hours of the day.

23. Prester John (Preste Juan) was a legendary medieval figure of fabulous
wealth and power, alleged to have been Christian ruler of the Indies.

24. The words which Moscatel attributes to Inés here are in keeping with
the sentiments which we ourselves have heard her express in her parody of the
outraged lady of virtue (see note 17). Ladies in serious Golden-Age drama often
make almost identical statements (compare the words of Inés, "que soy grande
para dama / y para esposa chica" with Doña Mencía's declaration to the enamored Prince Enrique in Calderón's *El médico de su honra:* "pues soy para dama
más, / lo que para esposa menos."

25. Many Golden-Age plays are set in Italy and are peopled, as Alonso's
remark suggests, with duchesses or countesses of Amalfi, Mantua, or Milan.

One example is Lope's *El mayordomo de la duquesa de Amalfi*. *Picardía* has a double meaning in Spanish: as a proper noun it refers to the place, Picardy; as a common noun it means "roguery" and can imply "sexual impropriety."

26. The verb *picar* in Spanish, "to prick, sting," can also infer, as here, "to stimulate sexually" (compare note 25, above).

27. It was the custom in seventeenth-century Madrid to empty slops from windows and balconies.

28. The "ladies" do not wish to reveal their place of baptism, for that piece of information would enable him to discover their age by examining the records of their parish church. Alonso's failure to enquire about their baptism betrays his lack of concern for their family origins, and therefore the dishonorable nature of his intentions. Had he had marriage in mind he would have taken great care to scrutinize baptismal and other records to verify that there was no taint of Jewish or Moorish blood in the family of the lady of his choice. Noblemen were obsessed with maintaining and demonstrating Christian *limpieza de sangre* ("purity of blood") in seventeenth-century Spain.

29. Etiquette was strict at the period. Chairs were offered to distinguished visitors as a mark of respect. Male visitors who were close family friends might sit on stools. Alonso is displaying his bold contempt for social proprieties by insisting that he would take a chair on his first visit (see José Deleito y Piñuela, *La mujer, la casa y la moda* [Madrid: Espasa Calpe, 1946], p. 91).

30. The word used for "Latin dictionary" in the original is *calepino*, a term derived from the name (Calepino) of an Italian scholar who compiled a Latin/Italian dictionary (1502). Alonso has yet to meet Beatriz, but he is well informed as to her latinate mode of speech (thanks, for instance, to the comments of Juan, Act I, sc. 1).

31. We offer only a selection of the learned words listed by Inés in the original. Amusingly, the maid cannot resist gilding the lily by quoting a latinism which Beatriz has not in fact employed on this occasion, "crepúsculos" ("crepuscularity").

32. Beatriz's reference is to the planet Saturn, associated with melancholia. In spite of her melancholy state, Beatriz will endeavor to put aside the elevated language of tragedy and adopt instead the common language associated with comedy. The phrase "calzar el trágico coturno" (literally, "to put on the tragic buskin") derives from the practice followed by actors in the classical theatre of wearing high-heeled buskins when playing tragic roles. By extension it came to be applied to the high-flown language used in tragedies, and to mean "to speak or write in an elevated manner." The English phrase "to put on the buskin" has the same significance. The phrase "calzar el zueco" (literally, "to put on clogs") came to signify the style of speech employed in comedy.

33. For the most part Calderón uses the *gracioso* to break the dramatic illusion and mock the conventions of cloak-and-sword comedy. See, for example, *A House with Two Doors*, notes 7 and 20. In this case, however, Alonso is the playwright's mouthpiece; but then, as we have shown, Alonso's behavior is more typically that of *gracioso* than of *galán* (see our Introduction, pp. xxxvii-xxxix, and Arellano, *No hay burlas*, pp. 301-2).

34. Arellano argues (*ibid.*, p. 303) that the reference in the original

("¡Lindo búcaro del Duque / o de la Maya seré!") is not to Mayan pottery but to a type of pottery from Portugal, made in the Lisbon area.

35. The reference to a hired mule is somewhat obscure. Moscatel may have in mind the two panniers carried by a hired pack-mule, which were often stuffed to overflowing.

36. Unlike Don Pedro, the audience fully understands Inés's reply: she has dropped the lamp deliberately to provide an "innocent" explanation for the noise made by the men in the china cupboard.

37. Moscatel associates Inés with the saint after whom she is named. Santa Inés was often depicted in paintings with a lamb in her arms as symbol of her innocence. He plays on the double meaning of *cordero*: "lamb" but also "meek," "ineffectual." He stands there sheepishly, forced to take it like a lamb while his master embraces his girlfriend.

38. The double meaning intended in the original is inevitably lost in translation. Inés makes a pun by means of the phrase "pie quebrado," which signifies literally a "broken foot" but also refers to a type of Spanish verse-form with short or broken lines inserted between longer lines of poetry. The famous poem by Jorge Manrique (d. 1579), "Coplas a la muerte de su padre" ("Verses upon the death of his father") is written in "pie quebrado." Inés suggests that Moscatel's "poetic" account of how his master sustained his broken foot was appropriately rendered in verses with "broken feet."

39. More double meanings insinuated by Inés. Traditionally she has never kept a secret but has worked hard to divulge it to all and sundry. Now, however, she promises to change her ways and keep Beatriz's secret religiously, as she would a saint's day, giving her tongue a rest. As we soon discover, Inés's double meaning indicates duplicity of purpose. Far from piously observing the feast of "Saint Secret," she tells tales to Leonor at the first opportunity. *Graciosos* and *graciosas* are notorious gossips (see the behavior of Arceo and the duenna Lucía in *Mornings of April and May*, Act I, sc. 4, and note 3 to that play).

40. In most Golden-Age plays the *gracioso* tells at least one anecdote (see, for example, Calabazas' story about the tailor in *A House with Two Doors*).

41. The exact sense of the original lines eludes us, probably because of textual defects. Hartzenbusch offers a reconstruction in *Comedias de Calderón*, 2:323, Biblioteca de Autores Españoles, vol. 9.

42. The proverb which Moscatel has in mind could be: "Cornudo y apaleado, mandalde que baile" (literally, "Cuckolded and thrashed, [now] command him to dance"). The saying derives from a popular story about a cuckolded husband which ends, after beatings, in a dance of reconciliation. Moscatel feels like the husband in the story: "cuckolded," in a sense, by Alonso, he has also just been kicked by him, and all that remains is for his master to order him to dance.

43. The Hircanian tiger, like the Albanian lion, is often mentioned in literature as a symbol of extreme violence and ferocity. See, for example, Góngora's *Soledad primera* (*First Solitude*): "¿Cuál tigre, la más fiera / que clima infamó hircano" ("What fiercest tiger, that ever defiled Hyrcanian clime"). There are also many allusions to the Hircanian tiger in Elizabethan drama (for instance, in *Hamlet* and *Macbeth*). The source of th allusion could well be Pliny, *Naturalis Historia*, or Virgil's *Aeneid*, IV. 1.367.

44. References, serious and burlesque, to the mythical phoenix (in connection with longevity, uniqueness, rebirth, immortality, and other themes) are innumerable in Golden-Age literature. See, for instance *No Trifling with Love*, Act I, sc. 3; Act II, sc. 3. As for mothers-in-law, they clearly had a bad reputation even in the seventeenth-century for living longer than their relations thought convenient. In the original Inés describes the phoenix as a "suegra mentira" ("false, lying mother-in-law"), doubtless to imply that mothers-in-law are given to deceit, as well as to remind us that the phoenix is an imaginary creature. The maidservant may also intend to hint that in wishing Alonso a life longer than that of the nonexistent phoenix, she is not being entirely sincere.

45. Hartzenbusch (*Comedias de Calderón*, 2:325) believes that some lines are missing here.

46. Possibly a reference is intended to some contemporary scandal involving a marriage annulment.

47. Alonso's speech offers another example of Calderón's fondness for accumulating and elaborating a whole series of images before reiterating their main elements as a finale (see *A House with Two Doors*, note 1, and *Mornings of April and May*, note 29).

48. Moscatel recalls the fate that befell him and his master upon their previous visit to Don Pedro's house (see Act II, sc. 5; Act III, sc. 1). Moscatel intends mischievously to mislead the audience into believing that he and Alonso may evade discovery again, that the denouement may not be upon them yet. If so, behind the mischief of the *gracioso* can be glimpsed the teasing intention of the dramatist. Compare and contrast Calderón's technique in *A House with Two Doors* (see note 29) and *Mornings of April and May* (see note 20).

49. Once a woman married, her reputation ceased to be the responsibility of her father or brother and devolved upon her husband. See Edward M. Wilson, *Spanish and English Literature of the 16th and 17th Centuries: Studies in Discretion, Illusion and Mutability* (Cambridge: Cambridge Univ. Press, 1980), chapter 6, "The Cloak and Sword Plays," p. 96.